THE FUN PALACE

For my children, Seán, Mark and Antonia,
and my grandchildren, Luke and Leah

THE FUN PALACE

An Autobiography

Agnes Bernelle

THE LILLIPUT PRESS
DUBLIN

First published 1996 by
THE LILLIPUT PRESS LTD
4 Rosemount Terrace, Arbour Hill,
Dublin 7, Ireland.

A CIP record for this
title is available from
The British Library.

ISBN 1 874675 28 7

Acknowledgment
The Lilliput Press receives financial assistance from
An Chomairle Ealaíon/The Arts Council, Ireland.

Set in Galliard
by Verbatim Typesetting & Design Ltd.
Printed in Ireland
by Betaprint of Dublin.

FOREWORD

Agnes Bernelle claims to have been born in Berlin in 1923. Berlin one can believe: but seventy-three years old? Nonsense; she can't be more than twenty-four, and a young twenty-four at that, a mischievous twenty-four. Enthusiastic, indefatigable, amorous, ambitious, loyal, resilient, funny, incredibly tolerant (except of intolerant people), forcefully feminist, instinctively rebellious, perennially skint yet imbued with ineradicable style, she emanates sheer Youth though every sentence in this book like a heron flashing its wings against a rainbow. But she must be the age she says, for she brings to us what seems a full century's worth of inimitable anecdote: theatre, politics, social contretemps, the joys and miseries of an 'open' marriage, of life in Weimar Germany, Hitler's Germany, England in World War II, the Riviera and (of course) Ireland. How many of us know how exiled German theatre-folk practised their art in London during the 1940s? Or have heard of the way young actresses were slotted into the war effort by the U.S. military? Or can guess what it was like to try to finance stage-shows and films in the post-war years of austerity? Agnes knows: she was there, and she did it. She met Marlene Dietrich when Marlene was a young mother making sandwiches in a Pimlico kitchen. She remembers her own mother escaping by the skin of her teeth from recruitment as a Nazi agent-provocateur. She tells how at the last minute she rejected a paradoxically indecent leotard for Salomé's 'Dance of the Seven Veils', thereby becoming the first nude-in-motion on the censored British stage. In short, *The Fun Palace* is the widest-ranging, most instructive, most appealing theatrical/personal memoir one could possibly imagine, and it doesn't even get past 1963. I want to read all about Agnes in Dublin (and elsewhere) since then: and so, I guess, will every one of her hundreds and hundreds of friends, in the 'profession' and out of it. Let's hope there's a second volume, soon.

JOHN ARDEN

ACKNOWLEDGMENTS

My gratitude for help and/or encouragement is due to: Paschal Finnan, Jonathan Williams, John Arden, Crióse Brogan, Maurice Craig, Brendan Ward, Nuala O'Connor, Victor and Alma O'Reilly, Charlotte Bielenberg, Hans Christian Oeser, Ann Ingle, Lorraine Brennan, Barry Egan, my publisher Antony Farrell, Amanda Bell, Brendan Barrington, Bernard and Mary Loughlin and their staff at the Guthrie Center at Annaghmakerrig.

THE FUN PALACE

'*Everything is so dangerous that nothing is really frightening.*'
GERTRUDE STEIN

I

It's curious—but I never could remember leaving Berlin.

I can't remember what time of day it was, or from which station we left—for surely we left from some railway station, one didn't fly much in 1936—and did we take much luggage, and who came to see us off? How did we feel as we settled down in the railway compartment when the guard's whistle made us into exiles with one sharp blast?

And yet I can recall almost everything else about that journey. The ship tossing and shaking us across the sea towards England, the immigration authorities at Harwich early next morning checking and rechecking our entry visas. My first English breakfast on my first English train. I can see it all even now, from the small glacé cherry on my first dining-car grapefruit, to the large sooty roof of Liverpool Street Station. I shall never forget arriving in London—but I never could remember leaving Berlin.

I was born there in 1923. My layette cost my parents several million Deutsch Mark, not because they were millionaires, though at that time they might well have been, but because I arrived in the middle of the Big Inflation, when banknotes issued in the morning weren't worth the paper they were printed on by the afternoon, and my father, who owned and ran several theatres in Berlin, paid his employees in groceries collected at dawn from the city markets. It was an uneasy lull between world wars, marked by the collapse of the German Empire, the hasty establishment of the Weimar Republic, and the abortive Spartacist uprising.

Of course, I knew nothing about all that as I slept in my frilly cot in our apartment in Schöneberg, a residential district of Berlin much celebrated in song, which featured in one of my father's musicals, *Maytime*.

We lived in a house overlooking the Viktoria Luise Platz—a small, pretty square which was not square at all, but round, and was, for a long time, the outside world for me. Unlike the private squares in English cities it had no railings, and was freely accessible to children less rich, and less protected, than I was. They swarmed all over it, playing hopscotch, cops and robbers and marbles. I envied them. I envied them their marbles in particular, and since I could afford to buy them rather than to win them from the other children, they became the currency by which I bought my way into their company.

We occupied only one floor of the house we lived in, which was not unusual then in Berlin. The residential houses were large and ornate, with massive entrance doors which, not like our own, were often flanked by caryatids, groaning under the weight of first-floor balconies. Our house had a lofty entrance hall with checkerboard marble tiles and a huge gilded mirror on each side. A long narrow corridor ran the length of the twelve rooms we occupied on the first floor. It was perfect for bicycling from my bedroom at one end to my playroom at the other. The bedrooms all had tiled stoves in the corners, which my parents had left standing, even though central heating had long since been installed.

The reception rooms could be made into one large continuous area by sliding their connecting doors into the wall, which was great for parties. The oval drawing-room had six tall windows, and after the many winter colds I caught during my over-heated childhood, my mother would muffle me up to my eyeballs, my hands in woollen mittens, my legs in itchy leggings, open all six windows wide, and take me for walks around the grand piano. I hated to be so mollycoddled and longed to be down in the square making snowmen with the local kids.

Apart from such minor irritations I think I was happy most of the time. I had been a late and much wanted child, and my parents could afford to deny me very little. Until I was three I had a pretty nurse called Ettie, whose cornflower-blue eyes regarded me with uncritical affection. I became used to being doted on, and to having my own way in every-

6

thing. If I didn't want to walk home from the park, I would sit on the pavement and howl. If I didn't want my mother to go out in the evening, I would try to grab and tear her dress when she came to kiss me goodnight. If I didn't want to eat my spinach, I would bring my fist down hard and make it fly all over the room, protesting loudly that I didn't know right from wrong yet, and therefore should not be punished. In truth, I was a monster.

My parents had no option but to retire Ettie, who promptly replaced me with an illegitimate child of her own. They brought in a strict governess; she arrived in a green hat and was called Fräulein Basner. From the beginning I detested her.

One of my most vivid memories is of her first evening with us. Through two translucent glass panels in my bedroom door I could see the shadowy figure of Fräulein Basner unpacking her clothes and hanging them in a closet outside. I was standing up in my cot, howling for her to come back in and read me another story. She took absolutely no notice.

A picture of my older brother on his pony was hanging above my bed, and now whenever I come across it in an old photograph album I know again the awful frustration and rage I felt so many years ago when I turned my tear-stained face to it in noisy supplication. I don't know if I really expected Emmerich to get off his horse and help me to attract Fräulein Basner's attention, but she did not respond to my yells, and so began the taming of this particular shrew.

Although at the very beginning she was nearly dismissed for spanking me, Fräulein Basner stayed with us until I was too old to have a nanny. We soon became devoted to each other, and the formal 'Fräulein Basner' became the more affectionate 'Bäschen'. When she left us, at the age of fifty, she would not look after any other children. Instead she advertised for a husband, and married a trombone player from the Potsdam Municipal Orchestra. We danced at her wedding, and lost touch with her when the war came.

In 1954, when I went back to Berlin for the first time, I got a message across to East Berlin where I had been told she was living. Returning late from a visit to the theatre, I found Bäschen sitting in the lounge of my hotel with a basket of

7

eggs on her lap. She had been waiting there for many hours. How she got across that border I never found out. We had a tearful reunion, and I invited her for a proper meal, but she had to get 'across' before midnight, and only took the time to tidy my room in the hotel before she left. I never saw her again.

Christmas was always a great event in my parents' house. All our extended family and many of our friends would come for dinner.

A tall tree was put up in the drawing-room, with real candles and a great deal of angel hair (lametta) hanging from its branches in long swathes of silver. Around the room were small tables stacked with presents for everyone and on every table was a plate of goodies: nuts, raisins, honey cake and marzipan.

I was usually too excited to sit obediently through Christmas dinner, which we had on Christmas Eve, as is the custom in Central Europe. We had carp with parsley sauce, or goose with chestnut stuffing, and a sweet made of poppy seeds—which I hated. After the grown-ups' coffee and brandy, the long-awaited moment came at last. My mother disappeared behind the double doors, which had hidden the drawing-room all day, and the sounds of 'Stille Nacht' came wafting through from our hand-cranked gramophone. The doors opened slowly and we rushed in to find our presents.

One particular Christmas I made straight for the tree, for underneath its branches I could see a wondrous object: a miniature Citroën complete with headlamps, indicator, number-plates and fat rubber tyres. I jumped into it and grabbed the steering wheel. In vain I looked for the ignition key.

'How do you start the engine?' I asked anxiously.

'You don't, Mädichen,' said Uncle Carl Meinhard, whose present it was. 'You have to pedal it.'

Pedal! I had to pedal it!!! I didn't even try.

My parents were embarrassed. Carl Meinhard was my father's partner, and a very generous man. He had had this tiny Mercedes specially built for me in the Citroën factory, a replica of their latest model, no less.

'Aren't you going to say thank you to Uncle Carl?'

I hesitated for only a moment, then went to my table, took a marzipan orange and handed it to Uncle Carl.

'Thank you,' I said in measured tones.

'Well thank you, my dear,' said Uncle Carl, 'but look here, this isn't a real orange.'

'It isn't a real car either,' I replied.

I am told I would never play with it, and eventually it was given away.

When I was five, my parents put me into a small Montessori school in the Palais Goldsmith-Rothschild on Unter Den Linden. This school had been started privately by the Baroness Rothschild to prevent her children from having to go to 'common' schools, and coming into contact with 'common' germs. Her family paediatrician, who was also ours, had selected a small group of sufficiently 'germ-free' tots of whom I was one, which suited my doting parents.

Each morning I was driven to school in a black limousine by a chauffeur in a smart, buttoned tunic, knee-breeches and a peaked cap. I fondly believed that the car belonged to my father, whereas it really was the property of the chauffeur. This was no affectation on my father's part. He needed a car and a driver in his busy life, but owning a car privately was not yet in fashion in Berlin in the twenties.

In the Montessori school I quickly learnt to read and write. The method is good, provided the school is consistent in its application. After one year my mother came to check on my progress. She found to her dismay that we, the original pupils, were being left more or less to our own devices, abandoned in favour of a new 'germ-free' class. This was not strictly the teacher's fault since the school was required by law to take in new children every year. The problem was that there was just the one teacher. 'Mann kann nicht mit einem Toches auf zwei Hochzeiten tanzen (Don't try and dance at two weddings if you have only one bum)' remarked my mother, who was always strong on proverbial wisdom, and as I was not receiving instruction she removed me from the school.

On my first day at home, I was upset and worried because I did not want to go to a bigger school. Not even the arrival of my father's barber, Herr Kyrieleis, could placate me. He usually managed to thrill me by moving his ancient razor up and down a leather strop as a prelude to covering my father's face with an excess of soapy lather, but on that day I could not be consoled by such trifles.

Bäschen produced a volume of Hauff's *Märchen* to cheer me up. Cheer me up indeed. There was no question that these tales were meant for children, but they were horrendously violent. The *Struwwelpeter*, a favourite with German children, was bad enough, but to play the flute on the bones of one's murdered brother or to have one's head hammered to the mast of a sinking ship with a rusty nail—this did not seem to me to be a suitable literary diet for a child. I called for an eraser and spent the morning rubbing out the words of each offending story until hardly any print was left. After that I felt better and began to think more positively about the 'other' school.

The 'other' school, though it accepted children of all denominations, was run by a Jewish lady, Fraülein Zikkel, and was certainly regarded as Jewish by the Nazis, who later closed it down.

Sending me there, a Protestant, continued a family tradition of religious reversals. A generation earlier, my Jewish father had attended a Benedictine school in his native Budapest. There was no better school in all Hungary, and my grandmother decided that only the best was good enough for her little Rudie. I don't know what strings she had to pull, or what charms she brought to bear upon the holy monks, but her little Rudie was accepted, the only Jewish boy in the entire school. Of course, at first he was taunted by the other boys, but my grandmother was a resolute woman. On the first occasion that presented itself—a nature walk—she whacked one or two of them with an umbrella and settled the matter once and for all. There was never any trouble after that. My father fitted into monastic life and was often found on his knees before the holy shrine, serving mass along with the other altar boys.

This kind of ecumenism has been the hallmark of my family. My earliest religious affiliation was to Martin Luther. Someone had given me a picture of him, double chins and all, and I stuck him to my bedroom wall and gazed at him adoringly for years to satisfy my inborn need for an idol.

In any case, my parents would have found it hard to give me meaningful religious instruction.

My Jewish father's child by his Catholic wife is a Protestant; and while I, his child by his second, Lutheran, wife, eventually became a Catholic, I suspect that if I had not been brought up a Protestant I would have become one sooner or later. This state of affairs has never particularly bothered any of us, and I can't help feeling that God, whatever religion He is, must prefer it to sectarian strife.

My formal education was not extensive. I never went to university, alas, but because I have lived in several different countries, held different nationalities, and been involved with several different religions, I have been loyal to the communities I have lived in and the associations I have joined. Thus I may be forgiven for refusing to feel German, though I was born in Germany; or Hungarian, though my father came from Hungary; or English, though I was brought up in England; or Irish, though I am living in Ireland now. Nor do I count myself as 'Aryan', like my mother, or Jewish, like my father, nor even a 'good Catholic', though our cook tried her best to make me into one.

My mother, Emmy, was born in 1887 in Wittenberge, which lies on the railway line between Hamburg and Berlin—as she would always emphasize, because she was the daughter of a railwayman. One of five children, my mother was pretty and ambitious. By the time she was twenty she had decided that life in a small provincial town was not for her. At that same moment, my father, who was seven years her elder, was negotiating the purchase of his second theatre in Berlin. It seemed unlikely that they should ever meet.

My grandparents did not approve when my mother left for Berlin. For a young girl to take such a step was unheard-of in those days. What would the neighbours say? Emmy arrived in the big city with one small bag, wearing the smart new outfit she had made herself. It did not take her long to find a position. The Bernauers were looking for a nanny for their son, and in that responsible but lowly position, my mother entered my father's household.

She always tried to hide this fact in later years. When my father wrote his memoirs at the end of his life, she made him take out any references to their original relationship. I have always thought the story touching and romantic, and hope that wherever she is now she will forgive me for revealing it here.

My half-brother, Emmerich, was only three years old when his mother was struck down with typhus at the age of twenty-seven. She caught the disease on a second honeymoon in Spain. On her deathbed she called for Emmy. 'Promise me,' she whispered, 'that whatever happens you will never leave my child.' My mother, who was holding little Emmerich in her arms and weeping, vowed to bring him up as her own.

Not long after Henny Remilly's tragic death, my grandfather, who considered his daughter's presence in the house of a widower unseemly, demanded her return. Emmy arrived in Wittenberge and true to her promise had Emmerich in tow. What indeed did the neighbours say—returned from the city in disgrace with an illegitimate child? My grandparents must have been relieved when Emmy took the boy back to Berlin.

It was then that she took control of my father's household. Calmly and efficiently she executed all the duties of a wife bar one. Pretty as she was, my father did not then regard her in any romantic way. Freed from the bonds of a too-early marriage, he threw himself into a bachelor's life with gusto. Ladies came and went. Actresses and other beautiful women frequented his parties and, more often than not, his bed. My mother loved him secretly for many years.

When Emmerich was old enough, Emmy became engaged to an old admirer, a Berlin lawyer named Paul Nordmann, who had been waiting patiently for many years. She gave in her notice to my father. To her dismay he did not make a comment. A week went by. One morning she saw a familiar overcoat hanging in the hall and heard male voices in the study; presently she was called inside.

'I thought I had been invited to Berlin to talk about your marriage to Paul Nordmann,' said her father, 'and now I am told that you are marrying Direktor Bernauer. He has just asked me for your hand'.

They had a fairy-tale wedding, and went on a fairy-tale honeymoon—my brother went as well—then came home to Viktoria-Luise-Platz to live happily ever after. But did they? Poor Emmy, not for long did she enjoy the 'good life' with her Rudolf for which she had waited so patiently. Her prince, though charming, was also a Jew, and in the beer gardens of Munich a man called Adolf Hitler was beginning to make his name.

My father had barely reached his teens when his parents decided to leave Budapest and move to Berlin. He waved goodbye to the holy monks and entered the Friedrich Gymnasium, where he learnt to speak and write flawless German. At university he studied philosophy and history of art, and because there was little money at home, he took a part-time job selling *Meyers Konversations Lexikon*—the German equivalent of *Encyclopaedia Britannica*—from door to door. At night he penned lyrics for the satirical cabarets, which were flourishing at the turn of the century in Berlin. These verses were set to music and later published in a collection called *Lieder eines bösen Buben—Songs of a Bad Boy*—from which I draw material for my shows and records to this day.

When after a year my father had failed spectacularly to sell a single set of encyclopaedias, he threw in his hand. Deeply embarrassed, he first bought a set for himself, so he could report at least one customer to his employers. This set was destined to travel across Europe and has come to rest on my bookshelves in Dublin.

My father, much influenced by the poetry of Heinrich Heine, also wrote lyrical verses in his youth. Grandfather Joseph surreptitiously sent his early poems to a literary magazine and was, if anything, more thrilled than his son when they were printed.

Joseph Bernauer emerges from my father's descriptions as a gentle and caring man and does not appear suitably cast for his role as a sales representative. Not long after his forty-fifth birthday, he fell off his bicycle and injured his liver. A year later he lay dying of cancer. This was the end of father's dreams of an academic career—he left the university of Berlin to provide for his mother and younger sister Gisela.

Attracted to the theatre from his student days, when he took part in crowd scenes, he decided to go on the stage. It seems almost unbelievable that a theatrical career was ever considered a safe way of earning a living, but the system of theatre in continental Europe made this enviable assumption quite natural. There were, and are even today, many steady jobs for performers, directors and designers in Germany and elsewhere in Europe. Every provincial town has its state theatre, most of them with artists on long-term contracts.

Whenever I think of the fate that forced us to emigrate from Berlin, it is not the country I regret leaving, or the possessions we had to abandon, but always the loss of this theatrical system, which was originally my birthright, and which might have provided me with a far more comfortable and rewarding career had I been able to stay there. After all, my parents had christened me 'Agnes'—Agnes Bernauer, after a classical play by Friedrich Hebbel—in the reasonable assumption that one day it would say on a German playbill '*Agnes Bernauer*, played by Agnes Bernauer'.

As an actor my lucky father first worked for the great Otto Brahm at the Deutsches Theatre in Berlin. There he made friends with Carl Meinhard. In 1901, when they were barely in their twenties, they put together a light-hearted entertainment which could be performed on special occasions in the homes of well-to-do members of the German bourgeoisie. They gathered together a small, but talented, company, 'the Bad Boys', and when they found that there was no suitable material available they wrote their own songs and sketches. My father invited Dr Wulff, the editor of *Lustige Blätter*, the German equivalent of *Punch*, to contribute some humorous pieces and to issue invitations for the try-out. His reputation would ensure a good attendance. And so it did, but in a most unexpected way. Instead of the bankers, factory owners and businessmen the Bad Boys had planned for, Dr Wulff had invited the entire artistic and cultural élite of Berlin, in the hope of showing off his own masterpieces—which turned out to be so bad that most of them had to be cut during rehearsals. The Bad Boys and their actors and actresses were thrown into a panic. They were only too well aware that failure on this night could mean the end of their careers, since everyone who could give them work was right there to witness it.

They need not have worried. That night saw the birth of a new style of cabaret entertainment—an hilarious satire of the German artistic and literary world. This required an eagle eye, a sensitive ear, a razor-sharp wit and above all an audience intelligent and informed enough to understand all the allusions. In his ambitious recklessness, Dr Wulff had provided the Bad Boys with just such an audience. The reception was tumultuous. The original plans for the show were soon abandoned. Since neither Meinhard nor Bernauer wanted to give up a serious career in the theatre, they held their Bad Boys evenings only once a year, at midnight, for invited guests.

These guests could be separated into three categories: those who would telephone before the show to ask if it was perhaps their 'turn' to be parodied; those who delighted in the distorted image of themselves presented on stage by the mischievous company; and those who wrote offended letters, asking if they were of so little importance that the Bad Boys had not found them worth holding up to ridicule.

The Bad Boys continued to prosper and my father became an actor in Max Reinhard's Ensemble at the Berliner Theater, which seemed to fulfil his ambitions at the time. As a director he was not 'called', but 'chosen'. Meinhard, always the entrepreneur, had gathered together some stars of the Berlin stage to send on tour during the silly season. They were waiting for a famous director to arrive from Vienna. In the meantime Meinhard asked his buddy, my father, to sit in at rehearsals for a few extra marks and to provide a focal point for the orphaned company until the great man could take over.

A short time into the first rehearsal the leading man stopped in front of my father. 'You don't like what I'm doing!' he said. 'No—I mean yes, of course I do,' stuttered my father. 'No, you don't. I can tell by your face. I wish you'd tell me how you would have me play this scene.' My father was mortified, but this was only the first of many such interruptions. The company would stop, whenever my father put on one of his faces, to take advice and direction from him. By the end of the week they refused to work under the famous man from Vienna, and by the end of rehearsals my father had become their official director.

In 1908 Carl Meinhard and my father rented the Berliner Theater and set out on a long and fruitful partnership in theatre management. Over the next ten years they bought the Komödienhaus, the Hebbel Theater and the Theater am Nollendorf Platz, which they managed, putting on plays ranging from classical drama to light-hearted farce. With so many theatres to finance they needed a great deal of money, and since there were then no grants or subsidies, my father hit on the idea of writing and producing his own musicals. This would keep the cash 'in the family', and instead of paying out royalties to other authors, he could use the money to subsidize two of their theatres which showed only serious drama. Thus *Maytime*, *The Chocolate Soldier*, *The Girl on the Film* and countless other operettas were born, while the theatres given over to classics and serious modern plays went from strength to strength under father's direction.

The Meinhard/Bernauer venture closed down in the year I was born. They leased their theatres to other people and dissolved their partnership. Father was then only in his forties, but considered that he had worked long and hard enough in the theatre. After all, he had started in management exceptionally young. He used to frighten me, and I suspect he frightened my brother before me, with the assertion that no one who had not 'made it' by the time they were twenty-three, would ever come to anything. I know he died, when I was thirty, with the firm conviction that I was, and would always be, a hopeless failure.

My father brought me up to be a gentleman. He could not help it, of course, since he himself was one of nature's gentlemen. His word was his bond, and he rarely had to sign a contract in all his long years running his theatres. He was the biggest single influence in my life. He often told me he had no regard for family ties and that he loved me not because I was his daughter but because I was his friend. If I misbehaved he sent me little notes telling me how much his 'friend' had disappointed him. I have been told by analysts that this put a strain on me but neither of us was aware of this danger at the time and I adored him without reservation, and would do anything to live up to his concept of me as another son. He consulted me at an early age on matters concerning his work and allowed me to sit in on script conferences. Construction and storyline were all-important in those days, and I have never quite rid myself of the urge to reconstruct a script—anyone's script—that seemed to me to be too shapeless or too long.

A dedicated movie fan from the age of five, I knew the titles and the casts of every German film in the twenties and early thirties. After his retirement, when my father began directing 'talkies' in Berlin, he would not only ask me for my casting suggestions but would often act on them. Film stars who appeared in father's films could not have known that they had been chosen by a nine-year-old.

Father never lost his academic bent, even though he had not finished his university courses. An afternoon with him in the Pergamon Museum was an experience to be treasured, but best of all were the morning sessions in his dressing-room. He had lost most of his hair at an early age. Being vain, he grew his side hair to a special length and slowly and carefully plastered it, strand by strand, across the top of his head until it formed a shiny dome. Whom he wanted to fool that way I do not know. I think he did it just to please himself, and it certainly pleased me, for it prolonged our magic mornings, when he taught me more than I would ever learn at school.

He was a very honest man, but at times he took his honesty to ridiculous lengths. Fleeing from the Nazis, he would not cheat them by smuggling out some of his cash, and went to London with nothing but his gold watch to pawn. He was also a very human man with human foibles. His biggest weaknesses were cards and women. He loved to play cards in Berlin's theatre club until the early hours of the morning. Not until I was almost grown up did I begin to understand some of the odd results of this obsession. Those little blue stickers, for example, that would drop to the ground from beneath our chairs and tables at certain times: if this happened on some hot summer afternoon when my mother was entertaining friends, she would turn pale and hastily place a foot on them. I must have been the only person present who did not know that these pretty little tabs came from the bailiff and had to stay until my father's gambling debts were paid. He must have always paid them, for no one ever came to cart our furniture away, at least not until we had to sell it during the Nazi era.

Against all my expectations, the 'other school', which I had dreaded so much, was a great success. I enjoyed the more challenging way we had to work there and learnt to socialize with other children, which was wonderful, because I was, technically, an only child. Brother Emmerich was seventeen when I was born and within a few years he would go to work and later marry Edith, whom he met when they were both fifteen.

Emmerich joined the Ullstein Group as a journalist, and as such he broke new ground. If he was asked to do a report on brewing he would get a job in a brewery. If he was asked to write about the building trade, he would become a labourer on a building site. It was always exciting to wait for him to come home in the evening in dirty overalls, and it was thrilling to be allowed to stay up late and celebrate when he became editor of the *Vossische Zeitung*—at the age of twenty-three! It was even more gratifying when father gave him a telling-off for refusing to cut his toenails. But none of this could keep me entertained for long and until I went to the new school I had to find my own amusement.

I spent many hours dressing up. My mother had the most exquisite beaded gowns. Her youngest sister Martha, for whom she had found a job as a seamstress with one of her own couturiers, Gerson Prager Hausdorff, one of Berlin's grandest fashion houses, had ended up marrying the son and heir.

Both sisters now got their clothes at knock-down prices, and after they had worn them a few times in public I was allowed to play with them. Dressed up like that I would stand in front of the tall mirror in my mother's sitting-room, play my little gramophone, and pretend I was the singer on the discs. I sang along with the recorded voices of pop singers and opera stars alike. Did I say 'pretend'? I was all of them.

I also had a splendid tent, hand-painted with galloping horses and Indian braves. Since we had no garden, I put it up indoors and retreated into it with a pile of cushions and an even bigger pile of books. When I had raced through my own books I would go into my father's study and borrow his. My mother always smiled approvingly when she caught me disappearing into my tent with finely bound volumes of Dickens or Tagore, and I doubt if she realized that the edition of the *Arabian Nights* she brought to my bed when I had the measles was not the children's classic she had read but the unexpurgated version.

This was not the only erotica in our house. Illustrated copies of the amorous adventures of both Casanova and Don Juan were hidden away where I could easily find them, providing me with a liberal and most imaginative sex education, which I shared generously with my friends. When Bäschen was busy somewhere else, they would join me underneath my bed, armed with torches, to leaf excitedly through the forbidden pages.

Of course there were more innocent pleasures to be had. My very best friend Vera Calmann—one of a long line of Veras in my life—lived in a flat above the Scala, the great variety theatre of Berlin. Vera's father was manager, so we children had the run of the place. We could plonk ourselves down in the front row and watch the programme as often and as long as we pleased. We saw some of the finest international variety acts over and over again. My favourite by far was the girl in the sky-blue satin shorts, who sidled coyly across the stage between acts, carrying a numbered card and wearing a fixed and manic smile. I dreamt of growing up to be just like her.

The conductor of the Scala was a matinée idol, the suave and handsome Otto Stenzel. Poor Vera had to sit through endless shows with me so I could ogle at gorgeous Otto and his Brylcreemed hair. I am sure I am not the only one of my generation who recalls it all with such nostalgia—the Scala, Otto Stenzel and the 'Number Girl'. How sad I was, when the war was over, to find them gone. The Scala had received a direct hit and I could find no trace of it.

My parents took me to plays and operas from an early age. The most lavish production I saw was Verdi's *Aida* in the open air, on an Italian beach. The vast sandy strand was a perfect setting for the story, played out against a midnight sky. There were real elephants on the stage.

I spent the next few years entertaining my parents' dinner guests with a parody of Aida's famous aria in Act One, which I decided was much too long and repetitious. Wrapped in my mother's chiffon scarves, I would wring my hands, which were covered with her rings, and roll my eyes to heaven. 'O Patria Mia,' I would warble, 'non ti vederai piu—non piu ti vederai, patria mia ...' until I was snatched up by Bäschen and carried off to bed.

I was forever acting and dressing up, and wanted to try my hand at production. Beginning modestly, I staged Lebende Bilder—living pictures, picking my 'cast' from amongst my schoolmates, and we put on a show for my ninth birthday. The sliding doors between our two drawing-rooms opened to reveal scenes of well-known fairy-tales: 'Sleeping Beauty', 'Mother Goose', 'Jack and the Beanstalk'. I appeared as Snow White with seven of my dolls dressed up as dwarves.

My next attempt was more public. I was ten years old and now in the Rückert Lyceum, a high school for girls. On a day in mid-summer, the school hired a barge to take us all out on one of the many waterways that surround Berlin. We would stop for lunch in one of the secluded waterside inns and enjoy the entertainment laid on by the senior forms. I did not see why the juniors should not make a contribution. I found a verse play in a children's annual that seemed suitable. It was about one Abu Hassan, a jolly rogue, who, together with his wife decides to con his sultan and sultana. Weeping profusely and making 'much ado', they go to the palace and each in turn claims that the other has 'expired', pocketing a handsome purse every time. A dilemma arises when both sovereigns arrive at their humble abode to find out which of them is dead.

I dressed my actors in my mother's Gerson Prager Hausdorff glad rags, and the sultan and sultana in particular were a splendid sight. There was no curtain at the inn, which I had failed to foresee, and when my actors, playing dead, arose to make room for the next scene, they had to drag their shrouds behind them. This made the play more hilarious than even I had anticipated. My success at that time was chiefly accidental, and I could not have foreseen the effect it was to have years later on my professional career.

In 1978, when I wanted the rights for Günter Grass's stage play *Onkel Onkel* for my first attempt as director at the Project Arts Centre in Dublin, I wrote to Kiepenheuer, Grass's publisher in Berlin. Would they consider me, an untried director, worthy of this privilege? Imagine my surprise when I received permission almost by return of post. The head of the publishing house, Dr Maria Sommer, wrote asking me if 'Agnes Bernelle' could be 'Agnes Bernauer', her erstwhile fellow pupil in Berlin, whose production of 'Abu Hassan' had given her so much pleasure during a school outing that she had chosen theatre publishing for her own career.

In 1930, when Joe May directed a film called *Eine Tolle Ballnacht* for UFA, the biggest German film company, he needed a little boy. When he did not find what he was looking for, he rang my father and asked if I could play the part. I was to wear a sailor suit. My hair was fairly short with the then-fashionable fringe and Uncle Joe said it would have to do. I was thrilled and felt that now at last I was a true professional. My one and only scene was with a well-known German comic, Jacob Tiedke, who was the butler. The unfortunate young woman who played my nanny could not act and so the scene was re-shot with a more experienced actress and I had two days of filming instead of one.

UFA invited me to the première of the film. There was a seduction scene in it, played between Robert Thoeren and my 'screen mother', Nora Gregor, on a couch. Compared to sex scenes in today's cinema, it must have been extremely tame, but when it appeared on screen, my mother told me to cover my eyes. I did so obediently but was nevertheless aware of what was going on. After the screening we were all asked to go on stage to take our bows and were given large laurel wreaths with satin sashes, our names marked on them in golden letters. It was a German custom on opening nights.

Not long after my film début, Paramount in Paris wanted a 'boy' just like me, with a sailor suit and a fringe. They offered a five-year contract which my father turned down. 'If

you want to be an actress later on,' he told me, 'you will benefit from growing up in a normal way.' I cried for days. I often
wonder if my father would have acted the same way if he had
realized how close the Nazis were and how slim my chances
were of growing up in a 'normal way'.

II

It was always an enormous thrill when my maternal Grandfather Erb came on a visit to Berlin. He had a long bushy beard and when he came to pick me up from school the children took him for Father Christmas. On the rare occasions when Bäschen went to visit her mother in Koenigsberg I was allowed to stay with him and Grandma in Wittenberge. I loved their little house with the dark, narrow stairs, the heavy Germanic furniture with the white doilies on the arms of the chairs, the grandfather clock in the corner and the Victorian children's books on the shelves; I loved their breakfast of sausages and cheese, eaten from small wooden boards in the shape of pigs. I loved going upstairs to Aunt Bertha's flat to eat the caramel sweets she made for me. I even loved the small enamel bowl on the old washstand that had to be filled by hand for my morning ablutions. And most of all I loved cycling through the little town with my cousin Rudie, something only big children were allowed to do in Berlin.

Once my grandfather took us to a fun-fair on a large meadow outside the town. I had never been to such a place before and found it enchanting. There were dodgems, coconut shies, shooting galleries, roundabouts and even a bearded lady, but most delightful of all was the Fun Palace, an extraordinary building, the like of which I have never encountered since.

First you had to go up what was called a 'shimmy stair', a wooden stairway divided down the middle. As you set your foot upon it the two halves began to move in opposite directions, one up and the other down. It took a while to get up this busy staircase; giggling and panting you finally arrived on a wooden walkway which ran around the little building like a balcony. Lulled into the false belief that all you had to do now was walk along it to get to the other end, you soon found yourself stumbling, falling and crying out in surprise, as the planks collapsed beneath your feet and flicked you up and down. Other lengths of flooring were even more slyly deceptive. You expected them to move, but they failed to do so and just when you were sure you had nothing more to fear they gave a sudden heave and tilted you on the floor. On finishing the course you entered a small chamber containing a single seat constructed like a garden bench; instead of wooden slats it was made of metal rollers. As soon as the door shut, leaving you in the pitch-dark, the metal rollers began to roll. It is impossible to describe the sensation. It was as if the earth was moving away from under you. Without even time to scream, I found myself sliding down a huge chute, made, I believe, of canvas, with people before and behind me. This was delightful and quite the best part of it all. I wished I would never reach the bottom, but reach it I did, to be collected by Grandfather and taken home for tea.

I have never forgotten the Fun Palace, because all my life I have been subtly reminded of it. Perhaps I have just about arrived at the top of the chute. Going down will be exhilarating and rewarding, I feel, but I hope I shall not get to the bottom too quickly and too soon—and will there be an old gentleman with a white beard awaiting me?

When I was nine years old, my grandfather travelled to the Rhineland and the Schwarzwald region to visit the towns and villages of his youth. His ancestors had crossed the Rhine from France during the persecution of the Huguenots by Louis XIV. Grandfather was born in Karlsruhe, but moved around a great deal because he was a railway carpenter. He met Grandmother during a time up north and settled with her in Wittenberge. He had never been back to his birthplace, and now he wanted to see it once more. He must have had a premonition. My mother, brother, sister-in-law and I went with him to visit some of his remaining relatives in Pforzheim and Karlsruhe, and later spent a few weeks holidaying in Glashütte, a small village at the edge of the Black Forest.

I had a great time that summer, especially in Glashütte, where I made friends with the children of local farmers and was allowed to take part in the haymaking and its attendant jollities. I also rallied the other children who were staying in the only village inn and founded a 'literary club'. This involved the compulsory wearing of pale-blue ribbons and equally compulsory meetings in a shed to listen to me reading excerpts from my 'works'—romantic novels I had taken to writing around that time. I must have been an insufferable bully, since I cannot imagine that any of those unfortunate children enjoyed wasting their precious holiday time on such rubbish. My playmates, the boys in particular, went on strike about wearing my ribbons, but none of them ganged up to throw me into the village pond.

All these activities came to a sudden end when Grandfather suffered a stroke. He had always been healthy and hearty, and only days before we arrived in Glashütte he had walked to the top of the Feldberg, a fairly steep ascent. 'I should never have let him do it,' wept my distraught mother. I was taken into a darkened room to say goodbye to him. He was as white as the sheet he lay on, and made horrible rattling noises as he gasped for breath. He was gone before the morning. It was my first encounter with death.

After Grandfather's funeral in Wittenberge, I retreated more and more to my favourite place, our balcony at Viktoria Luise Platz, and spent a great deal of my solitary leisure time there.

From this balcony I watched with awe as the great airship Zeppelin, followed closely by the bulkier Hindenburg, flew over Berlin. On this balcony an older playmate told me about bombs, a new and alien concept to my world. The thought that human beings could aim such horrifying instruments of death and mutilation at others, that they could drop these obscenities on sleeping cities, was chilling to me even then. I have never been able to divorce the concept or the reality of bombs from the memory of this moment on my beloved balcony. It is an irony of fate that in the war that followed it was that sturdy structure and not this more fragile being which was destroyed by bombs.

It was from this balcony also that I watched the long

columns of voters setting off to put Hitler into power and I spent many hours grieving there, not only for my Grandfather Erb, but also for my Uncle Berzi Gonda, who died of a sudden heart attack when I was ten. Who would bring me yellow feathers for my dolls from his factory now? Who would give me a banana every time we met? Had I but known it, his early death saved my favourite uncle from untold suffering. His wife, Aunt Gisela, and one of his daughters ended up in Belsen. My aunt, a spirited woman, remarried there, but both she and her new husband perished. My cousin Ilma miraculously survived five years of suffering, and just before the end of the war, when she and other living corpses were about to be driven into a Polish lake, she heard gunfire and saw the camp guards jumping from the train. American soldiers came out of the bushes and liberated the prisoners just in time.

Whereas my Jewish relatives on my father's side were either killed or tortured in the camps, members of my mother's 'Aryan' family married men in Nazi uniform. I think my mother had expected more sympathy from her family for her Jewish husband, who had always been there to help her brothers and sisters educate their children and to take them travelling abroad. After the war she quickly forgave them and spent a great deal of time sending food parcels to those of her family who had survived. Alas, there weren't all that many. My favourite cousin Rudie had fallen during the last week of the war; brown-shirted Ernst Weise was killed long before; my Uncle Franz, Rudie's father, who had escaped the draft because of his age, was taken to Russia and put to work in a factory; he never returned. My mother's family, more fortunate than my father's during Hitler's time, paid dearly for their privileges afterwards.

When my father retired he bought a villa in a place called Abbazia in Istria, which was then part of Italy. Until 1933 we spent several months there every summer. Our journey to Abbazia from Berlin each year came very close to resembling a royal progress. Our party usually consisted of my parents, myself, my nanny, my brother, his girlfriend Edith, assorted female cousins who were brought along to find rich husbands on the Riviera di Levante, our cook, three cats, the luggage and my hand-cranked gramophone. Those members of my family who were not travelling came to see us off at the station, bearing gifts.

Once when the train broke down after puffing and panting over the Brenner Pass, our party got out onto the small platform of a mountain halt, wound up my gramophone, and started a merry dance in which most of the other passengers joined.

I vividly remember watching from the wide luggage net, above the seats, into which I had climbed. I always spent the best part of any journey in one of those nets, and refused to come down until we arrived at the tiny station above Abbazia where we would be met by the local taxi and whisked downhill to our house.

Originally Abbazia—renamed Opatia when it became part of Tito's Yugoslavia—was an Austrian possession, much loved and frequented by the imperial court of the Hapsburgs. Claimed by Italy at the Treaty of Versailles in 1919, it now sported the flags and emblems of Mussolini, but its spirit of gaiety and opulence was largely unchanged and many members of the Austro-Hungarian aristocracy had managed to hold onto their villas. My father, though respected at home as an artist and impresario, must have been a parvenu by their standards, but he was graciously accepted once he became the owner of the charming Villa Belvedere, so called because of its wonderful view across the bay of Istria.

My first call upon arriving was always to the garden, a sweet-smelling Eden bursting with delicately scented shrubs and flowers. I would climb high up into our fig tree and pretend I was Jane of Tarzan fame.

I know, of course, that we are given to idealizing the past. 'The good old days' we all remember so well were often nothing of the kind, but Abbazia really was a dream! Tall palm trees lining every path and exotic blooms everywhere.

A picture in an album shows me howling in the water, but I learnt to swim happily enough a few years later in the silken Adriatic sea. And what a thrill it was the first time my instructor took me 'off the hook' and I discovered I was swimming on my own.

Each day we walked through the small resort to the Lido,

a specially imported sandy beach, which had been cleverly laid out between the rocks. The way down to it led through a little park where a band used to play. While I gathered the pistachio nuts that had fallen on the path, munched 'caramelli mandoli' (sugar-coated walnuts on a stick), Bäschen fell in love with, and became engaged to, the leader of the band. After that I could hear her every morning doing slimming exercises in her room.

Poor Bäschen—all that noisy huffing and puffing may have helped her to lose weight, but it did not, after all, get her to the altar. Her Italian lover died of flu the following year. I don't remember sharing in her grief. Selfishly I was too glad she would not be leaving me.

When my brother was twenty-one, my parents gave a ball for him at Villa Belvedere. Almost ill with excitement, I watched the preparations being made. Small as I was, I did my best to help out in the garden. I swept the marble dance floor, supervised the Chinese lanterns, helped to decorate the tables set out on the lawn, and fussed around the specially installed bandstand.

At six o'clock they said I should go to bed and have a nap. I didn't want to miss a moment, but they assured me that no guests would come till after dark.

'And you will wake me up at midnight Bäschen, promise?'

'Of course, of course—now go to bed.'

When I awoke the sun was up. The last guest had left hours before. The debris of the ball was all over the garden. I did not help with the clearing up.

Villa Belvedere was usually filled with summer guests. My father, who loved writing plays but hated writing them alone, always had one or other of his co-authors to visit. My mother invited her family, all of whom brought me toys: a garden swing, a huge teddy bear on whose lap I could sit in my rocking chair, a wooden cannon with exploding shells which I could train on unsuspecting guests—but none of these possessions could outdo the Christmas orange I was given once in Abbazia.

My favourite among my summer friends was Tutzi, orphan grandchild of the verger of the little·church that stood next door to our house. She would come across in her faded cotton dress to play with me, and I would listen eagerly for the soft patter of her bare feet outside my veranda. One year I was getting over a tonsil operation rather slowly and my parents felt that the warmth of an Italian winter would do me good. I looked forward to Christmas with Tutzi. It would not be quite as grand as usual—none of the family were with us—and the house, the tree, and everything would be a little smaller, but there should still be enough glamour left to dazzle her. But Tutzi had no time to come. There was a great deal to be done over Christmas in the little Protestant church and Tutzi had to lend a hand. She worked from early morning until late at night and I hardly saw her.

To make up for it she had me invited to the special children's service a few days after Christmas. Full of suppressed excitement I presented myself at the parsonage door and was taken into the church by a well-scrubbed Tutzi in her Sunday best. I had never seen her wearing shoes before! We sat down at the back of the church, sang Christmas carols in Italian, and listened to the words of the gospel: 'Suffer the little children to come unto me …'. After the sermon all the children were asked to come up to the front, one by one. The pastor had a large basket by his side which was brimming with golden oranges. Each child was told to take one—even me. As I tiptoed back to our pew I thought my heart would burst. I held my precious present tightly in my hand. It made me feel I really did belong.

This was our last holiday in Abbazia. For seven happy years we had passed our summers here. For seven summer seasons my parents had strolled to the Lido Beach to swim with their friends. They had danced on the terrace of the Palast Hotel, driven through the town on flower-covered floats at Carnival time, won dancing competitions, and been crowned with paper crowns as 'Mr and Mrs Abbazia'. It was as well they did. The good time was running out for them.

It was in 1930 that I myself had a taste of impending doom.

From a hoarding near our school a gigantic portrait of a man with a black moustache was staring down at me. It was winter, and some of the boys from my class were hurling stones, disguised as snowballs, at his ugly face.

'That's Adolf Hitler,' they chanted, 'and he is coming to kill all the Jews.' I knew my father was a Jew, and stood and shivered in the snow.

On 19 September 1930, the National Socialist Party increased its representation in the Reichstag from 12 to 107 deputies, making it the second-largest party after the Socialists. Hitler himself was banned from taking his seat because he was an Austrian. There was an uproar at the opening session when the Nazi deputies arrived in their brown uniforms. In spite of this, Hitler was given German nationality. From then on, and throughout the next three years, the Nazis did their utmost to promote political unrest. But although their party was gaining ground by devious and complex political manoeuvres, there were some serious setbacks too. It was not surprising that the ultimate outcome of this struggle was not expected by many people until it was too late.

In 1933, when Marshal Hindenburg became President, Hitler was the head of the largest party in the Reichstag, but he was far from satisfied. Intrigue continued and finally broke the tired old Marshal, who, weary and discouraged, all but gave up the fight. The pressure on him was too strong, the unrest in the land too great. 'The people must decide,' he said, and fixed the date for a plebiscite. On 14 November, 1933, Germans had the chance to vote for Hitler or get rid of the Nazis once and for all.

All day long the voters marched. They carried banners, and red flags with swastikas, and all wore stickers saying 'Yes'. Just underneath our balcony was a halting site where volunteers would hand cold drinks to overheated marchers. We stood on the balcony and watched the endless columns passing beneath us. Martha, our cook for many years, suddenly rushed down to join the marchers—and to vote herself out of a job. Soon my parents would be unable to pay her wages. But she was a simple soul, who did not fully understand what she was doing.

Even before the count was finished Hitler's victory was plain. Huge torchlight processions passed through the city. I could hear the noise of marching feet, and listened to the shouting and singing as I lay in bed.

Next day my father and Carl Meinhard tried to leave the country. They were seized at the frontier and put into jail. My aunts and cousins sat in our drawing-room, endlessly drinking cups of coffee, and talking in frightened whispers as if someone had died. No one told me anything, but I knew. Like most children I always knew exactly what was going on in the house.

A few days later my father and Uncle Carl were released unharmed, but their passports had been confiscated.

It was not long before our German nationality was officially withdrawn. With one stroke of the pen we were stateless and could not leave the country.

Once the Nazis were in power many things began to change for us. Though Hitler's mania would engulf Jews from every walk of life—progressing from the burning of their books to the burning of their people, as Günter Grass described it, initially it was the most prominent who suffered. Overnight my brother Emmerich lost his job as editor. My father's name was taken off every poster, every programme of his productions. His plays and songs were still performed, but not credited to him. Soon his associates were too afraid to give him work in films.

Few of my father's Jewish tenants could now pay him their rents, but even before they had officially come to power, the Nazis had dealt my father a fatal blow. It was the scandal of *All Quiet on the Western Front*. This beautiful film based on the novel by Erich Maria Remarque was first booked by my father in a venue that was part of the theatre complex he owned at Nollendorfplatz. He had spent his available cash converting the Mozartsaal into a cinema. *All Quiet on the Western Front* was expected to run for at least twelve months to bring back this investment. On the opening night a group of Brownshirts, led by Joseph Goebbels, turned up outside the Mozartsaal. They let off stink bombs, and released white mice into the auditorium. The following night they did the same. Father appealed to the Chief of Police, but even he was powerless against the Nazis. The project was abandoned and the entire investment was lost, at a time when my father was not allowed to earn enough to make up for it. Not long after this incident the entire complex at the Nollendorfplatz was auctioned off by the bank for the paltry sum of the outstanding mortgage. A year later, two more of my father's theatres suffered a similar fate.

Now my mother came into her own. With the minimum of fuss she rearranged our lives and cut down expenses. She sent away the cook, and, armed with a cookbook and some Hungarian recipes she had brought back from Abbazia, she calmly took her place. Only once before had mother cooked a meal. She often told the story of that night:

A cook called Maria Schultz had worked for my parents long before I was born. My father gave many lavish dinner parties for private as well as business reasons. Just before one of these dinners Maria fell seriously ill. There were about thirty guests expected and it was unthinkable to cancel the dinner at such short notice. Telephone calls to various domestic agencies had not produced results, and so, in what she later described as a 'blue funk', my mother put on an apron and went into the kitchen. Maria was more distressed than my mother. There seemed to be no calming her. She could not bear the thought of letting people down and she had little confidence in my mother's cooking. It was only when she was told that she could act as a 'back-seat' cook that she followed the doctor's orders and went to bed, but sent exacting instructions to my perspiring mother, and had the maids scurrying to and fro between her small chamber and the kitchen.

A five-course meal eventually arrived with Mother smiling and apparently unruffled at the table. From time to time she made some excuse and left the dining-room hurriedly. None of the guests, who gave the meal their lavish praise, ever knew that Maria had died peacefully before the dessert had reached the table.

Back in the same kitchen after many years my mother did become a splendid cook. I have a little book at home in which she wrote the recipes she had collected; it is old, fading, and falling apart, and I keep it in a plastic case. I often search its crumbling pages for some dish or other I remember well.

We could no longer stay in our twelve-room flat and moved into a smaller one. I have to smile when I think that we called it 'small'; by most standards it was palatial. But we could not take all our furniture with us, and since we needed ready cash, we had a sale before we moved away. The dealers came and haggled over, and finally carted away, some of our prize possessions. Most of my books I sold for pocket-money, and my dollhouse was given away. At the end of that exhausting day we packed our bags and left the house forever. We could not know that it would not survive. Its splendid stucco body perished in the war. All that is left to remind me is a photograph, provided by the Stadverwaltung Schöneberg, and a small drawing done by Erich Kästner. This shows the bank on the corner where *Emil and the Detectives* caught their thief. Just above the bank he has drawn my mother's bedroom window, with its odd scalloped curtains. How that little drawing used to intrigue my children later on in London, when I read them bedtime stories.

It would not be true to say that I was unhappy in our new surroundings. However disturbed my parents must have been during the 'nazification' of our lives, a child of my age could cope much better. Children rarely look too far ahead or take too many backward glances. To me, life appeared to go on much as before. We had remained in Schöneberg. My father's plays and musicals still brought us enough money to live on and though I had to pass the horrid pictures in *Der Stürmer*, the Nazi paper, with Jews depicted like ghouls, which were put up on corners of our street, I could still stroll to school each day through the Stadpark Schöneberg. By now the school I walked to every morning was the Rückert Lyceum, a high school for girls, very different from the one I had known before. There were at least five hundred pupils, and whereas Fraülein Zickel's private school took up only one floor, this one took up a whole building. It had five floors, big, airy classrooms, wide corridors, drinking fountains on each landing, a music room, a painting room, a playground where we spent our breaks and a large assembly hall.

There is a good description of the school in Hildegard Kneff's book, *The Gift Horse*. Until I read this, I did not know that she had been at my school, a year ahead of me. All things considered, I enjoyed the school as much as any I went to. I got used to giving the Hitler salute, right arm raised, each time I passed a teacher in the corridor. This was the rule, and I learnt to cope with it as with other 'Third Reich Regulations'. I tried my hardest not to be different, but more than that, I longed to wear a uniform and march behind a flag like all the other girls. Since I could not join the Hitler Youth, I joined the VDA, a spurious association for Germans abroad, when my form mistress suggested it. I was not a German any more, and not yet 'abroad', but now I had a uniform—a skirt and tie just like the Hitlermädchen in my class—though mine was blue, not black like theirs. I even marched behind the flag on 'Demonstration Sundays', but deep inside of me I must have felt some guilt, for one day I stopped conforming.

Not long after the Nazis came to power, our Protestant pastor was removed from his teaching post, and the singing master Herr Kölle was given his classes. Herr Kölle was a rabid Nazi, knew nothing about the spiritual side of any religion, and spent his time ranting about the evils of Freemasonry and the iniquity of the Catholic Church. This had the opposite effect on me to that which was intended.

If Catholics are Christians like ourselves, I thought, how can they be so evil? I sought out the small number of Catholic pupils in our school, and began to question them. One of the group, a tall, handsome girl called Gisela, who was in a higher class, became my friend. I started to go to Mass with her, as I had often done with Martha, our cook, and Maria, our parlour maid. One day, kneeling in front of the altar rails, I saw what appeared to be a glowing flame beckoning me from the holy book. It seemed to call me to join the Faith. 'Well, and why not?' I thought. This church is not a sect, or breakaway religion started by some mortal man. It seemed to me a fairly safe commitment to be a Catholic, even though the beckoning flame on the Bible was probably nothing more than a reflection of the candle on its metal mount.

How much guilty embarrassment was involved in my decision to change my religion, I can never be sure of. I had watched as the Jewish pupils at my school had to leave one by one while I was protected by my father's foreign birth. Whenever he filled in the countless questionnaires that parents had to answer in those days about the 'purity of blood', he always put 'Hung-aryan' in the space provided, and since we always got away with this rather doubtful joke, I soon became the only non-Aryan pupil at the school.

When I told father of my decision to become a Catholic he did not seem at all displeased. He told me that for some time now he himself had been taking instruction from a Berlin friar, Pater Rauterkus. He had kept this very quiet; not even mother knew. He did this because he had never been able to shake off his monastic upbringing in Budapest. I don't believe the Jewish community has ever forgiven him: his name is never mentioned in any book or publication that celebrates prominent German Jews.

My headmaster's reaction to the news was very different. Here he was, sheltering an undesirable—a non-Aryan blot on his otherwise pure establishment—and here I was deliberately adding another stigma to myself. He urged me to reconsider. The Catholic Church was not popular with the Nazis. I myself had often witnessed the arrest of our local priest after Sunday Mass by men in Nazi uniforms who had been sitting in the front pews, busily transcribing the sermon in shorthand. I stuck to my guns, secretly delighting in the headmaster's discomfiture.

My mother was now the only Protestant in our household, and when she took me on holiday back to Abbazia in 1938 to stay with friends, our hostess Margit Neuhausler, who was taking instruction in Catholicism, persuaded my mother to do the same. When they 'graduated' from their class there was a ceremony in the local church. The dozen or so Jewish converts were to be baptized together. I was to be my mother's godmother. We waited by the font, holding candles. Suddenly the priest beckoned to my mother. He had only just realized that as a Protestant, she would have been baptized already. This put her in a different position to the other converts, whose sins would now be washed away by the holy sacrament. He told her she would have to go to confession, but since she had not been instructed my mother did not know what to do. After what seemed an age she rejoined us by the font, sputtering with rage. At fifty-one she had had a lifetime to confess. But her dismay was nothing compared with that of her Jewish companions who felt deprived and discriminated against.

Years later, I woke up one night and thought: 'My parents are living in sin! Both of them are now Catholics and should be married in a church.' I spoke to them severely the very next day and they agreed that I should go and see the priest in our local London church. 'And how long have your parents been living in sin?' asked the priest. 'Thirty-five years, father,' I answered him. 'Go home,' he said gently. 'They are married.'

In 1934 my father was called to Vienna to work on a film script with his friend Rudolf Oesterreicher. Austria had not yet been annexed by Hitler and was still counted as 'abroad'. He realized that he would need a travel document. He called the Hungarian consulate in the hope that they would give him a passport. Twenty years earlier he had given up his Hungarian nationality. Living, working and owning property in Berlin had made it simpler to be German. He had been home once as a young man to do his military service, but the consul could not help him unless he could prove that he had been back to Hungary during those twenty years for even just one day.

He came home to us sadly, but my mother was optimistic. Had he forgotten how they had gone to Budapest for the opening of one of his plays? Did he not remember the argument they had? She wanted to go—he didn't. They had gone.

My father hurried back to the consulate. 'Good, good,' the consul beamed, 'but prove it! The official entry stamp must be in one of your passports!' But German passports were always called in when they were out of date. There were millions of them stored in the cellars of the Reichstag building in Berlin.

Once more my father called on the chief of police. This time his old friend was able to help. Two policemen were sent into the cellars to search for the passport. It took some time, but to everyone's relief they found what they were looking for.

Our family, including Emmerich and Edith, were given new papers at the Hungarian consulate. I do not like to think

36

what our fate would have been if the passport had not been found!

Now that we had papers we could travel abroad again. Emmerich and Edith went to Holland. Father went to Vienna, but later that summer he met us in Bad Ischl, a charming Austrian resort, very popular with the composers and librettists of Viennese operettas. Many of them had summer houses there. At the time we stayed with Rudolf Schanzer, with whom my father had written several plays. Uncle Rudie was as kind as he was witty, and it was good that we spent that summer of 1935 together, for we never saw him again. He was murdered by the Nazis in Italy, where he had fled shortly before the war.

That holiday stays in my mind for many reasons. It was a kind of watershed for me, an interlude between childhood and adolescence. The experiences of the past three years had made me grow up faster than other children of the same age. I was not much more than twelve years old, but I was already thinking seriously about the problems of our lives. I would take solitary walks to work things out. I did not share my father's view that the Nazis were a passing phase. More than my father at that time, I was in touch with life in Germany. Bad things were happening to Jews, yet I never noticed anybody objecting.

There was no doubt in my mind that since I had one Jewish parent, I would never be allowed to work as an actress. I begged my father to leave Germany for good, then I could finish school abroad, and learn to speak a foreign language properly, without an accent. An accent, I knew well, would be a serious handicap. I did not fancy playing comical French maids or foreign-sounding gypsies all my life!

My father, who could never deny me anything, hesitated only briefly. He was now in his fifties; it would not be easy for him to start again—and in a foreign language! A few weeks later he was on his way to London.

For the moment, my mother and I had to stay behind. Since no one was allowed to take money out of the country, he pawned the gold watch he carried on his wrist for ready cash in England. He would have to earn a great deal more to keep the three of us.

That year I waved goodbye to many friends who went abroad ahead of us, not only Jewish ones. My friend Maria had sailed to America some time previously on a glamorous ocean liner with her glamorous mama. They were on their way to Hollywood. I was sent wonderful accounts of this enviable journey written by her mother in green ink—she had once been a young aspiring actress at my father's theatre. The first time I saw her, she was standing in the tiny kitchen of her Berlin flat, making sandwiches for Maria's seventh birthday party. She wore a white overall, and her beautiful face, devoid of any make-up, was framed by a halo of shiny golden hair. I have always remembered that moment as The First Time I Saw Marlene Dietrich, though I could not then have known that she would become a superstar in Hollywood.

I have had similar experiences with other famous people. When we lived in Victoria Luise Platz, I used to love sitting on the wide window ledge in our dining-room, watching the street below. Every afternoon, at three o'clock, an elderly couple passed beneath our window. The man had wild grey hair and an unruly grey moustache. There was no way in which I could have understood his importance or the meaning of his work, and yet in the computer of my mind these moments were recorded as: When I Saw Albert Einstein Passing By.

My father was beginning to earn enough money in London, ghost-writing film scripts for English productions, to allow him to look for a suitable boarding-school for me. I recently came across a letter I wrote him at that time. I cannot imagine how he put up with its pomposity even in its original language:

Geliebter Pappi,
Your evaluations and the headmistress's letter to you astonished and disappointed me considerably. The vision these conjure up of the school in Berkhamstead little resembles that which I gained during our conversations on the subject, nor does it comply with the vision of what I consider desirable in my present situation, or for my future plans. Such a school, it strikes me, I could attend as a day-girl, without having to part from you in London, as there must be of necessity many such large establishments there. Everything I have gleaned about this school tells me that it is meant for English pupils

only, and that I could never hope to forge a true relationship with the curriculum, would lose all confidence and fall hopelessly behind. And, since I am someone who is really concerned to learn, I beg you to abandon your well-meant plan to send me to this large establishment.

I blush to think my father actually kept this dreadful letter to the end of his life. I remember that he answered it kindly and found me a smaller school.

Of course it is much easier to be pompous in German! I fancied myself as a poet in those days, and would scatter my literary pearls around with indiscriminate abandon. I wrote a poem which began, 'Oh man, you being—helpless—small ...' and gave it to my father for his birthday; he kept a straight face. I wrote an ode which started, 'I am trying to forget you, yet my efforts are in vain,' and presented it to our French teacher, who was recovering from a nervous breakdown.

The school my father ultimately chose was Holmwood, in north London. It more or less 'complied with my vision' because it was small and cosy. Amongst its former pupils, I have since discovered, was Christabel Bielenberg, the author of *The Past is Myself*.

Shortly before I left Germany, my mother took me to see a march of Hitler and his notorious storm-troopers. We joined the crowds that were lining the pavements on Unter den Linden, and as he came past, standing in an open car, arm raised in his famous salute, we were close enough to touch him. 'I could kill him now if I had a gun,' I thought.

We had seen Hitler only in photographs and news-reels, looking sallow with his black moustache and hair falling over his ugly face. We were not prepared for the difference it made to see him in colour rather than in black and white. His light blue eyes, his pink complexion, and above all, his auburn hair made him look much less repulsive than we expected. We knew that his mass appeal lay in his talent for rabble-rousing, but we had never understood why his physical appearance had not put off the 'rabble'. Now we knew. I hate to admit it, but Hitler was almost attractive when you saw him in real life.

I was now getting excited at the thought of going to London. Boarding-schools and school uniforms were not then part of the German experience, except for the daughters of the aristocracy, who were sent away to school to be 'finished'. I had romantic notions about such finishing-schools, fed to me by a diet of teenage novels in which the beautiful, blonde heroine goes to a school in an ancient château, discovers buried treasure in the cellar, gets trapped down there and is finally rescued by the handsome nephew of the principal. Holmwood School in Finchley was not quite like that, I suspected, and when the clothes list arrived, I knew. I had only recently been allowed to lower my hem-line and wear silk stockings. Imagine my dismay when I read that I was expected to wear black lisle stockings, a black velour hat, a very short gym-slip, and flat-heeled, heavy, lace-up shoes. There was also the mention of a blazer. There is a word in German that sounds exactly the same. It is spelled *bläser*, and means trumpeter, or herald. 'Good heavens,' said my mother, 'does this mean you'll need a chap with a trumpet to walk ahead of you, calling: "Taratata—here comes Agnes!"?'

My mother gave up the flat in the Innsbrucker Strasse, sent the furniture into storage in London, and installed herself in the only Jewish boarding-house left in Berlin. I said farewell to my classmates, who clubbed together and bought me an ivory necklace. Both Veras wept buckets and one of them inherited my male budgerigar who promptly laid an egg. It was autumn 1936 when my mother took me across the sea to England.

III

Soon after we arrived we drove over to Finchley. As we got out of the taxi, I saw a grey-haired lady in a short gym-slip in the front garden of Holmwood School. She was viciously attacking a small white ball with a curved wooden stick; she called out to me in an incomprehensible stream of syllables ending with dribbling … dribbling … dribbling. Dribbling was in fact the first English word I learnt.

My parents left and I was taken to the principal's private drawing-room. Presently I was enfolded in the musty embrace of this ancient lady, who still wore ankle-length Edwardian dresses and had a preference for foreign 'gels'. Fierce as she could be with 'native' pupils, she always made allowances for me. If I as much as sneezed, she called for the doctor; if she took us on an outing it was always I who rode with her in the hired Daimler; and how she liked to show me off on Parents' Day! Poor Miss Patch, I did not make it easy for her.

At Christmastime we always had an exhibition and parents came to see our 'work': handcrafts, painting, needlework, book-cover illustrations. My contribution in my second year was the cover design for an imaginary novel called 'Fatal Lady'. It showed a mini-skirted blonde in fishnet stockings, perched cross-legged on a globe. A number of males were dangling from each hand like puppets on a string. Miss Patch hurried some important parents past my masterpiece and steered them towards the woodwork display. There, in the centre of the table, was the box I had fashioned for my father's collar studs. It showed a naked nymph in hot pursuit of an escaping satyr.

By then the other girls had grown accustomed to my 'continental' ways, but on my first night in the 'dorm' it had been another story. I did not speak a word of English, but I wanted badly to communicate. I remembered a song my father had once taught me, parrot fashion. 'As I walk along the Bois de Boulogne,' I began to sing, 'with an independent air,' I sauntered up and down the middle of the dormitory, '… you can hear the girls declare … he must be a millionaire …'. I swung my towel with great enthusiasm, hitting a senior girl in the eye. '… You can hear them sigh and wish to die … you can see them wink the other eye,' I winked, '… that's the man who broke the bank at Monte Carlo!' The other girls were not amused. To show off in this way and to display one's middle-European vulgarity was simply not done in the London of the 1930s.

The mistress on duty saved me from further embarrassment by coming in and turning off the lights and closing the door behind her. In an instant all was commotion and flashing lights. Torches were brandished. Girls in pyjamas flitted from bed to bed, and I did my best to join in. Suddenly we heard footsteps coming up the stairs. Torches were turned off. The girls leapt back into their beds. I did the same. The others knew the distance in the dark, but I had no such experience. I jumped into bed on one side, overshot, and fell out again on the other, crashing against my washstand. Something broke with a sickening crunch—was it my back? The mistress switched on the light and examined the damage. The iron towel rack, against which I had flung myself so recklessly in the dark, was broken. The only mark on my back was an enormous bruise.

I could not have done anything better to be 'accepted' at Holmwood. For days queues formed outside our dormitory. Everybody wanted to see the amazing back that could shatter iron. Delighted, I sat on my bed, clothes and underwear raised over my head, while the inspections took place. I added 'iron' and 'bruise' to my vocabulary. The language barrier no longer mattered.

I soon found out that I could make myself understood by using both French and German words, giving them English-sounding endings. It was the mixture of Saxon and Norman origins of the English language that came to my aid, though I myself did not understand very much of what was said to me. And then came the day when we opened our *Henry V* school edition in English class.

'O for a Muse of fire ...' begins the chorus on page one. The Shakespeare school textbooks are heavily annotated in the margins. Without these notes my English classmates would not have understood much more than I did. I stared at the first page, and in an instant, like a bolt from the sky, I was struck with perfect understanding of that speech. It was as if I had known this ancient tongue in another life. From that moment on, three weeks into term, I was able to speak English.

I could not resist trying to re-educate everyone during my first term. Their quaint English ways seemed ridiculous to me. Eating peas off the underside of the fork, slurping soup from rounded spoons, and, worst of all, not to be allowed to mention any part of your body below the waist—what nonsense! Vera Callmann, who had followed me to Holmwood School, had a stomach-ache. What was the point in mincing words? It was her stomach that was troubling her, I told Miss Patch. But she was shocked at my use of that word at table. Obstinately, she insisted on these antiquated manners, and in the end I abandoned my attempt to bring enlightenment and logic to the school. By the second term I had even acquired a kind of serenity. My continental contrariness had been knocked out of me, and I became docile and compliant— even popular I think. My nickname at school was 'Hardy' of 'Kiss Me Hardy' fame! This did not mean that we were lesbians, and though we did develop strong passions in our middle teens, these were directed not at pupils but at staff. I, for example, adored the drama teacher.

In my three years at Holmwood my air of innocence kept me out of trouble. No one credited me with some of the practical jokes I used to play. I learnt to imitate Matron's handwriting, and on the occasional days when she was indisposed and confined to her room, I would plaster the school with directives signed by her. 'This toilet is broken and is not to be used until further notice,' it said once on every lavatory door. That day I was the only person in the school who was not in terrible discomfort.

When I was not busy putting sherbet powder into the junior boarders' chamber-pots, I was writing 'operas' using hit songs of the time, based on the plays of Shakespeare. To the tune of 'Oh I must phone Annie tonight' I had Lady Macbeth warble, 'Oh we must kill Duncan tonight—I will make his servants tight!' or 'Duncan now is murdered, I know what we'll do, we will wash this blood off right away, come to bed now soldier, little man, you've had a busy day!' The guests at the banquet exclaimed, 'Two lovely meat pies! (Two lovely black eyes)', to which the ghost of Banquo replied, 'Heaven, I'm in heaven, and I am so dead that I can hardly speak, you will never find the happiness you seek ....'

We performed these in the dorm after our end-of-term midnight feast, and sometimes the gym mistress came and joined us. It was a far cry from the débacle of 'The man who broke the bank at Monte Carlo', and showed how well I had travelled the road towards integration.

Of course, I was still determined to produce my literary masterpiece. In my new language I was no longer quite as reckless in trying to write poetry, but prose was another matter. I was reasonably confident that I could write novels. Didn't I often get top marks in English, and have some of my essays read out in class?

"What exactly do you mean by disregarding my orders?" Fitzgerald's fist banged on the table. "They were expecting you with the explosives in Camden Town!"

I came across this gem recently in an old exercise book. What I thought I was doing writing about the IRA I can't imagine. I knew nothing about Ireland, had never been there, and the only Irish person I had ever met was Miss Entrican, our science teacher, with whom I was on the worst possible terms. She had a very beautiful, low voice, which invariably put me to sleep during her classes. She believed—falsely as it happens—that I was bored by her subject, or her method of teaching, and began to persecute me. I retaliated promptly. When I came top in science at the end of the summer term Miss Entrican nearly had a seizure. Since I had been banished from her physics class for insolence, and since I had spent most of that time upstairs in the dorm reading Agatha Christie, I was supposed to fail.

While Miss Entrican was forever suspicious of me, Matron, with far more justification, never was. When we had a rash of minor thefts in the school, Matron really came into her own. She would line us up in the dining-room and berate us ferociously, threatening God knows what punishment if the culprit did not own up. I was amazed years later, when I had tea with Miss Patch, to be told that all the missing items had been found in Matron's own room, including a staggering number of packets of sanitary towels.

We still could not afford to have my mother join us in London, in part because she had to be in Germany to collect my father's income from his continental publishers. On one summer holiday, when I went to Germany to visit her, I sailed on the *Bremen*, a splendid ocean liner on the last lap of a homeward journey from South Africa. After we left Southampton we hit a ferocious storm, and the fog and the wind kept us marooned in the English Channel for an extra fourteen hours. While my mother had visions of her little darling spending a horrid night being seasick alone in her cabin, her little darling was dancing the night away with a group of handsome German students on a dance-floor that looked like a boxing ring, surrounded as it was by heavy ropes.

Back at Holmwood, while I progressed in leaps and bounds in my use of English, my French, learnt in Berlin, was deteriorating fast. This was not the fault of Mademoiselle, who came every Friday to teach us the language. As usual I wanted to conform and—illogical and silly as this was—I longed to speak French with the same faulty grammar and English accent as my classmates.

Mademoiselle and I were the only Catholics in the school. Committed to abstain from meat on a Friday before the ban was lifted, we could not have the steak and kidney pudding, which filled the dining-room with such a mouth-watering aroma once a week on that day. Instead we were given a green, suspiciously unwashed-looking salad, topped by a cold and jellified substance, which, the cook assured us, had started out as 'egg'.

For strategic reasons I was placed beside Mademoiselle at table, and I remember once watching with horrified fascination as she manoeuvred her fork past her feather boa and swallowed the caterpillar that had made his home on a lettuce leaf.

The feather boa was part of Mademoiselle's distinctive dress. She was a real period piece. Her high-necked, ankle-length, brown crèpe-de-Chine dress encased an hourglass figure, which owed its shape to some fancy whalebone stays of the kind we had not seen since *Gone with the Wind*. The brown feather boa, forever tickling her nostrils, concealed the wrinkles on her aged neck, and her heavily painted face looked out from underneath a coal-black curly wig.

I shuddered to think what she must have looked like stripped of all her finery, and I tried to picture her seated at her dressing-table, a scrawny old crone with a few wisps of white hair, much like the countess in the opera *The Queen of Spades*.

Mademoiselle loved the English gutter press, and conducted her lunchtime lessons in the dining-room entirely by way of the daily papers. She also adored violence, and always managed to find accounts of horrendous assaults and accidents which we had to translate into French then and there. She revelled in gory descriptions of people being torn limb from limb, and children being mauled by angry lions through the bars of cages at the zoo, but above all she loved sex. Jane of *The Daily Mirror* was our staple diet at mealtime. This alluring, blonde cartoon heroine was usually shown wearing the scantiest of black lace undies, and being observed by men with binoculars: '"Jeanne a perdu son soutien-gorge." Répètez après moi, Aniez,' Mademoiselle would boom as the soup arrived, 'What 'as she lost?'—'Her bra Mademoiselle,' I would answer correctly. By the time we reached the custard and prunes, Jane was in the bathtub, without even her soutien-gorge. 'Elle est tout à fait nue, she ees all nakid Aniez, un Monsieur la regarde par la fenêtre, a gentilman ees regarding 'er through the window ...'. Miss Patch, sitting at the next table, may have cringed, but she never did anything to stop Mademoiselle. After all, she was only bringing us culture.

If Miss Patch made decisions which were contradictory, it was because she had a touching ignorance of the ways of the world. She allowed us out of school each summer under the most bizarre conditions. We all had white piqué mini-dresses to play tennis at school. Those of us who had small bosoms and long legs looked downright sexy in those outfits. Each summer, Miss Patch would rent a coach and send her seniors off to Wimbledon in these provocative clothes, chaperoned only by one hapless teacher, and without tickets for any of the courts. We would scatter in all directions as soon as we arrived, determined to pick up any man who looked as if he might buy us strawberries and cream and let us use his ticket for the Centre Court.

The girls in my dormitory had formed great relationships with the choirboys at the local church by means of nods and winks during Sunday service. This had developed into dropping little billets-doux in the aisle and picking the answers up surreptitiously. At the same time, Jonathan, the local dentist's son, had taken to standing underneath our window and shouting, rather than whispering, sweet nothings at Yvonne Mackintosh. These scandalous goings on were discovered and there was consternation in the drawing-room. Miss Patch issued dire instructions from that hallowed place. We were never to be left alone again. Some member of staff was to be with us in the rooms at all times. I was righteously indignant to be lumped together with the real offenders. After all, though I may have helped to compose some of the love notes, I had not attended the Anglican services, and Jonathan was far too spotty for my taste. I much preferred the youth who sold the tickets at the tiny local railway station, who always slipped me a sugar heart with my return ticket from Woodside Park to Finchley Road at weekends. My father suggested I should consider the punishment as payment for something naughty I had really done, which had not come to light. 'That way you won't mind so much,' he said. It was a useful suggestion which I still follow on occasions.

Although my father had found work in London, writing scripts and directing B-pictures, as these low-budget films were called, his earnings were not spectacular. He had to maintain himself and pay for my school fees. He had only been able to take a two-room flat in a house in Golders Green, where I spent weekends and half-term holidays with him. There was not much room, and even less money, for my mother, who had to pass most of the time in the Berlin boarding-house, spending what was still coming in from my father's publishers on her own upkeep and on such items as clothes for me and father. Sometimes she came over to London to be with him. Not being Jewish herself, she had nothing to fear by going to and fro, or so we thought.

I benefited from this arrangement. To use up more of the German money, mother took me on lovely holidays. We went to Lake Balaton, to Bad Kissingen, the famous spa, and even once more to Abbazia. Another time we met father in Amsterdam to visit Emmerich. He was writing revues for Rudolf Nelson, which were staged at the Tuschinsky Palast Cabaret. Every three weeks Emmerich had to write a new edition, and I can't imagine how he did this without going off his head!

Emmerich was particularly gifted in this genre, and I can still quote from his hilarious rhymes. Unfortunately, like most of the really clever wordsmiths, he cannot be translated. When he left Nelson and went to the United States he never wrote another line. Even if the new language had not hampered him, I can't help feeling that he had exhausted that particular talent in Amsterdam. When I said goodbye to him and Edith in Amsterdam I could not have foreseen that more than twenty years would pass before we would meet again. They sailed from Europe before the war could trap them and deliver them back into the Nazis' hands. They arrived in California by way of Cuba, Florida and New York. There, after twenty years of marriage, they produced a daughter, Evelyn, and, to their own amazement, bought a house and settled down. I was well into my thirties before I went to stay with them.

In many ways I was more worldly than other children of my generation. From the age of nine I tried to copy my father and his colleagues by writing *risqué* songs and sketches. I knew quite a bit about the world, although nobody had ever told me anything directly. Perhaps it was understandable that the grown-ups in our house, where much was freely discussed, did not always notice the small girl hanging around with eyes and ears open to pick up every scrap of scandal. I knew about the female cousin who had been 'allocated' to my Uncle Kurt in a house of ill repute. I met the six-foot lady my mother had befriended in hospital, who had gone there to have a sex-change operation. I knew that when she was invited to convalesce in our flat she was caught chasing cousin Kate around the grand piano. In spite of all this I managed to remain a virgin until I met Desmond Leslie at the age of twenty, and I was incredibly naive in many ways when I began to attract the attention of the opposite sex.

In my early teens I lost my heart to Roger Graf von Norman, a constant visitor to our household. Though he was very young he was in love with my mother. She was clearly flattered by his attentions, but did not take him seriously. Roger was in the Nazi party, and the bizarre situation would occur, that he would arrive in our flat on the Innsbrucker Strasse in a brown uniform, a swastika on his red arm band, with a large bouquet of roses, having just stood guard outside some Jewish shop to stop people going in. He was always much put out when my mother wouldn't ask him to stay for tea on these occasions.

I remember that I attracted men when I was just thirteen; no wonder, then, that I did not understand them. On holidays at Balatonföldvar in Hungary, when dancing with a young man, I found it odd that he should carry what I thought to be a 'torch' in his trouser pocket.

At Bad Kissingen, a chap by the name of Hasso von Kösling attached himself to mother and me. We met every evening in the Municipal Gardens to walk about and take the waters. It never occurred to me that he did not come there because of my mother. She had always been a beautiful woman, and men were drawn to her until she was well into her seventies. One day, she came down with gastric flu. 'Hasso will be waiting,' I said. 'Then off you go and don't mind me,' my mother said and went to bed.

This should have been the young man's wish fulfilled. The moon was full, the jasmin was in bloom, romance and sweet perfume were in the air. He could hardly believe his good fortune when his beloved, hitherto so heavily chaperoned, came towards him on her own, her silken locks and chiffon gown ruffled gently by the breeze. He held his breath. 'My mother has the runs and cannot come!' the vision blurted out—and fled.

By the time we spent a last summer in Abbazia, I was fifteen. I had my first proposal of marriage from an Italian prince, but fell in love with a thirty-nine-year-old Viennese dentist who was between concentration camp and emigration.

He was one of the lucky-Jews who had been released from a camp and deported to Italy. While he was waiting for a visa to the States—an American woman friend had offered to marry him to bring him there—he was getting a suntan on the Lido. I admired his trim figure and good looks and refused to notice the bald patch that was starting on the back of his head. I lost my appetite and started to pine on the rare days when I did not manage to bump into him on the Lido or the promenade.

I knew that he was fond of dancing and so I made my friend Luciana—who was 'already' seventeen—take me to the tea-dance at Hübner's Grand Hotel. He was there all right—with the well-dressed redhead I had seen him with before. Someone asked me to waltz. On the way to the dance-floor, as we passed his table, I stuck out my tongue at him.

Looking back, I feel convinced that he was having an affair with this attractive woman twice my age. Nevertheless, he must have been flattered by my adoration, for, in spite of my infantile behaviour at the tea-dance, he asked me to meet him in the park one night.

I made an excuse to our hostess and slipped out. The night was dark, the air was soft. This time I did not blow it. I let myself be kissed. It was my first real kiss, tongue and all— and I fainted clean away.

When I recovered and he had walked me back to the house where we were staying, I crept up the stairs avoiding the grown-ups in the drawing-room. My heart was beating like a drum. Did it show? Could they tell? Was I now one of them? I could not have felt more guilty if I had lost my virginity. When we left Abbazia, my dentist gave me a snapshot of himself, upside-down, doing handstands on the Lido. I never heard from him again, but the snapshot, pressed tightly against my heart, would console me through the nights of terror in the London Blitz.

We came home that summer to the anxiety of the Munich meeting between Hitler and Neville Chamberlain. Czechoslovakia had been overrun by the Germans and most people in Britain expected to go to war.

My father was one of the few who always defended Chamberlain. England had not been ready for war, he would say afterwards, and Chamberlain had deliberately won a year's respite for the country to begin to arm. It is conceivable that my father was right about that. After all he had never been insensitive to the fate of small nations. The day Hitler invaded Austria he was having his lunch in a restaurant on the Golders Green Road. Suddenly he heard a tumultuous noise. It sounded to him as if thousands of voices were shouting and chanting. When he went outside, he found nothing but a half-empty street. The waiters he questioned thought him very odd. They had not heard any noise. It was the very hour that Hitler entered Vienna, the city where my grandmother was born.

For the time being Britain was not at war and I started on my final year at Holmwood.

War was declared the day my exam results were due. On the fourth of September 1939 I stood outside the house in Golders Green to await the postman, while indoors my parents listened to the news.

It was a miracle that we were all together at that moment. Only a week or so before my father had been abroad, while I was staying with some family friends at a charming little château at Chatou. I was to have remained there a year to perfect my French. While the heads of governments were wheeling and dealing about the fate of Europe, I was on a blissful camping holiday with the children of my hosts. Our tent was pitched near the beach at Cabourg. Since we had forgotten to take the containers of drinking water Tante Madeleine had so carefully prepared for us, we had to make do with the red plonk we had remembered to bring. We did everything with it—the rinsing, the washing-up, our teeth— and were in a permanent state of intoxication. I remember that Tante Madeleine screamed when she opened the door to us on our return and saw me with purple cheeks swollen by bee stings, and all of us reeling from the wine. Uncle Jean, her husband, who had been with us as chaperone, had a great deal of explaining to do, but was cut short by the interesting item on the radio—Hitler and Stalin had signed a non-aggression pact.

There was some rejoicing at this news amongst my French friends, but I went upstairs to pack. I felt sure this was some clever ploy of Hitler's to give him a chance to invade the Russians. Reluctantly Uncle Jean and Tante Madeleine drove me to Paris, and put me on the boat-train. They thought I was foolish to leave Chatou after only two months—but a week later I would not have been allowed back into England. The Hungarians joined the German side and I became an enemy alien.

My mother's arrival in London a short time before me had been even more dramatic. She had not been due to visit us until later that year.

Rummaging through some old trunks after her death, I came across a photograph of a distinguished-looking old gentleman. It had an inscription to my mother, in German, and was signed, 'Ever yours, Gottfried von Eckerhardt.' I was amazed that my mother had kept it all this time and had packed it away so carefully, knowing who and what this man had stood for. She must have done it out of gratitude for the part he had played in her timely escape from Berlin. I knew him quite well before the war, this dapper little man who was so full of old-world charm and yet so very dangerous. Whenever I came to join my mother in Berlin on my school holidays, he would shower me with sweets and little presents. It now seems incredible that none of us ever questioned the presence of this 'Aryan' junker in the Jewish boarding-house. Apart from him and my mother, the other residents were all Jews and were staying only to await their exit visas.

One fateful day in the summer of 1939, Herr von Eckerhardt invited my mother out to dinner. Bored and lonely, my mother was only too delighted to accept the invitation, but when they reached the restaurant, her expectations of a pleasant meal were rudely dashed. Two sinister men in SS uniforms were already seated at their table. Introductions over, the two strangers ordered their expensive meal and turned their attentions to my mother.

'We know all about you,' they told her. 'You have a Jewish husband in London, and a half-Jewish child in an English school.' The waiter brought the soup, but my mother had lost her appetite. 'We'll give you a chance to redeem yourself. We know that you make several trips to London each year, and that you always bring presents with you when you go. All we ask is that you take some papers and small packages from time to time, and deliver them to our people in London. You will not be suspected.'

Unable to swallow a single bite, my mother got up from the table. 'You must excuse me, but I am not feeling very well.' She left the restaurant as fast as her shaking legs could carry her. Outside stood a large black limousine. The two SS men managed to overtake her. 'Allow us to drive you home,' they said, bowing deeply and clicking their heels. One of them opened the car door, and the other took her hand and pressed a large roll of banknotes into it. Almost paralyzed with fear, she let the banknotes fall to the ground. The two men bent down to gather up their money. This was my mother's chance. She raced through the Stadtpark, which separated the town hall from the part of Schöneberg where her boarding-house was situated. Fortunately there was no road for traffic through the park. Mother ran for dear life and managed to reach the house before the limousine, panted up the stairs, grabbed her winter coat and passport and took a taxi to the station. In mortal fear she spent the night in the waiting-room, watching the door. Nobody came for her. She caught the first train out of Berlin thinking they would stop her at the frontier, but neither the SS men nor Herr von Eckerhardt had expected her to act so quickly.

My mother arrived in London the next day collapsing into her astonished husband's arms. The doctor was called. She was too ill for many days to tell him what had happened. A short time after she recovered the Germans marched into Poland.

After the declaration of war, there followed a few months of inaction. Both Britain and Germany were poised for air attacks but nothing much happened until the winter. We were all issued gas masks and given the drill of how to behave in an air raid. As an enemy alien there was not much I was allowed to do for the war effort, so I became a temporary nanny to two little boys. I was pushing baby Michael's pram around the playground and keeping an eye on John, his elder brother, who was flying a kite, when a German bomber appeared in the skies over London. The air raid sirens began to wail, and we made for the communal shelter, me feeling very responsible for the safety of my two small charges. When their mother arrived in the shelter, I was quite put out that she had not trusted me to 'save them' from the German bombs.

This was the first of the heavy air raids we lived through during the early years of the war. I used to sit under the kitchen table and tremble as the horrible screaming bombs came roaring down from the sky. I felt totally trapped and could not imagine how I would survive the terror and mental anguish of this situation, even if I was not killed. We have all seen pictures and news-reels of refugees trying to escape from somebody's bomb attacks, and watched the slow moving columns of ragged and scared humanity. Sitting under a table gave an even greater feeling of helplessness and despair. Living on an island, there was nowhere to escape to.

One night, when I was particularly terrified, I climbed to a little room at the top of our house. It was the only room without black-out material on the windows and therefore had to be kept in total darkness. I put my hand out to reach into my bookcase where I had stowed my schoolbooks, and came away with the Acts of the Apostles. I took the book downstairs to the light and opened it at random. 'Not a hair of your head shall be harmed,' I read, and a marvellous feeling of reassurance came over me. I knew then that I would be spared. I never again felt fear and went calmly through the Blitz and the subsequent attacks by doodle-bugs and V2 rockets, even when the house would shake and tremble, incendiaries would land in the back garden, and the motor of the doodle-bugs would stop just above my head. My parents, who had not received the divine message, decided to join those citizens of London who made the trek to the Underground to shelter, sitting on cold platforms with nothing but a sheet of newspaper between stone and their bottoms. Later on in the war, the London County Council erected proper bunks in the tube stations and allocated these to people who applied for them. Some Londoners spent years sleeping below the streets of their city, while the more reckless waited for the trains to take them into the West End for a night out amid the noise and dangers of falling bombs, or to take them back again to the uneasy comforts of their own beds at home. I owed my place amongst them to my mother's mink.

My parents, who had left behind so much in Germany, naturally cherished the few treasures they had been able to save. Fearing that they might return from the tube shelters in the early morning and find their little house bombed to bits, they decided to preserve what they could easily take with them. The treasures moved to the tube every night consisted of myself, my father's fur-lined winter coat with the beaver collar, and my mother's elderly mink which she wore with diamonds and pearl drop earrings as we made our way down the stairs to the platforms. Since Golders Green had its station above ground we would take the train as far as King's Cross.

Imagine the scene at the station, always teeming, as it was, with the good working-class people of St Pancras, when my parents carefully unfolded their *Evening Standard* and sat themselves down on the sports pages. Dressed in these exotic garments, they talked to each other in thick guttural German accents while overhead the German bombers droned in an effort to blow us all to kingdom come. Embarrassed to the point of hysteria, I would slip away with my section of the *Evening Standard* and take up position on the opposite platform, pretending I had nothing to do with these 'enemy aliens'. It says much for the good nature of the plain people of London that no one addressed a hostile word to my parents, but accepted them cheerfully in their midst. I wonder if now, fifty years later, the mood would be the same?

After a week of considerable mortification, I refused point-blank to shelter in the Underground. My parents, who protested that they had gone there only for my sake, gave in and we spent the rest of the war in our own beds at home.

Home was no longer the two-room flat in Golders Green, but a small suburban house in a street off the Golders Green Road called Sneath Avenue, a name which always used to embarrass me. It had a small but pleasant back garden, with an elm tree that sheltered many birds and squirrels my mother used to feed. We had been able to fill the house with what was left of our Berlin furniture, which my mother had so wisely sent into storage in London well before the war broke out.

I was now going through a period of intense frustration. I had only just left school but life had come to a standstill for me before it had properly begun—not only because war had broken out, and our Hungarian passports made us technically into enemy aliens, but also because I could not get permission from the Home Office to take up any but the most menial work.

There was a Citizens' Advice Bureau in our district. I went in. I may be an enemy alien, I thought, but I am still a citizen. 'Please can I have some advice,' I asked the ladies, who were most understanding, especially Miss Callard, the tall one in the big black hat. 'Going on the stage at this time in our history may be a little difficult, even for an English girl,' she told me, but she said I could learn shorthand free of charge if I were willing to gather the local kids whose schools had been evacuated and run classes in the adjoining church hall. For the next six months I did my best to cope with Pitman's famous hieroglyphs, and became headmistress, senior teacher and nursemaid to twenty children between the ages of two and sixteen. I myself was only sixteen and a half and had to put my hair in a scrawny bun and wear my mother's lipstick to keep discipline in my 'school'.

On Fridays I brought in a small piggy bank and my pupils filled it with sixpenny pieces. This was my salary, and I recall the pride with which I walked down Sneath Avenue carrying the brand new lavatory brush I had bought my mother with the first money I had ever earned.

IV

There are moments in my life from which all others spring. My meeting with Miss Callard and her ladies in the Citizens' Advice Bureau in 1939 was such a one, and everything that has happened in my life can be traced back to it in a chain of events and encounters.

One day the ladies asked me to entertain some overseas students. My repertoire in those days was scant: Kipling's 'If' and a hit song or two. But my mauve lips and fingernails were sensational and I was talent-spotted by Egon Larsen, a journalist and writer, who passed me on for an audition with Fritz Gotfurt, another author from Berlin, with whom he was writing and producing a revue at the FDKB (Freier Deutscher Kulturbund, or Free German League of Culture), which was a German anti-Nazi, anti-fascist, refugee organization. As Professor Hugh Rorrison writes about it:

> The initial impetus came largely from the communists ... the refugees in Britain were not allowed to form political organisations, so the FDKB was originally a surrogate for political activity ... it became the social and cultural force of the German Community for the duration of the war.

The membership of the FDKB consisted of writers, painters, sculptors, musicians and actors. The group operated out of a three-storey house in Upper Park Road, which had been lent to them by the Church of England at the instigation of the Bishop of Chichester. On the tiny stage, built into the drawing-room, a company of well-known German actors and cabaret stars performed satirical revues. Fritz always said that he engaged me only because I looked and sounded so hilarious reciting 'If' at my audition. But I think it was because they really needed a juvenile. I played 'too much and too soon', and always at the expense of the audience, but it was wonderful how much experience I gained in a very short time from the seasoned artists around me. Some nights, at the height of the Blitz, the place would shake and rumble, but the audience never stirred except to applaud. Most of them were elderly people who had lost everything they possessed except their lives, and they were quite willing to risk even that for a few hours of entertainment.

The first production I appeared in was called *What's in the News?* (*Was bringt die Zeitung*), a satirical appraisal of the press performed in a mixture of English and German, and in Refugeespeak, a humorous mixture of both. The revue was always well attended, not only by the local refugees, but more often than not by English showbiz personalities, including Walter Hudd, Beatrix Lehmann and the Boulting brothers.

I learned almost everything I know about putting over a song from my experienced colleagues. I even wrote my own lyrics when our authors were too busy. Working on the shows at night was a happy release for those of us who spent our days in mundane back-breaking jobs. Our salary at the Little Theatre was small; we were lucky when our share came to two shillings and sixpence for a weekend.

Apart from the training and experience I gained at the FDKB, I also found my closest friend there. Dorothea Gotfurt, wife of Fritz, was twenty-nine—fourteen years my senior—and extremely beautiful. She had been Miss Berlin in 1925, perhaps the only and certainly the last Jewish beauty queen in Germany. After an unhappy early marriage she had run away to England with Fritz. They had arrived in London in 1936 and had hoped to be able to rescue her small son from the Nazis. But in those days, as the defendant in a divorce case, Dorothea had no rights over her child and the father had refused to let him leave. After several highly risky trips back to Berlin, Dorothea had finally persuaded her ex-husband to send the boy to school in England. She had gone with Fritz to the station to meet her son off the train but he never arrived. Phone calls to Berlin had gone unanswered. The Gotfurts learned much later that the night before he was to leave, the child and his father had been dragged off to a concentration camp.

I remember the photographs of a beautiful, dark-eyed boy which graced their rented rooms in Hampstead during the war. Later, when Fritz made a career in films and they were able to move to a flat in St John's Wood, the photographs disappeared. I never dared to ask Dorothea but Fritz told me once that when the war had ended he discovered that both father and son had been killed at Auschwitz. Dorothea never talked about it until her last year of life, but I knew that it never ceased to prey on her mind.

In St John's Wood, where I also lived for a long time, we saw each other almost daily and our friendship deepened over the years. Whenever I needed advice I always went to Fritz, who gave it unstintingly in his sardonic way. Dorothea, who had supported them both during the lean years by making gloves, was later able to write plays and made a name for herself with her translations of Agatha Christie and others into German.

Another moving spirit of the FDKB was John Heartfield (formerly Herzfeld), the originator of photomontage. A small man with a mischievous face, he enjoyed nothing more than to 'take the piss out of pomposity', as he would say. He put on some funny evenings at the League and I can still see him in a white nightie and blonde wig parodying *Gebet Einer Jungfrau*, the German equivalent of *A Maiden's Prayer*.

After several years working happily at the FDKB I was most upset when my father forbade me to take part in the next production. An article had appeared in one of the daily papers attacking the League for its Soviet sympathies. Father had suffered some bad experiences in Berlin with Communist-backed unions and now he feared that my involvement with the League could harm me in the future.

In spite of my tears and protestations, he refused to change his mind, not even when Hans Fladung, one of the League's founding fathers, a famous Communist activist who had been badly tortured and beaten by the Nazis, arrived on crutches to argue with him and stumbled on our doorstep to fall into the front garden. Hans's main objection was that now I would be free to work for Peter Herz, who ran a semi-dilettante Viennese cabaret in Swiss Cottage and who had been pursuing me for a long time.

When father refused to give in to me, I am afraid I did play at Peter Herz's, as I really felt I could not survive without my weekend theatre work. I was at that time entirely unpolitical; later, when I was more mature, I found that I was leaning more and more to the left. Even today, after the fall of the Iron Curtain and the reprehensible regimes that fell with it, I cannot help wishing that the liberated nations had not thrown themselves so wholeheartedly into the arms of capitalism but had opted for more aware and caring governments.

In my teenage years I often bewailed the fact that I knew nobody to give me a little push or use any influence on my behalf in the 'big' world. My father was too proud to tap any of his connections. He felt that his more successful fellow-refugees had enough of a struggle to establish themselves. My mother once made an effort on my behalf, but it did not turn out well. Looking back on it now it seems that I over-reacted, but being barely sixteen I could not help myself.

Richard Tauber was singing in Lehar's *Land of Smiles*, his most famous role at the Golders Green Hippodrome, and my mother bought two tickets. She introduced me to Tauber before the show. He remembered her from Berlin, and knew who my father was. My mother told him that I was anxious to make my way in the theatre, but that we didn't know many people here. Could he help?

Tauber was very courteous. He gave me his famous lopsided smile, and told me to come back and see him in the interval. Then we could talk about it. As soon as I entered the dressing-room he grabbed my breast. I pushed his hand away and fled to my mother. I did not mention this incident to anyone for many years since it gave me the same unpleasant sensation when I remembered it. Eventually, I met Richard Tauber again some years later, and even worked with him, when I wrote the lyrics for my father's production of *Gay Rosalinda* at the Palace Theatre, and Richard was the conductor. The last thing I remember about him was his funeral at St. James, Spanish Place.

Schools were now reopening and most of my pupils no

longer needed me. Since I could not make a living at the FDKB, I had to look for work during the day. My shorthand had never progressed beyond the most basic stage, and this gave rise to some painful experiences during my job interviews. Clarissa Davidson, a kindly Jewish socialite who had befriended me, made an appointment for me with a business friend of her brother's who was looking for a secretary. To test me, he dictated a letter which was full of highly technical expressions. Rubber tubing, spriggets and other such devices abounded, as did precise figures of diameters and other dimensions. He rattled off this letter at a ferocious speed. There was no way I could keep up with him, but what was worse, I had boobed in the very first line. He had instructed me to address this to Messrs so and so in the city, and in my ignorance of business usage I had written, 'Mrs'. Halfway through the letter I threw down my pad and pencil, and without so much as a goodbye, I ran out of the apartment building. I did not dare telephone Clarissa for many months.

Nevertheless she made one more effort to find me a job. She arranged for me to have an interview with Lady Kemsley, wife of the press lord, at the Dorchester Hotel.

I had laddered my last pair of silk stockings and could not afford to buy another. I wondered on the way up to her suite if she would notice my bare legs. Lady Kemsley was looking for a teacher/ companion for her daughter from a former marriage. Ghislaine at eighteen was two years older than me, and much taller. She was very worldly; some might have called her spoilt. What on earth made her mother think that I would be able to keep her in check and teach her German I cannot imagine. Perhaps she was just desperate to unload responsibility for beautiful, wilful Ghislaine, for she engaged me, bare legs and all.

Ghislaine and I liked each other, but it was a lopsided relationship. I was too young to be her governess, and too proud, or perhaps I should say too conceited, to be her glorified lady's maid. As a companion, I had no real authority over her. She refused point-blank to learn German, and simply dragged me from couturier to couturier for her fittings and from Bendix to Fortnum and Mason for tea and éclairs.

I did not lack friends of my own at that time. Some of my

friends were as passionate about theatre as I was and as frustrated because of the lack of work for newcomers during the war. We decided to form our own group—Prospect Theatre. We had great plans to produce modern classics by Büchner, Brecht and Kafka. Had we been able to raise the necessary capital, we would have been well ahead of the avant-garde theatres that eventually established themselves in London.

At the same time I was madly in love with an unattainable man. It was a young actor, Alec Clunes, who was about to open a theatre club, the Arts Theatre, in Great Newport Street. I came to know him at a fund-raising concert at the Rudolf Steiner Hall, which I had been asked to organize.

The first half of the performance was carried mainly by the members of Prospect Theatre doing short pieces, or at least that is what we had agreed to do. Christopher Willard chose to read a never-ending piece of poetry. I groaned as he turned over page after page of tightly written verse, and inwardly cursed him.

A year later I was to regret my reaction when I heard that Christopher had been killed in the war. If only he could come back and read his poem again, I thought, I would not mind if it took him forever.

Alec Clunes, who was compèring the show, had done splendidly before the interval. I had succeeded in getting the young Palestinian pianist Shulamit Shafir to take part, and she was to play for the whole of the second half. Her mother, who was also her manager, took one look at the piano stool and declared: 'Shulamit cannot possibly play sitting on that stool. It is much too low, and anyway she needs some tea before she goes on. Are there no facilities for making a pot of tea in this hall?' I dashed out into Baker Street, which was almost deserted on this wartime Sunday afternoon. Where would I find a cup of tea and a higher piano stool? I don't know how I managed it, but in no time I was racing back to the hall with a paper cup of scalding tea, trying not to spill any. Up the many stairs I panted, only to find that Alec had sent Shulamit and her mother away. 'You're better off without them,' he told me. Perhaps he had a point, but who was going to do the second half?

I cannot tell what happened, because I have deliberately

blotted out the memory of that débâcle. The show must have worked out somehow, because my passion for Alec did not fade afterwards. On the contrary, when I discovered that he was fond of cats, I raised heaven and earth to find a small black kitten and left it at the stage door of the Arts Theatre on the day before the opening night, with a note attached to the basket, anonymously wishing him luck. I did not need any thanks. My love was enough. Then I called on Ghislaine at the Dorchester and made her book an entire row for the first performance of *Twelfth Night*. Ghislaine did her best, and that night I arrived proudly with my large party at the Arts Theatre in the back row of the stalls. These were the only seats we were able to get at such short notice. Unfortunately it is difficult to hear or see well in the last row of the stalls, especially if you are surrounded by debs and guardsmen who do not care terribly for the immortal bard. My party giggled and chatted all the way through the performance but it did not make any difference to me. By then my evening had been ruined anyway, for as the curtain rose on love-sick Orsino, the noble Duke lying on his couch and calling for music, 'If music be the food of love, play on …' loud mewing came in answer to his call, and a black kitten wailed its way across the stage. The audience burst out laughing while I dissolved in tears. In the interval I crept out of the theatre and out of Ghislaine's life.

I did a little better when I went to see Charlotte Francis and Geoffrey Goodheart, who had bravely taken over the St Martin's Theatre in 1940. I say 'bravely' because it was, at the time, the only West End theatre in operation, with the exception of the Windmill—which 'never closed'—and Alec's Arts Theatre Club. The Shaftesbury had been bombed in the early months of the Blitz, and with it went a new production of *The Chocolate Soldier*, one of my father's operettas (originally *Der Tapfere Soldat*). That was the end of our hope of a substantial weekly royalty income that could have been given directly to us without going through the publishers in Germany, who were collecting all my father's foreign money and had no means of getting it to us. All the other West End houses simply closed their doors.

Francis Goodheart Productions had little money to spare

and gave me £2 per week to work for them. I had my own room and telephone. When Charlotte, whose dictation was very fast and erratic, discovered how bad I was at shorthand, she reduced my salary to thirty-five shillings. Actually it was not just a shorthand typist they required. They could afford to employ only one person and I became secretary, production manager, play-reader, understudy and stage doorkeeper. This suited me very well. I understudied all the female parts in our productions, although I never got to play them. Actresses were simply too healthy on the wartime diet. I took home a play or two to read each night and had my evaluation typed out neatly when I returned to the office in the morning. And I battled with the Home Office to procure work permits for foreign stars.

When we put on Herbert Marshall's production of *Thunder Rock*, I would wait for the young Cyril Cusack in the stage door-keeper's lodge, to smuggle him into his dressing-room undetected by the stage management when he was late—as he often was in those days. On opening nights it was my job to look after the critics and see to their drinks. On one occasion I was detailed to sit with James Agate, the doyen of them all, to humour him. I was not looking forward to the prospect of having to make conversation with the 'great man'. Apart from his reputation as a merciless reviewer who could demolish a play or a performer with a single caustic remark, he was physically daunting, a large man with a big, round face and a booming voice. But against all expectation Agate was gentle and understanding. Aware of my feelings of inadequacy, he kept asking me questions about our production that I could answer promptly, thus putting me at my ease. It might have been different had I been a boy. It was a fact he himself never denied that he propositioned every young man he met as a matter of course; but I was a girl and by the time I had to usher him into the private bar to join the other critics we had become firm friends. No wonder I adored my job. It was the next best thing to acting, I was inside a theatre and did not care what hours I had to work.

During the run of *Thunder Rock*, Cyril Cusack and I would often go home together on the tube. We both got out at Golders Green station and walked together down the deserted Golders Green Road during the air raids while bits of shrapnel from ack-ack guns whizzed past our heads. I used to keep, in a sewing box, a jagged piece of metal that missed us by inches. Unfortunately, Francis Goodheart Productions did not last the war. They had managed to keep going while there had been little or no competition, but gradually the other West End theatres reopened, and one day Francis Goodheart ceased to exist and I was out of a job.

Throughout this time I had been taking acting lessons. Elisabeth Bergner, who knew my father from his Berlin years, had spoken about me to her own renowned elocution teacher, Flossie Friedman of the red hair and aquamarine eyes. Flossie, who had a heart of gold, taught me for many years without taking any fee because I was a Jewish refugee. It was she who erased the last traces of my German accent, or at least I flatter myself that she did. She made me exercise my consonants and vowels endlessly. 'Red leather—yellow leather,' I would repeat after her, speeding up the words until the consonants were hopelessly entangled. And how is this for vowel sounds: 'Miss Bradley, her hat still on her head, sat on her bad flat bed and wept sadly'? She taught me audition pieces and made me sing 'Over the Rainbow'.

Although I did not start singing lessons seriously until much later, an Italian singing teacher known as Maestro Mario offered to teach me for free, but when I went to his studio he pushed me on to his settee and in the ensuing struggle lost his wig. The sight of Mario without a hair on his head was so comical and disconcerting that I burst out laughing and never went back.

In any case my voice was adequate enough to put a song across, and so I decided to take up Inky Stevens's offer to audition for the Nightlight Club. Inky Stevens was one of the top public relation experts in London. We had met when he was looking after the publicity at the St Martin's Theatre. He often told me it was a shame that a pretty girl like me should waste her youth behind a typewriter. When I explained that I was finding it impossible to obtain a work permit, he introduced me to Violet Dean, Basil Dean's sister, who ran a club off Leicester Square. By now I had collected a small repertoire of songs and poems, though, mercifully, 'If' was no longer one of them. The old ladies and gentlemen of the various Jewish and German refugee associations would offer me a booking here and there to do a solo show for them. I was now a sort of 'baby star' at the Free German League of Culture—so why not try the Nightlight Club?

After the audition Violet Dean told me that she thought I had some talent, but I had no material strong enough for cabaret. My songs were all published numbers that could be bought in any music shop. 'Come back when you have a repertoire of your own,' she said, 'and I will put you on.'

At first I was doubtful of my chances to develop such a repertoire. Fritz and Egon weren't keen to write in English, Inky Stevens had no time, and I had no money to pay anyone else. Cabaret writers were few and far between, and very expensive. In the end I wrote my own songs. Violet had explained to me more or less what people did, and I had been her guest at the club on several occasions to watch the cabaret. Mostly people sang satirical and *risqué* songs. That should not be a problem, I thought, and started off with the man who wouldn't make love to me because 'he lived with his cousin in Middlesex'. When I had written half a dozen songs in this vein, I put on my mother's best evening dress, sewed silver sequins onto the front and sang my songs in the Nightlight Club. It must have been incongruous. When I saw a photograph of myself 'in action', I realized that here was a lamb in wolf's clothing.

No one laughed. I carried on smiling to the end, but inside I felt like death. 'Never mind,' said Violet Dean, 'you are very young, my dear, too young for that kind of material.'

'But you asked me to get some cabaret songs,' I protested.

'It doesn't suit you at the moment. Give it time.'

I cried for the best part of the day, mainly on band leader Geraldo's shoulder—his office was next to mine in the St Martin's Theatre. He had taken it to carry on the administrative work for his jazz band, or orchestra, as it was called, and it seemed that the Geraldo Orchestra needed a great deal of administration because he was in the office himself nearly every day even when he must have been leading the band until the early hours of the morning. I had got to know him as a friendly neighbour from whom I could borrow things like carbon paper and paper-clips when I ran out of them, and as I had a tea machine in my office we often shared a lunch break and a sandwich or two. Geraldo was not his real name and he was much more English than he let on. He had very shiny black hair which must have used up a lot of Brylcreem and which reminded me of my own father's shiny pate. Perhaps it was this similarity that made me turn to him in my misery at having failed as a night-club singer.

I now had to look for another job to be able to help my parents. Mother still had to take in lodgers. This time I wanted a less demanding one because Fritz and Egon were working on a new revue for the FDKB and I needed enough time off to play Miss Ariel in *Mr Gulliver Went to School*, the most ambitious and successful musical show we attempted there.

Della Kempinsky, wife of my colleague Gerard, came to my rescue. She was working at the Esplanade Hotel off Maida Vale in some managerial capacity, and introduced me to its colourful owner, a burly Russian called Westermann. He engaged me as a part-time telephonist with very flexible hours.

While I worked there the entire Polish government in exile was living in the Esplanade. So was the astrologer German Louis de Wohl, whose psychic powers were employed by our government to provide day-by-day readings of Adolf Hitler's horoscope. Hitler believed in horoscopes, so his next move could often be anticipated.

Another Pole, Paul Stockhammer, who had owned a large fishing fleet in his native Gdynia and now ran a fish factory in London, was a frequent visitor to the Esplanade bar and restaurant. He often stopped for a chat at the switchboard, and suggested many times that I should leave the hotel and come and work for him in his fish factory; he would pay me a lot more than that scoundrel Westermann. I always refused, telling him I could not be disloyal to my boss. But Stockhammer was not the man to give up easily. One morning when I arrived for work, Mr Westermann greeted me with a hangdog expression. The hotel was not doing so well, he said—this was news to me. Many people were not paying their bills—this I could well believe. Much as he regretted it he would have to let me go. 'But don't worry,' he said to me, 'I have arranged another, better job for you. Your new boss is waiting in the lounge, go and talk it over with him.' The new boss was Paul Stockhammer. I wondered how much Westermann had made him pay for me.

Determined not to go to the fish factory and not to work full time because of my theatrical commitments, I compromised and went to work for Paul Stockhammer part-time in his flat in St John's Wood.

Paul was an excellent linguist, and since I did not speak Polish, he would dictate his letters in German and I would transcribe them into English. A warm-hearted and generous man, he was loved and respected by the Polish community in London. People wrote to him, not only for financial help, but also for his advice on private matters. After a while he trusted me enough to leave his entire correspondence in my hands.

Once he threw a party which most of our correspondents attended and I found it fascinating to meet them all in person. There was the couple whose marriage I had attempted to save, the two young people I had encouraged to get engaged and the ex-schoolboy whom I had advised on his first sexual adventures with ladies of easy virtue. Little did they realize how much I knew about them. Paul, on the other hand, was very much at sea and often had no idea what his friends were talking about.

He did know, however, about my own ambitions and my permit troubles, and was determined to help. He knew a wealthy businessman from Palestine who had managed to get an unconditional working permit for one of Paul's friends. Perhaps he could do the same for me.

When Mr Gee came to London he used a flat in Kensington. Paul introduced me as promised. The rest, Paul said, was up to me.

Unfortunately Mr Gee fancied me and did his best to seduce me. When he failed to do so he held me with promises without actually trying to get me a permit. When he took me to lavish lunches with bank officials and other sharks of the business world he liked to give the impression that I was his mistress, and though I was soon irritated by this relationship, I dared not break it off in case he could and would really make good his promises.

I now started on a round of auditions and somehow always got the part. Possibly this was because there were few up-and-coming young actresses in the English theatre during the early days of the war. Little good it did me, for I still had no working permit. To obtain it required a strong letter from the management to the Department of Labour, and since I had never been important enough for managements to put themselves out for me with the Department, my permit was invariably refused. The frustration made me physically ill.

Eventually I landed the role of Irma Potasch, the juvenile lead in a production of *Potasch and Pearlmutter*, which was to go on a lengthy tour. When I explained my problem to the management, they said they knew just what to write. They handed me a sealed envelope and told me to take it in person to the Labour Exchange. Sick with doubt and apprehension I carried it around in my pocket for days. Then I steamed open the envelope and read the letter. My worst fears were confirmed. The management was almost begging the Department to 'help this young actress who is badly in need of a job.' I knew there was no point in handing this in. I walked around town for hours clutching the resealed envelope and then I went into a phone box and rang Mr Billinghurst at the Department of Labour.

I told Billinghurst that I was representing Charles Killick, the manager in question. We badly needed a working permit for an actress who was to play the lead in our next production and without whom we could not possibly go ahead. Mr Billinghurst said that we were very ill advised to use that particular actress. 'She's no good, she's never got a job in a play in her life.' 'No! because you've never allowed her to take one,' the management cried with some spirit. When Billinghurst told me that this actress was an enemy alien and had to report to the police each week, it became very clear to me why I had always lost my jobs. But this management was not to be intimidated. I decided to change my tactics.

'I am sure', I crooned, 'that you are a reasonable man. I will have to cancel the production if I can't have Bernelle, and you would not want to throw so many British artists out of work. I will send this actress to you this afternoon and you will give her a permit as a special favour to me.'

As soon as Billinghurst had put his signature on my permit I snatched it from the table and I was out of the building and racing down the Strand, panting with fear that he might come after me and take it away again.

Before the show went on tour there were more formalities to observe.

In 1940 the British government had introduced internment for aliens. As it was impossible and even ludicrous to lock up all the Germans in the country, the government set up tribunals to decide who was dubious and had to go to a camp, and who could be trusted.

My parents and I had been ordered to report to our local tribunal centre. It happened to be the church hall in which I had run the school for the Citizens' Advice Bureau. At that time I had often used the small kitchen where the local police officers had their tea break, and it so happened that the officers who conducted the tribunal were the very ones with whom I had often shared a cuppa. They were amazed to see me. 'It's the schoolteacher,' they said, 'What are you doing here?' I explained, and in no time at all they had stamped our identity cards with the desired letter B, which meant that there would be no internment for us. The only restrictions that were imposed on the B people was that they could not keep a wireless and could not venture more than five miles from their homes. It was this last restriction I had to deal with now. The tour would take me all over the country and I had to get a special permit from our local police station.

One of the officers had called at our house shortly after the tribunal to ask my father for my hand in marriage. He explained that I would have less trouble if I were a policeman's wife with a British passport. My father was touched, but had told the policeman that I was still too young for marriage. Now I was hoping that my officer would not be around when I called to get my permit. I did not want to embarrass him. Fortunately he was not on duty and I duly filled in the application form. Some of the questions were laughable. 'Do you normally have offensive weapons in your house?' 'Yes,' I wrote, 'I normally keep a submarine in the bath.' It may have been risky but they didn't mind the joke and gave me permission to travel.

We rehearsed in one of the West End theatres and every morning we went to the stalls bar for our coffee break. I had been brought up without even a whiff of coffee and never did acquire a taste for it, but I can never be in a theatre without wanting a cup in the interval. A simple case of association— just like Pavlov's dogs.

I adored every day we rehearsed in London. It was wonderful to stand on a big stage at last! In my lunch hour I could stroll in the Charing Cross area—theatre land as it was and still is—browse around the second-hand bookshops, see the stars entering and leaving at the Ivy and Arts Theatre restaurants, treat myself to eels in parsley sauce at the marble counter in Sheckey's, or meet my friend Humphrey Jennings, the documentary film director, and let him take me out to lunch at Rules near Covent Garden. He would shortly be called to the front and would never come home again. Occasionally I had a date with bearded Jack Bilbo, the *émigré* painter from Germany, at the Café Royal. Bilbo had asked me to sit for him. 'But it must be in the nude,' he insisted. I was still a virgin and very 'uptight'. This will liberate me and prepare me for life, I thought, and agreed. So after rehearsal I would go to Jack's house off Leicester Square, and pose for him stark naked. I felt very brave and a little anxious and was always relieved when his wife came in with two steaming cups of tea and I could put a shawl around me. Jack would not let me see the picture while he was working on it, but one day he laid down his brush and turned the canvas around. There it was, as large as life: a brightly painted cube. Thus liberated and also informed about 'modern art', I entered the last week of rehearsals.

What I felt the first time I entered a theatre by the stage door is impossible to convey. Even now, after hundreds of jobs in theatres, I still get a thrill when I enter a theatre backstage and know that I am part of the company and 'belong'.

After several weeks we went on tour. I saw a great deal of Crewe Station. We seemed to pass through it almost every time we changed towns. I fell in love with all the male members of the company in turn. They treated me very kindly, but rejected me firmly, since they guessed that I was still a virgin—all, that is, but my leading man, who was seventeen and a virgin himself. Whenever there was a particularly heavy air raid we would hop into bed together and cling to one another until it was over. Of course there was some fumbling and much cuddling, but we both finished the tour some months later in the condition in which we had set out on it.

I came to know many English towns. Coventry was almost completely destroyed by the time we arrived. There and in Hull I went for long eerie walks through devastated areas. When we were in Cardiff the ack-ack crew went off to play darts in a neighbouring town. Somehow the Germans got wind of it and came over to give the place a proper strafing. The dive-bombers frightened even me. I climbed into our landlady's garden shelter and sat there all night, convinced that we would find neither house nor theatre the next morning. Would I ever see my stage-clothes again? It is of such trivial matters that one thinks in moments of danger. To my surprise, house and theatre were unharmed and sets and costumes still intact, and we carried on with the tour. After Exeter we had to say goodbye. I was not then experienced enough to know that however close-knit a company of actors becomes during the run of a play, they will inevitably lose touch once the production has come to an end. One is forever forging ties only to lose one's 'family' time and time again. This is one of the emotional drawbacks of an actor's life and one I found hard to get used to. My juvenile leading man went back to his steady girlfriend, an older woman, and I went back to Sneath Avenue. A month's work at Huddersfield Rep followed. The second permit was always easy. Huddersfield was a weekly repertory company and I was expected to act at night in an Agatha Christie play, while rehearsing *Love Lies Bleeding*, one of the funniest farces on the repertory circuit, during the day. Unfortunately the offer had been made at the last minute, and I found myself travelling up to Yorkshire holding the Agatha Christie script in my hands. I was supposed to learn my words on the train; there would be no time for a rehearsal, I had been told. The director, who met me at the station, explained the moves on the way to the theatre and since I had to be on stage in an hour, there was just time for a bag of chips. Fortunately I have always had a facility for learning lines, but am utterly hopeless where names and figures are concerned.

When I arrived backstage, the company was tense with apprehension—would I give them their cues correctly? I did! In fact I got through the part without a hitch until the end, when I came to the speech that explained the entire convoluted plot. It went something like this: when Stephen realized that Albert had lured Betty to Brighton in order to mislead Richard and make him think that Oliver had never told Valerie about Genevieve and Albert's murder ...

. I did not remember a single name. The rest of the cast watched with breathless admiration as I substituted the most outlandish-sounding people for the actual characters in the play. The audience was less enchanted. They left the theatre that night totally bewildered. 'Couldn't make it out, could you?' some of them were heard saying. 'Rum bird, that Agatha Christie—didn't know what she was doing when she wrote that play.'

V

About the time I met my future husband, I was working in a new cabaret venue, By Candlelight, off Maida Vale. It was another refugee place. The shows were witty enough, written and directed by my father with an Austrian journalist, inappropriately named Rudolf Steiner.

By Candlelight addressed itself to a more affluent section of the refugee community than the cabarets in which I had performed before. Father and I were able to earn a little more money, but I was not happy about his involvement with the company. Only once before had he left his beloved arm-chair by the fire at Sneath Avenue, where he spent most of the day with our cat on his lap and a pipe on the ashtray beside him, even though he was only in his sixties. Years before he had directed Wanda Rotha in *Rain*. I recalled that it had not been a happy experience for him. Not working in his native language, directing actors who did not recognize the great producer of former days in the old gentleman with the German accent and the hearing problem. By Candlelight was better in some ways. The actors knew of his reputation and followed his direction. But I considered that it was not his style and always felt resentful. He was, after all, only an employee of Steiner. He ought to have his own place, I used to tell myself. I often wondered if he felt the same, and I discussed this problem with Mr Gee, who had become enough of a friend to receive some of my confidences. He said that he could easily raise enough finance to set father up in his own small theatre. I so much wanted to believe him that I started looking around for suitable plays for this fantasy venture.

At around this time I had a very urgent call from Gee and

rushed to the West End to meet him. His mother had died and he was in very low spirits. I felt sorry for him and when he asked me to accompany him to Manchester on a business trip I agreed to go. We were playing only at weekends and I had no excuse to refuse. We sat all night in a dismal train, blacked out as much as was possible because of the threat of air raids, Gee reading the *Financial Times* by the dimmest of lights and me reading a play that I wanted him to back for my father. We arrived at the station hotel at five o'clock in the morning. It was cold and grey in Manchester and it was just about the worst time and place for a seduction—if that was what Gee intended. He had booked us into a double room. The first thing I did was to lock myself in the lavatory. I stayed in there for ages, still clutching my script. I came out only after Gee began to bang on the door and shout. To my horror he was stripped naked. I had never seen a naked man before and burst into tears. Gee tried his best to calm me down and get me into bed, but failed. When the sun rose, he abandoned the attempt and went off to his business meeting. Manchester had not been a good idea, we agreed on the way back to London. 'Next time I will take you to a nicer place— a good hotel in town.' 'Yes,' I agreed without enthusiasm, 'you do that.' Fortunately, even the well-connected Mr Gee could not find a hotel room in wartime London.

I always say that I got married on the first day of peace by accident. Maurice Craig once asked me which was the accident, the marriage or the date. With hindsight, I now say both. And it was Mr Gee who was to blame.

He rang me out of the blue and asked if I would come to a party in Mayfair. The party was given by Lady Elwes, the mother of the painter Simon Elwes. I had never before been asked to a Mayfair party. I agreed to go, but had no idea what to wear. My mother's evening dress was once again brought out of mothballs. We had some of my Aunt Martha's jewellery for safe-keeping—my mother's had long since fallen under the hammer—and dressed from top to toe in black velour and decked out with aunt's diamonds, I arrived at Lady Elwes's house. None of the female guests wore anything that went further than their knees. I felt embarrassingly overdressed and rushed into the nearest loo to pull my skirt up over my hips in several layers. Since it was a fairly tight skirt it stayed put without pins but I looked monstrously large below the waist. At least I was conforming.

When I emerged from the bathroom I could not find Mr Gee. I pushed my way through the crowd and reached the buffet. I did not know a soul. Two young men in uniform were helping themselves to the food. To hide my embarrassment I offered the one on the left some spaghetti. 'No thanks,' he said, 'they're cold!' We got into conversation and discovered that neither of us had been invited directly. This seemed to forge some kind of bond between us and he hardly left my side all evening. He told me he was a Spitfire pilot on leave and regaled me with stories about his exploits in the RAF—'... and there I was upside down with nothing on the clock.' I did not know then that this tall story was a well-known conversation piece in wartime. I lapped it all up, even the *risqué* jokes that followed. Mr Gee found us deep in conversation on the drawing-room sofa. Far from being put out or jealous, he seemed delighted. He bent down and hissed in my ear that my young friend was Winston Churchill's cousin and since he had taken a liking to me, why didn't I invite him back to Mr Gee's flat afterwards. Gee had asked quite a number of 'important people' and there would be another jolly party with plenty of booze. Desmond Leslie, for it was he, agreed readily and we could have taken leave of our hostess there and then. The party had thinned out and the drawing-room was almost empty. But that was just the trouble. If I got up from the sofa to make my way across the room my new conquest would see the vastness of my hips. I sat rooted to the spot, but when we were the only people left, I had to get off the sofa whether I liked it or not.

Desmond told me afterwards that he had quite a shock when the slim young girl he had been chatting up turned into a black-bottomed monster, but he was now committed to taking me to Kensington. As soon as we were inside the door, I rushed to Gee's bathroom and hastily pulled down the layers of dress. Desmond was more intrigued than ever. What an extraordinary girl this is, he thought to himself, who can change her shape in a minute. He sat down at the piano and played some jazz. As I stared at his back I seemed to hear a voice inside me whisper: 'You're going to marry that chap.' 'Nonsense,' I thought, 'I'm not getting married before I have made a name for myself. Doesn't my father always tell me, no artist should spend her time pushing prams.'

Some hours and several bottles of champagne later, Gee gave Desmond money to take me back to Golders Green in a taxi. In the dark interior of the cab he took me in his arms, 'Will you live with me?' he whispered. I gave myself up to romantic fantasies. We would live in a swish apartment in Park Lane. In the drawing-room before a log-fire Desmond would recline in a large armchair, his aristocratic slippered feet resting on a snow-white sheepskin rug. I would light his Black Sobranie cigarette for him, he would tousle my hair ... as he was doing at this very moment. 'Yes,' I breathed, and closed my eyes. For the next week we spent every possible moment together to make the best of his leave. At home they christened me 'the submarine'—one who surfaced only occasionally. Desmond was staying at a hotel near Marble Arch, and the day he took me there to lunch we held hands under the table. We even talked about marriage and thought we might get engaged if we both survived the war. There was a phone call for Desmond and he went off to take it. He was smirking when he returned to the table. 'Your pal Mr Gee is a dirty old man. He wants me to use my influence to get him a room in this hotel for a dirty weekend with a floozy. But now he wants to talk to you.'

When I got to the phone Gee was furious. He wanted to know what I was doing at Desmond's hotel having lunch with him. 'That's exactly what I'm doing,' I said and hung up. I don't know how I managed to finish my lunch and was hardly aware that I was following Desmond upstairs to his room.

I was still in a state of shock when Desmond emerged from the bathroom in a silken robe and started to peel off the layers of dark blue underclothes my mother always made me wear. 'Passion-killers they call those,' Desmond said, amused. He did his best, but I was barely responding. I will lose him anyway, I told myself, once he finds out that I am the floozy.

I pleaded with him to take me out of London. I said it would be different once I was away from all the pressures.

'What pressures?' he said.

'Don't ask. Just take my word for it.'

We agreed to go to Henley-on-Thames and made a date for a day when there would be no performance. One night when we did have a performance a large hired limousine was waiting for me outside the theatre. It had been ordered by a Mr Gee, and to my horror it took me to Desmond's hotel. Gee was already in the lounge and when we waited for the lift to take us to the second floor, I thought I would die. I was convinced that Desmond would step out of the lift. My relief at reaching the room without bumping into Desmond was so apparent that Gee could have been forgiven for mistaking it for the enthusiasm he had always expected from me. He was to be disappointed. Once again he ended up with a weeping woman in his bed. I don't remember how I got out of the hotel room. Mercifully there was no sign of Desmond.

My friend Georgette was playing in the local rep in Henley and I told my parents I was off to stay with her. When I was ready to go my mother stopped me at the door. She made a dreadful scene. The first one of its kind, but not the last. Until that day I had not known that she was, and always would be, consumed with jealousy of any of my female friends. I was going to miss the train. In desperation I blurted out the truth. 'I'm not going to see Georgette, I'm running off with a man!' That's torn it, I thought. To my amazement she relaxed, and let me go, relieved that her little girl only wanted to lose her virginity.

I arrived at the station just in time, and can truly say that I eloped with Desmond on a laundry ticket. Our train journey into the setting sun was most romantic. We kissed all the way and Desmond crushed the orchid he had pinned on me against his breast. At Henley-on-Thames, as we went through the ticket-barrier, he handed the collector a piece of paper then grabbed me by the hand and shouted, 'Run!' We sprinted away as fast as we could and did not stop until we could no longer hear the ticket-collector calling after us.

'I gave him my laundry ticket,' said Desmond. 'I always travel on my laundry list.'

I didn't know if he expected me to laugh, but I was not yet used to his ways. The sun had gone down. Romance was no longer in the air. A feeling of panic took hold of me. Here I was in a strange town with a man I hardly knew, who could not afford a railway ticket to Henley-on-Thames.

Once we had booked into the pleasant hotel by the river I shut my mind against doubts and fears. This was to be my unofficial wedding night, and by God I was going to enjoy it.

I woke up the next morning to bright sunshine, safe and sound in Desmond's arms—or so I thought. The telephone on the bedside table rang shrilly. Who on earth could that be? Surely not a call for me: no one knew where I was.

The voice on the line was Gee's. He had had me followed for days and demanded my immediate return to London.

'Forget about theatres and permits,' he said angrily. 'If you don't come back instantly, I will make sure that you and your family will be in serious trouble. You are enemy aliens after all, and I have my connections.'

'Who is it and what do they want?' asked Desmond sleepily.

I almost shouted at him. 'It's Gee, you idiot. I am his floozy. He's found me out and he's threatening me with his connections.'

Desmond was suddenly wide awake. He took the receiver out of my hand.

'How dare you threaten my fiancée,' he said into the telephone. 'When it comes to threats, my family has better connections than you have.'

That was the end of the conversation.

I heaved a big sigh, not just out of relief. I was convinced that Desmond would now leave me in disgust.

'Don't be so idiotic,' he said. 'How can you be a floozy in such underwear.'

That was the end of Mr Gee for some time, but I saw a great deal of Desmond from then on. Whenever he could get away from camp he would appear at Sneath Avenue and if both my parents were out we would make passionate love. Sometimes it was like a French bedroom farce, with Desmond hastily leaving my room clutching his air force uniform and disappearing into the bathroom only minutes before my parents came up the stairs. Fortunately they did not twig the situation then, and they approved of him. I wish

I could say the same of Desmond's family, few of whom had even set eyes on me at that time. Lady Marjorie, his mother, was the one who mattered most. Separated from his father, Sir Shane, she lived during the war at the family home, which they called Castle Leslie, at Glaslough in County Monaghan. His elder brother, Jack, heir to the house and the baronetcy, was a prisoner of war in Germany. His sister Anita was an ambulance driver in the Middle East, and his Uncle Seymour—the Prince of Beggars as he was known in his capacity of fund-raiser for Queen Charlotte's Hospital—did not approve of Desmond's liaison with a penniless refugee who, horror upon horror, was on the stage. Seymour adored gossip and always sent snippets of information about our doings to poor Marjorie, who, isolated as she was in the country, got the impression that I was a ruthless foreign adventuress.

Desmond had quarrelled with his former girlfriend, an heiress, and meeting me had made the break final. She had been considered eminently suitable and her loss had been much lamented by Desmond's family.

Whenever Desmond came to London on forty-eight hours leave we would end up in some night-club and would sit all night over the jug of water supplied free of charge to every table. Having spent our last penny on the entrance fee we could not afford to buy drinks. If the club closed at four there would be an hour to kill before Desmond's milk train back to Taunton where he was stationed. Often we spent that precious hour sitting on a bench in Hyde Park while the night sky was criss-crossed by searchlights and the air around us was rent by exploding bombs. On these occasions Desmond would bring his laundry to town and I would wash it for him at Sneath Avenue. Once when he handed me his bag, in the foyer of the Churchill Club, the lock broke and the bag fell open, scattering socks all over the floor. Hastily I knelt down to pick them all up and stuff them back into his kit bag when a young couple about to leave the club swept past.

'Enid,' said Desmond, 'meet Agnes.'

I looked up from my lowly position, socks in hand, to see a tall blonde girl in a mink jacket looking down at me with ill-concealed distaste. It was none other than the 'eminently suitable heiress' Desmond was always talking about. I prayed that this story would not get back to Ireland, but it may have done, because when, much later, we announced our engagement, Desmond's mother promptly went into a nursing home.

Whenever I could scrape enough money together for the fare to Taunton, I would visit Desmond and spend a weekend in a B & B near the airfield. Sometimes there was a dance in the mess and I met his superior officers and danced with the squadron leader.

One day this man telephoned me in London to tell me that Desmond had fainted on parade, and advised me to get in touch with the Air Ministry about it. The RAF doctor suspected a heart murmur.

'Not very safe,' the squadron leader told me; 'he could have an attack in the air and prang his kite. Very valuable planes, Spitfires, you know?'

My reaction was one of resentment. It was not my place to stop Desmond flying. I loved him and was concerned about him, but he adored flying Spitfires and would be heartbroken were he to be grounded.

'You'll have to do your own dirty work, I'm afraid,' I told the squadron leader.

Not long after this I was ordered by the government to report to a munitions factory. I felt that I had something more important to contribute to the war effort than turning screws. I could speak in English and German and still remembered most of my French and Italian. None of this was going to be very useful in a factory. I had visions of ending up like Charlie Chaplin in *Modern Times*.

My local doctor sympathized with me. He gave me a medical certificate that said my kidneys and gall-bladder were in a sorry state, which happened to be true after a recent bout of jaundice. I had to go to the Labour Exchange every week with a fresh certificate. After some months I grew tired of the whole business and opted to be examined by one of the government doctors at the Military Hospital in Mill Hill. If he passed me for factory work, I would go and make munitions.

There were a couple of soldiers sitting with me in the doctor's waiting-room. We were handed questionnaires to fill in. These were literacy tests of the most basic kind and I flew through mine without any trouble. Just to be on the safe side I employed a method which had stood me in good stead during my school exams. I added a footnote. This time I wrote that I was a foreigner, had not been speaking the language long and wished to apologize for any mistakes in English. The military doctor, Dr Ling, was impressed. No wonder—the soldiers were still huffing and puffing over their papers while Dr Ling gave me the briefest of medical examinations and had a long chat with me about my theatrical background and aspirations.

I don't know what Dr Ling wrote in his report to the Labour Exchange, but I was declared 'unfit for factory work' and was free to take up any job in the theatre I could find without a permit. I called down every blessing on Dr Ling's head and took myself off to Birmingham to play Jacqueline in Terence Rattigan's *French Without Tears*. When I arrived at the Alexandra Theatre, the director took one look at me and said, 'If she's playing Jacqueline, Joan cannot possibly play Diana. This one is not plain enough, we'll have to reverse the roles.'

I was shocked. I would have preferred to play the mousy part instead of the scene-stealing leading role and embark on the career of a well-loved and much-admired serious actress, not a flibbertigibbet glamour puss. Joan Miller took the change-over in good spirit. She was helpful and friendly and occasionally came to my digs to borrow my hairdryer or to wash her hair in my basin. All of which confirmed my suspicions that my own bountiful hair type-cast me in glamorous roles.

I think I made a good fist of Diana. The notices were favourable and I was happy at the Alexandra, but I was right in thinking that ultimately the change-over would not be to my advantage. I had been given to understand that my job at the Rep would become more permanent if I did well in *French Without Tears*, since they could do with another juvenile character actress. But I had done too well. Now I had made my mark as a leading lady, and there wasn't room for two. I never held it against Joan Miller; the decision wasn't hers, but my job in Birmingham ended after seven happy weeks.

When I came back from Birmingham I made an attempt to join the army. I had 'overcome' Billinghurst from the Labour Department and had won my battle with the factory with the help of Dr Ling, and now I felt I should turn my back on the theatre and do what I could for the war effort. Alas, the army turned me down. I tried the St John's Ambulance Service. No dangerous enemy aliens thank you, they said. The only organization I was allowed to join was the Civil Defence as an air-raid warden, and I spent many nights during the Blitz patrolling Sneath Avenue, clutching a stirrup pump. This at least was better than cowering helplessly under the kitchen table. I attended briefings, held in the Lido cinema, and got to know all about the missiles we could expect to land on us: Butterfly bombs, land-mines, incendiary devices and other horrors. I could not help smarting under the shame of not being trusted to do anything more than patrol our own small street and alert the neighbours in their garden shelters when a fire started in their homes. My position changed dramatically after America entered the war, with the arrival of an American, Colonel Dave Winton.

Armed with a list of prominent German refugee artists, which he had put together in Hollywood, Colonel Winton telephoned my father. Carefully underplaying the true nature and importance of the operation he was setting up, he casually offered my father a job as a script-writer and translator. A possible radio station was vaguely mentioned. This would require some singers and broadcasters who had perfect German, and had to be trustworthy politically. My father— also casually—mentioned me. I was interviewed, first at the Savoy Hotel by the band leader Carroll Gibbons, who played the piano for me in a private suite and made me sing some English hit songs, and later by Winton himself in his office in Grosvenor Square. He said there would be a job for me in American broadcasting. I was to go to a studio in Buckinghamshire at the weekend and do some recording. It would be as well not to mention anything about it to anyone.

I had no idea what I was letting myself in for: I was being recruited for an operation which, had the Allies lost the war, could have been fatal for all of us. No one who became connected with the OSS, the American Office of Strategic Service, could have known that we were playing midwives to the dreaded CIA, which grew out of the OSS after the war. Our American head, General Donovan, may have had some idea of what he was setting in motion. None of us in the lower echelons were even aware of his name at the time. I discovered his identity only afterwards when a book appeared called *Under Cover Girl*, with a foreword by the General, which revealed much about our 'secret' operation.

I set off for Bletchley by train, happy and excited that I was going to do some radio work. I was met at the station by a heavily camouflaged army car. The American driver whisked me to a charming country house in the middle of nowhere, and told me it was where I would be staying the night. I don't know to this day exactly who my host was on that occasion, but subsequent 'idle talk' convinced me that it must have been the head of MI6, a distinguished-looking grey-haired man who was putting me up because our permanent headquarters at Newton Longville were not yet ready.

No sooner had I unpacked than a jeep full of American officers arrived at the door. They had come to take me out for the evening. My host admonished me not to talk to anyone in the local pub except my escorts. I was happy enough with their company and went off gaily in the jeep. Little did I realize what my presence in Buckinghamshire meant to them. They were highly trained personnel with the recently established American Intelligence Unit, working on the 'Enigma' project and on black propaganda behind a high security screen. They had not seen a woman since their arrival in England some months ago. No wonder they crowded around me, and did not want to let me go until way past closing time.

When we arrived back at the grey-haired man's house there was no sign of life. The place was in darkness. The officer in charge was too scared to ring the doorbell and I was too embarrassed to cause a disturbance. I was bundled into the jeep and driven at high speed to the 'secret house' a few miles away where all these uniformed boffins were billeted. There was only one single room in the entire building—the quartermaster's own. Everyone else slept in dormitories, set up in the reception rooms of this once-elegant mansion. The quartermaster gave up his bed for me. He impressed on me the need to lock the door: 'There are too many frustrated wolves around here,' he said. I did as I was told and slept undisturbed all night. No civilian, let alone a female one, had ever as much as set foot in this high-security fortress, nor would again for the duration of the war in Europe.

The following morning the quartermaster's young batman knocked on the door. 'Yes—who is it?' I called out sleepily. There was a loud crash and the young soldier, who had dropped the breakfast tray he was carrying, was seen running back to the kitchen, crimson in the face. 'He's got a dame in there!' he blurted out to the astonished cooks.

An hour later the 'dame' was being driven to the 'secret' studio to record her very first radio programme. As we were driving through the gates of the large park that surrounded the building, my producer, Charles Kebbe, and his commanding officer, Ira Ashley, volunteered the information that we were at Woburn Abbey, the Duke of Bedford's country estate. The studio had been built into the chapel in one of the Abbey's wings, which would explain its stained-glass windows.

Many years later, when the BBC took me back to Woburn Abbey for a television interview, we looked for this chapel in vain; the wing and the studio had been demolished. But back in 1943 it was there that Ira Ashley gave me my first briefing. He explained to me my role in Radio Atlantik, or Soldatensender West as it was also called. I was to be 'Vicky', the presenter of a radio request programme. The 'requests' would be chosen by our military superiors, whom I would never meet. I was to talk between these records, but I would also be asked to re-record the English lyrics of some of these songs in German. Later on, when the other singers had been signed up, we would be doing the recordings in our own little studio in the basement of the cottage at Newton Longville, as soon as our future living quarters had become operational, as Ira called it. I was always to start the programmes by saying, in German, 'This is Vicky with three kisses for you'— then I was to make the sound of kisses three times—smack, smack, smack—and after that there would be a short musical introduction taken from the popular jazz tune 'The Smooth One'. Ira told me that I had done well and I would be engaged permanently by the OSS. And bingo! Here I was in the army.

Ira then gave me a lecture on security. I was not to tell anyone what I was doing or who I was working for, except my parents, who were also recruited by the OSS and would be billeted at Newton Longville. My father was to write scripts and translate English songs into German. My mother was to be a chaperone to the household, which would consist of four singers, myself, Hilde Palmer (sister of the film star Lili), Lisl Ullmann, an Austrian actress, and a Czech girl called Trudi Benar—all refugees from the Nazis. There would also be our English pianist, Pat O'Neill, and several American officers, including Charles Kebbe, Ira Ashley, Stefan Schnabel—son of the famous pianist Arthur Schnabel—and a sound expert from Hollywood.

To avoid any awkward questions, we were to spend most weekends in our homes in London, to give the impression that nothing out of the ordinary was going on. We were never to speak to the locals in the village, except to give them the time of day or discuss the weather. We were never to telephone anyone from Buckinghamshire, or post letters in the local post-box. If we should by any chance be stopped by the British Army or police, we were to make up some story to explain why we were present in this high-security area. As enemy aliens we had no excuse to be there. Should we be arrested, the OSS as well as the War Office would deny any knowledge of us. We must not mention them under any circumstances, or count on their assistance if we got into trouble. It was not a very reassuring prospect, and we were lucky that none of us ever did get into trouble, although once we very nearly did.

The American soldier who used to drive us to and from the studio noticed one morning that a British army patrol was eyeing us suspiciously. Three blondes and a brunette in the back of a military vehicle looked to them more like an unofficial joy-ride than an army transport. They suspected our driver of breaking regulations and began to give chase.

Our driver enjoyed the situation and accelerated as much as he dared on the bumpy country roads. Forgetting the possible consequences to ourselves, we entered into the spirit of the chase and did our best to look guilty and furtive. Eventually the army patrol caught up with us and came to a screeching halt in front of our vehicle. The soldiers demanded to see our driver's credentials. He refused, wanting to draw out the scene as much as possible. By now we had stopped giggling and were praying that we would not be asked for our credentials also. But our driver waved some highly confidential pass at the Tommies which made it impossible for them to ask any further questions. They were furious, but they had to let us go. Their faces showed clearly that they didn't believe for one moment that we were engaged in a military operation.

By now we were firmly installed in the thatched cottage which was our headquarters. The OSS even provided an excellent cook. My mother had her hands full to make sure that some decorum was observed between the sex-starved Americans and the attractive female singers. Even so, there were clashes of personality and torrid love affairs to ruffle the domestic calm. I was the odd woman out because I was heavily involved with Desmond. He was still stationed in Taunton. It was not long before he noticed our frequent and unexplained absences. He did not ask too many questions, but one morning as I stepped off the train at Bletchley I saw him standing at the top of the stairs.

'Gotcha!' he said, a triumphant grin on his face.

'For God's sake, pretend you don't know me,' I hissed, keeping my eyes resolutely averted, but it was too late. The army driver who was picking me up had already spotted us. I didn't know what the penalties for breaking security were, but I was terrified that my superiors would suspect me of treason. I decided that the only thing to do was to be honest. 'However did you find me?' I asked. 'Easy,' he said, 'I searched your handbag for clues and found a return ticket to Bletchley in your purse.' Ira had, after all, failed to brief me properly in matters of security. Charles Kebbe and Ira spoke to our commanding officer on my behalf, and since Desmond was a British Spitfire pilot, they decided to trust him. He was even allowed to come and spend some of his leave in Buckinghamshire, so we could meet now and then. He bought two bicycles and made his base in a pub in the next village. Whenever I could, I cycled over, and was further initiated into the joys of sex. At least I was catching up on the other girls. In the cottage I shared a room with Hilde Palmer, and we became firm friends, chatting the nights away and telling each other our innermost secrets. Kebbe, who directed our recordings, was a very attractive man and seemed to have fallen heavily for Hilde. He was always giving her the songs with the cleverest lyrics and the snappiest tunes—at least that is what we others thought. Kebbe worked extremely hard, and when he was not producing us, he would be whisked away in a staff car to report to our superiors in Bletchley, who would send him back with further instructions and programme material for our station. He had very little time to court Hilde during the working week, and at week-ends she was in London. Eventually Kebbe was granted weekend leave. He screwed up his courage and asked Hilde to meet him for dinner at the Savoy.

I thought it would be kindness to give him some inside information. 'If you want to impress her,' I told him confidentially, 'bring an orchid to your rendezvous, I know she simply adores them.'

'How can I,' Kebbe said sadly, 'I shan't get off from here until the last moment. I will just have time to get to my London base to shower and change. There will be no time to go looking for orchids!'

I had an idea. Desmond was in London on leave. I would ask him to buy an orchid and leave it for Kebbe to collect at reception. Kebbe was most grateful and I telephoned Desmond and told him to buy the most beautiful orchid he could find.

I could hardly wait for Monday morning to find out how Hilde and Kebbe had fared on their romantic evening. Hilde was rather diffident about it all. She admitted that Charles Kebbe had actually proposed to her, but said that she had not been able to make up her mind.

'Why ever not!' I cried, 'he's gorgeous and you know you've always fancied him!'

'Well yes, I have,' Hilde admitted, 'but on Saturday night when we got to our table, he handed me a box, and what do you think was in it? An orchid—made of feathers! Can you imagine? I had to pin it on and wear the horrible thing all night! How can I marry a man who goes and buys feather orchids?'

'Hilde,' I said, barely able to hide my dismay, 'you can relax. It isn't you who will marry the man who bought the feather orchid—it's probably me!'

On one of my weekend visits to London, I was told by a theatrical agent that Gabriel Pascal was casting a film with Vivien Leigh and Claude Rains. Like another Hungarian before him—my father—Pascal had coaxed George Bernard Shaw to give him the rights to one of his plays. Father had made a musical of *Arms and the Man—The Chocolate Soldier*—and Pascal was about to turn *Caesar and Cleopatra* into a mammoth film.

I asked Kebbe for a day off and presented myself at Denham Studios for the audition. Desmond, who had travelled with me, was not allowed to come to the audition because he was not a member of Equity, the actors' union. I waved goodbye to him at the gate.

'Wait for me in the canteen,' I said and went to join the crowd of hopefuls who were to file past Pascal. There must have been well over a hundred of us.

Pascal was lording it on a throne-like chair, surrounded by his acolytes. From time to time he indicated someone in the crowd and his assistant noted down the name. When my turn came to pass the throne, I suddenly saw Desmond sitting next to Gabriel Pascal. I heard his voice as he pointed a finger in my direction. 'That one. The curvy one with the squashy lips!'

Pascal nodded.

I was outraged. I had yet to learn that Desmond could worm his way into anywhere, a skill he passed on to me in a minor form. I forgave him when I was told I was definitely 'in'.

I had been cast as one of Vivien Leigh's handmaidens. A great deal of fuss was made of us over the next few months. We were considered the *crème de la crème* among rising young actresses. Our group included Kay Kendall, who died so young from leukaemia, Virginia Keely, who was taken up by film producers in Paris, and Patricia Owens, the only one of us who made it to Hollywood. There were many tests and endless costume fittings. Oliver Messel had created exotic dresses for each of us. I remember him moulding mine to my body so that I had to be cut out of it. The wigs created quite a problem. A friend of Oliver's had made them. They were unusual and elaborate, but Gabriel Pascal decided we should use our own hair, saying we looked more sexy like that. Oliver threw tantrums every time the subject came up. As a result it was 'on with the wigs—off with the wigs', depending on who had the last word on that particular occasion. We were recalled countless times and I had to ask for leaves of absence more often than I can remember. Fortunately Ira and Charles Kebbe raised no objections. My presence at Denham only improved the security.

After a great deal of messing about, the first day for shooting our scene finally came. I had booked myself in to the local inn at Uxbridge for a fortnight to be near the studios, and Desmond had also taken leave and was joining me there. I arrived from Newton Longville in time for dinner. Desmond looked positively green. He had arrived the previous night and had been much upset by a dream. His own squadron was attached to a unit of exiled Polish pilots, one of whom had recently committed suicide. This man had appeared to Desmond in the dream and wanted to write a message to the world on his body with a flaming pencil. Desmond had tried to run away, but the Polish airman pursued him, the flaming pencil in his outstretched hand.

'You ate too much dinner and had a nightmare,' I reassured him. 'Have something light, some fish or something, tonight, and you'll be all right. You've been under a great deal of strain lately with all these raids on Germany. Now you can relax and I'll give you a good cuddle when we get into bed.'

A good cuddle was all we had that night because Desmond was still very disturbed. I had barely fallen asleep when I heard him shouting, 'He's got me—he's got me.' I switched on the bedside light and found Desmond half hanging out of the bed with his face and hands on the floor.

I calmed him down as best I could and stroked his arm, where, according to him, his dream pursuer had written the message. There was nothing there to be seen or felt, and I switched off the light. I went on stroking his arm in the dark and suddenly felt something coming up on his skin. It felt like a row of blisters. I was now in a cold sweat and found myself praying, and praying in French of all things. There is something wrong with this family, I said to myself. Look at Desmond's father, Sir Shane, a great eccentric if there ever was one. They're all hopping mad. Under no circumstances can I go on with this relationship, let alone marry Desmond and have his children.

Next morning we ordered breakfast in our room. I tried not to look at Desmond's arm, but could not help risking a glance when he was getting dressed. All along the inside of his arm was a line of messy capital letters, which spelled the word *merde* in blood and pus, as if they had been carved into his flesh with a knife.

I had to be in the studio for the first day of shooting and tried not to think about this unpleasant manifestation. I pretended to myself that all was normal in my life, picked up my costume in 'wardrobe', my wig in 'hairdressing' and sat down in the make-up chair. The make-up man put a towel around me and began to cover my face with panstick. My head began to ache as if my skull was about to burst. My eyes began to water.

'Are you all right?' asked the make-up man. 'Your forehead is burning.'

They had to send me back to Uxbridge in a studio car. The doctor came and took my temperature. It had shot up to 104! He ordered me home immediately. Home at that moment was the empty house in Golders Green. My parents were at Newton Longville. Desmond telephoned our family doctor who tried to find a rational explanation. 'It's all a question of an overactive imagination,' he said.

Then he told me of an experiment he had once read about in the *Lancet* where people had been shown a red-hot poker and were then blindfolded. When they were touched on their skin with a cube of ice, burns and blisters had appeared.

'It must have been the same with Desmond,' the doctor said. 'He was so convinced that his Polish friend had touched him with the flaming pencil that he reacted by producing blisters.'

I felt comforted and began to recover from my attack of nerves, for that is what it was. I forgot all about leaving Desmond, particularly since he was nursing me tenderly and kept me in fits of laughter most of the time, as only he knew how to do. When I was well again, I discovered to my dismay that our scene had been shot, and so I never did get to appear in Pascal's epic. Sadly, I returned to work for Soldatenseder West.

VI

Gradually we had come to understand the purpose and importance of what we were doing. Small as it was our unit was the entire personnel of a freedom station that was purporting to come from inside Germany, or at least from somewhere in Occupied Europe. We had the entire 'dirty tricks department' of British and American intelligence behind us. This clever hoax gave us endless possibilities to bamboozle and confuse the Nazis, and to help Allied agents behind German lines. Our radio waves were beamed to a large mirror, situated somewhere near the coast. From there they were reflected and bounced over to Germany. This way no one could be exactly sure where they came from, and it was almost impossible to 'jam' our station. There were reports of the broadcasts hailing from a barge on the Rhine, from a cellar in Dortmund, from a mobile van in the Black Forest.

It had been claimed that the idea was General Eisenhower's, but it was our mysterious, and to us 'invisible' boss, who is said to have thought it up. Officially he was known to us only as 'the beard', as no one in our outfit was allowed to know the identity of those above or below them. Every day Charles or Ira Ashley would be driven to the location in which 'the beard' lived with his staff, submit my father's scripts for his approval and bring back new instructions, new codes and vital messages to be included in my programme. It did not take us long to badger enough information out of the Americans to know that 'the beard' was British and that his name was Sefton Delmer. In peace-time he had made a name for himself on the *Daily Express*, but he had also worked in Berlin and spoke perfect German. To make our broadcasts appear as authentic as possible, he had invented a querulous German officer who was ostensibly running the station. This fictitious old boy wanted Germany to win the war, and that was the clever part of it. Hearing standard Nazi propaganda convinced the Germans they were listening to the real thing, and that led them to believe all we told them. We put out items about high Nazi officials getting extra food and extra clothing or smuggling their private wealth out of Germany. The old curmudgeon always sounded patriotic, but believed that the Nazis were spoiling his country's chances to beat the Allies. Our station caused an uproar in Nazi circles and the Gestapo scoured Germany in an effort to hunt us down.

Our main attraction was the constant stream of jazz. Jazz was forbidden in Germany. Hitler considered it to be alien and decadent. This made the German forces want to listen to us, and since the music was interspersed with items of news and other subtly disguised pieces of propaganda, they would invariably get the information we wanted them to have. Our news items were more accurate and informative than the official German ones. Eventually these bulletins were read out by real German soldiers, prisoners of war, who volunteered for this service. They were always brought to the studio blindfolded and remained so until they actually stood in front of the microphone to record their text. It was fascinating to meet and talk to them. One, Henry Zeisel, was a fine musician and eventually was even allowed to accompany me on the violin. Neither Henry nor I were supposed to know each other's names, but he managed to find out mine, and, better still, to get my London address. Our researchers amassed a wealth of detail about real people in Germany and about their relatives who were serving in the armed forces. They used to read the field post, which was often intercepted by our agents, and they interrogated prisoners of war. As a result my request programme went out to genuine German citizens. Often I was able to give anxious wives and mothers news of their loved ones at the front. Similarly, worried soldiers were given information about the whereabouts of their families after a heavy air raid.

Soon we received genuine record requests. They came in

letters addressed to 'Vicky' c/o Soldatensender West and were posted somewhere in Occupied Europe. I found these letters eerie and could never understand how they had reached the War Office. I was told that they were passed on by the Swedish Embassy, but could never quite work out how they had arrived there in the first place. Another peccadillo by our fearless agents perhaps?

But it was not only information and coded messages that I had to give out between records. Sometimes I was allowed to make jokes, at the expense of the Nazis of course. Once I told the good German citizens to put their samples of morning urine into small bottles and post them to the Ministry of Health in Berlin. The German postal service was clogged for weeks.

If we wanted to incite panic-buying of goods we had only to mention shortages of certain items. And since we were supposed to be a patriotic station I would always start by criticizing unprincipled hoarders. The good Germans would rush to the shops immediately and empty them. If we wanted to lower the morale of the soldiers, I would simply tell a certain battalion that, although it was surrounded and possibly trapped, all was not lost, and I would play them a cheerful tune. I like to think that because of my programme some of the Germans surrendered when they were still alive to do so.

After a time we became more ambitious with our programming. By 'we' I mean our little troupe in Newton Longville—sound expert, writers, singers and pianist. We began to manufacture whole troop concerts. Pretending that our songs and sketches were performed by soldiers and nurses at the front, we acted and sang them ourselves in the most endearing and amateurish way. One of our soldiers even managed to fall into the drum with a resounding crash on his way up onto the stage. The Allied invasion of Europe was now imminent and coded messages were sent out to our agents behind the enemy lines in the form of record numbers and labels. I could never tell how effective all this was in influencing the progress of the campaign, but I was told of one incident where my programme had actually been instrumental in capturing a U-boat. I did not know about that until after the war when I began to receive phone calls from

English journalists asking me to talk about it. I was then still pledged to secrecy so I always replied that I knew nothing of what they were asking me and that they had got hold of the wrong person. I was amazed when these reporters then quoted General Donovan himself. In the book, *Undercover Girl*, I had been mentioned by name. The Americans had apparently broken security long before the British, but I did not abandon my silence for many years. Not until almost fifteen years after the war, when Sefton Delmer wrote his own memoirs, *Black Boomerang*, and the BBC decided to make him the subject of an episode of *This is Your Life*, was I given permission to talk about my war work in general and the submarine incident in particular.

The story goes that a German submarine commander whose vessel had been lying undetected off the coast of Scotland had surfaced and surrendered without a fight. When he was interrogated he claimed that it was Vicky's programme that had made him do so. She had played a special record for him, 'Yes Sir, That's My Baby', in German and had congratulated him on the birth of a son—'and I hadn't been home for more than two years', said my victim angrily.

Until the end of the hostilities in Europe when our unit was disbanded, we regularly manufactured German records from the English or American originals. Besides my father, Egon Larson in London did some splendid witty translations, and other writers in the United States were working directly for Marlene Dietrich, who sang her most famous American hits in German versions which I frequently played. We would re-record the original disc until the start of the vocal, then either Hilde, Lisl, Trudi or I would sing the German translation to the accompaniment of the piano and some drumming from the Hollywood sound expert. These vocals would then be inserted into the record in place of the original English words. In that way we duplicated scores of hit records in German. It is a great pity that none of these witty recordings were allowed to survive. Egon Larson managed to 'smuggle out' two of his own translations on tape: 'Jenny Made Her Mind Up' by Ira Gershwin and Kurt Weill, and 'Bewitched, Bothered and Bewildered' from *Pal Joey*, both sung by me. He gave me copies shortly before he died and I am keeping them safe until some archive in Germany, England or America shows an interest.

When the BBC was preparing Sefton Delmer's *This is Your Life* programme, they asked me to take part. Like all the other subjects of this feature, Sefton knew nothing about what was to happen. He had been lured to Shepherd's Bush studios on the pretext of an interview about his forthcoming book. We were told to stay in our dressing-rooms out of sight while Sefton was hurried past our doors. I overheard the producer arguing with what he later told me was 'someone from the Home Office'. 'I'm not going ahead with the programme if I can't have Vicky,' I heard him say. 'Surely you can allow her to break security now, after so many years.' He must have won because the programme went on as planned. 'Here is someone you may recognize from the sound she makes,' said Eamonn Andrews, the presenter, to an almost speechless Delmer on stage. 'Und hier ist Vicky mit den drei Küssen …' I warbled off-stage. Then, smack, smack, smack, I imitated the sound of kissing and went out onto the set to meet my 'military' boss face to face for the first time.

The show went down very well with the invited audience. Most of the participants had friends or family out front and there was to be a party afterwards. 'There are some people over there waiting to see you,' the assistant director said when it was over. I took one look at the bedraggled group of males he had pointed out. In order to get to the studio in good time I had left Desmond to bring our sons and their friend Robert McNab along to the show. For some reason they were all wearing their very worst clothes. I had expected Irena, our maid, to check their appearances, but there they were, spattered with paint, buttons missing, jeans torn at the knees and sleeves half hanging off. Robert looked worse, if anything. 'I don't know these people,' I told the young assistant and turned away to talk to someone else. Then I made my way cautiously to the lift, hoping to escape my family, but when I got to the fifth floor, the starlight roof, where the party was held, there they were, engaged in animated conversation with Eamonn Andrews.

'I found out who they were,' he beamed, 'and I thought you'd like me to bring them up!'

But not everything that reminds me of the OSS is amusing. Some years after the end of the war I found myself in Paris lunching with some American friends. General Donovan, my former chief, was with us. In the intervening years our wonderful OSS had been changed into the dreaded CIA under his leadership. It was the one and only time we met face to face. After the meal we were strolling down the Champs Elysées in the sunshine when the General suddenly drew a letter from his breast pocket and handed it to me. What I read showed quite clearly that the Americans were about to interfere in another country's destiny by sending in their troops to bolster a corrupt régime. It was the first warning I had of things to come, and in the years of American intervention that followed I often thought ruefully of this moment; but just why General Donovan chose to share it with me I have never been able to explain. Could it have been vanity and the desire to show off his control over world politics to someone he trusted not to break security?

I handed the letter back to the General in silence. Another time my disillusionment was even more personal. It was on an early visit to Berlin that I found myself in Plötzensee. People who had fallen foul of the Nazi régime, such as the generals who staged the unsuccessful bomb attack on Hitler, were executed there and strung up on hooks from the ceiling. Subsequent German governments have turned Plötzensee into a shrine and it is always included in official sightseeing tours. We left our coach to look at the meat hooks, and then went into the adjoining room. There, along the walls, was the documented history of two ordinary German civilians who had been tried for treason. I picked one of them at random and, walking along the wall, I began to read. I don't know what made me choose this man and not the other, but to my horror I read that he had been executed for listening to foreign broadcasts. Had it been our station or the 'white' propaganda put out by the BBC? What difference did it make? For years I had entertained my listeners with funny war stories—the submarine, the specimens— and now I was sharply reminded of the reality behind the laughs.

In 1944 the Allied troops in Europe were making swift and spectacular advances. Things were definitely heating up, not only at the Second Front. At Soldatensender West we were busier than ever, exhorting the Germans not to lose heart. Under threat of imminent defeat, the Germans now bombarded England with rockets. We called them V2s. They were a particularly large, vicious weapon since they made it impossible to warn the population of their approach. They travelled faster than sound and you knew they had missed you if you actually heard the explosion, which came only after they had gone off. The so-called 'doodle-bugs'—small, unmanned planes containing a large amount of TNT—had been bad enough. Too often they managed to break through the protective air cordon near the coast and came sputtering all the way to London, belching smoke and fire out of their tails. If the engine stopped, you had to dive for cover. I remember watching the first one sailing over Piccadilly Circus. Later I was less fascinated whenever I heard the engine stop and cut out directly above our house—or so it seemed to us—as we cowered under the kitchen table expecting this horrible 'bug' to drop on us and blow us to smithereens.

With doodle-bugs and rockets you could never be sure when you took leave of your nearest and dearest in the morning whether or not you would see them again that night. But most Londoners did not worry unduly about these things until they happened. I had never worried about Desmond when he was flying on his missions to Germany. If I had thought about it too much I would have gone mad. Even so I was relieved when he was invalided out of the RAF in 1944, and arrived on our doorstep in the middle of one of the noisiest air raids we had had for ages. We could hardly hear what he was saying when we opened the door to him. 'Well, here I am!' I think it was.

Well there he was indeed, not living with me in the smart Mayfair flat I had envisaged on our first taxi drive, but moving into our semi-detached in Golders Green, slouching around in his pyjamas and dressing-gown until late in the day and working my father up into a state of righteous indignation: 'What would the neighbours say?' That was hardly the attitude of a liberated man who had brought up his daughter to be free and unrestricted by convention. The Victorian rectitude he had always dismissed as hypocrisy now came to the surface, fanned, no doubt, by a father's jealousy. I loved Desmond with all my heart and had committed myself to him for what I thought was forever, but I doubt that I would have got engaged to him at that moment if I had not also loved my father and wanted to save him from pain and embarrassment.

Demobbed from the air force, Desmond worked for an official radio station the Americans had set up in England, editing news bulletins and propaganda broadcasts, using their official transport shamelessly for our own convenience and generally raising hell. Once the Allied armies reached Berlin, both our jobs came to an end. I said goodbye to Kebbe, Ira and everyone else at Newton Longville. As a farewell gesture I was taken to lunch at the 'secret house' where I had spent my first night in the OSS.

When my parents and I returned to our house in London for good, we found Henry Zeisel and two more prisoners squatting on our doorstep. They were to have been shipped back to Germany that very week, but had managed to escape from their escorts and had found their way to Golders Green. 'We don't want to go home,' they said and pleaded with us to hide them in our attic until it had all been sorted out with the authorities. We hadn't the heart to refuse them and they camped with us for several weeks until I managed to persuade the Home Office to let them stay in England.

VE Day, the official end of the war in Europe, was a momentous occasion. A huge victory parade through London with Winston Churchill at its head was planned for the afternoon. In the event he was late, but it could not start without him.

The night before it seemed as if the entire population of London had assembled at Piccadilly Circus and, after much singing, shouting and flag-waving everyone moved off towards Hyde Park Corner. Desmond and I found ourselves walking behind a huge red flag with a group of Marxist interns from St George's Hospital. When we reached the hospital they did not stop but marched straight through the gates, up the stairs and down the middle of the public wards, cheered on by the patients. Finally we collapsed in an alcoholic daze into the opulent armchairs in the chief surgeon's private sanctum.

Next morning, VE Day proper, Desmond and I rose early. While the majority of the citizens of London were nursing gigantic hangovers, we bicycled through the abandoned city, our baskets filled with bottles and glasses, dispensing drink to the odd passer-by. Only one bottle, a litre of vintage wine, we guarded most carefully. It had been given to us by Dr Wittkowsy, a refugee of my acquaintance. We were to hand it to Winston Churchill in person. 'I have kept it throughout the war for this very day,' the doctor told us proudly.

When we arrived at No. 10 and chained our bicycles to the railings, we found the door almost completely obscured by a huge crowd. This time it was an orderly crowd, mostly defence personnel, top brass in the civil service and many politicians and dignitaries. Desmond, as usual, managed to talk his way inside. He demanded to see his cousin Winston, and we were shown into the drawing-room. After a few minutes Mary Churchill came in. She explained that her father was too overcome by emotion to see anybody. He was weeping, she told us, and she would have her work cut out to get him into a fit enough state to lead the march. We understood perfectly, handed her the bottle, and, our mission accomplished, set off again on our bicycles. The story got back to Lady Leslie that her son Desmond and his actress friend had held up the Victory Parade.

I was once again looking for a job. The BBC seemed the obvious place to turn. Hadn't I used my recording voice to help defeat the Nazis? Wasn't I 'Vicky, the girl with the pin-up voice'? I applied for an audition and prepared four short pieces in English, German, Italian and French. I was convinced I could not fail. When the letter came, I tore it open in happy expectation.

'Dear Miss Bernelle,' it said, 'Thank you very much for coming to read for us. Unfortunately there is no point in you ever applying again as your voice is entirely unsuited to broadcasting.' It was signed by Marius Goring, then head of the German department of the BBC.

Desmond, who had not been home to Ireland since leaving Trinity College to join the RAF, now decided to visit his mother at Glaslough. Both his grandparents, Sir John and Lady Leonie Leslie—she was one of the famous Jerome sisters from New York and aunt to Winston Churchill—had died during his absence, and his mother, now Lady Leslie, was more or less alone in the large house in remote County Monaghan.

He sent me amusing letters almost daily, but several months went by and he did not return. I began to get edgy. It was apparent that his mother was deliberately keeping him from me with many tasks and diversions, and he did not seem to mind. His family had never wanted me. Perhaps I was taking on a hopeless relationship. How could I, a foreigner and an outsider, and still very young, take on the weight of an entire family, particularly one that lived in a castle? His father, Sir Shane Leslie, had been very friendly when I met him once or twice for tea in London, but he appeared to be an outsider himself, a black sheep, disinherited for the benefit of his eldest son Jack, the prisoner of war. Did I really want to marry a man against his mother's wishes?

I was now playing small parts in British films and was meeting new people. Derek de Marney, the leading actor in *Latin Quarter*, flirted outrageously with me on the set and I had to admit to myself that I found him attractive. Obviously there were other fish for me to fry. A girl my age had no need to tie herself down where she was not wanted. After much heart-searching I wrote to Desmond and broke off our engagement.

Desmond wrote back by return to say that it was ill-mannered to end an engagement by letter and that he was seeking permission for me to travel to Ireland so I could do it in person. Even though the war was not over and I was an enemy alien, Ireland was neutral and Desmond had some strings to pull.

The temptation was too great to resist. I had spent my entire youth in blacked-out, bomb-scarred England, and to travel to a neutral country and see how normal adult life was lived, with lights in the streets and food in the shops, would surely be bliss. There would be ice-cream and bananas. In no time at all I was saying goodbye to my parents and sailing across the Irish Sea.

Desmond was at the quayside at Dun Laoghaire to meet me. He gave me no time to break off our engagement 'in person' and took me in a taxi to the Gresham Hotel, where, he told me, a large gathering of his friends was waiting for us in the dining-room. One of them, Jojo O'Reilly, now Countess Sliwinska, I had met once before in London. A talented writer and painter, and, in the fullness of time, mother of twelve children by assorted fathers, she became one of my best and most loyal friends.

The dinner at the Gresham was scrumptious. The shops I was not to see until the following day, but I recall that I bought ten pairs of fur-lined suede boots, unobtainable in London, and sold nine pairs of them at a fair profit when I got home. Nelson's Pillar, blown up by the IRA in 1966, still dominated O'Connell Street; you could still eat cheaply at the Green Rooster and have seafood pie at the Red Bank and Melancholy Babies at the ice-cream parlour in Grafton Street.

But it was not only the food I found exciting. I saw some beautiful buildings: the Four Courts, the Custom House, the General Post Office, the lovely, unspoilt eighteenth-century squares with their subtly coloured brick façades and the marvellous fanlighted Georgian doors. The soft aroma of turf smoke permeated everything and I still regret its gradual disappearance from the streets of Dublin.

There was so much to see and absorb that I did not get round to the problem of breaking off my engagement. 'It can wait until the day I leave,' I told myself.

Desmond introduced me to some fascinating people. He took me to the Gate Theatre to see Mícheál Mac Liammóir playing opposite Cyril Cusack's wife Maureen in Housman's *Prunella*. I thought I had never seen a young actor as beautiful and lithe as Mícheál and was thrilled when Desmond said we could go backstage and meet him. We found him at his dressing-table removing his make-up. I could not believe that this portly, though handsome, middle-aged man was the same person who had seemed so youthful on the stage.

We went to the races at Leopardstown and to the Phoenix Park where he introduced me to the President, Seán T.

O'Kelly, a tiny man, much beloved of his people. I was not in the least put out when during our interview he gave my bottom a little pat. There had been no mention so far of Desmond's mother and I did not expect an invitation, but when she heard on the grapevine that I was in Dublin and had even been taken to meet 'her nun', a Sister at the Loreto Convent in St Stephen's Green whom she considered her special friend, curiosity got the better of her. Word was sent and I found myself sitting in a train on the way to Glaslough muttering darkly that I would be 'polite to the woman—but nothing more.' She, meanwhile, was thinking exactly the same. Fortunately for everyone, neither of us was able to stick to our resolve once we had met face to face.

There was little petrol for Lady Leslie's car—neutral Ireland was experiencing shortages—and we were met at the station by Dawson, the butler, in his coachman's outfit, cock-aded topper and all, in a splendid horse-drawn carriage. Desmond made him drive the long way round so that I could admire the lakes and woods.

Castle Leslie is a large Victorian mansion built by Lynn of Lanyon and Lynn in grey sandstone. It is much brighter and far less Scotch baronial on the inside than the exterior leads you to expect. Tall windows let in the sunlight and open out onto the lake. The Italianate ceilings and fireplaces came out of an earlier house on the same site, as did most of the furniture and the paintings. These things were added to at the end of the last century by 'old Sir John', the painter, who had travelled widely in Italy and had brought back many precious things, including a Della Robbia mantelpiece.

We passed through the oak-panelled entrance hall into the 'gallery' and from there out onto the steps where we stopped for a moment to take in the breathtaking view of the lake. I was enchanted and overcome by a feeling of destiny and did not notice the woman sitting in the corner, her face hidden under a large brown hat, observing us silently.

At last Lady Leslie rose and took me by the hand. 'Can't imagine what that naughty Uncle Seymour thought he was doing when he wrote to me from London,' she said, 'You do not look a bit like the person he has been describing. Could have saved myself some anxious moments.'

From there on she could not do enough to make me feel welcome. I was to call her Marjorie from now on. She seemed ashamed of the small engagement ring which Desmond had barely been able to afford. She searched for her wedding veil and wanted me to take it back to London. She asked us to name the day then and there, but I made excuses and said that I did not want to get married in wartime.

We spent a magical week at Glaslough. I had been given the blue room with windows overlooking the lake. It is this lake and the siting of the house that lends Castle Leslie its unique beauty. I have never found another estate in Ireland with the lake so close to the house. Sitting at the dressing-table I could watch the ever-changing moods of the lake and see the swans ruffle the surface, which only minutes before had given a mirror image of the surrounding woods. I still had not given Desmond back his ring. The longer I put it off the less urgent it seemed. Was I falling in love with him all over again? Or was it just the lure of the house and the lake that had captivated me?

One night Desmond came to my room and demanded that I follow him down to the pleasure grounds to dance naked round the Japanese tree. Marjorie's bedroom over-looked the pleasure grounds and I was terrified that she would wake up, see us there and be scandalized. In the end I decided to risk it and there we were, like two fairy children, our bodies white in the moonlight, holding hands and danc-ing round the tree. My fears and apprehensions were forgot-ten. I knew without doubt that I loved Desmond and would marry him. Fortunately nobody mentioned our tryst in the pleasure grounds the next day and if Bridget, the all-seeing and all-knowing housekeeper had seen us, she wasn't telling.

VII

While I was away my father was asked to supervise and direct a new version of Strauss's *Gypsy Baron* for the provincial touring circuit. An extra part had been written into the operetta, the part of Maria Theresa, Empress of Austria, who had two good scenes in the second half. I auditioned for it and was engaged. I was also asked to write new lyrics for some of the songs. We were to be five months on tour, spending one to three weeks in most of the major cities in Britain. The war was expected to end very soon. In August 1945, the Allies had dropped the first atomic bomb on Hiroshima and the Japanese were bound to surrender. Unfortunately they did not do so immediately and a second bomb was dropped on Nagasaki. I felt only horror and despair at the time. Nothing could make me accept this act of inhumanity committed in all our names.

Before he could make all his arrangements for our tour of *The Gypsy Baron* I asked the production manager if it was all right for me to bring Desmond, my fiancé, with me. He was deeply shocked. In no way was he going to aid and abet immorality. If I was really engaged to this man I had better marry him before we started on our travels.

We had no choice but to fix the wedding. We picked 18 August 1945—the first day of peace, though we could not have foreseen this. I was married in a white dress made out of ancient brocade and satin Desmond had found in a large chest in Glaslough. Joyce Davis and her sister, friends from Holmwood school, and Hilde Palmer were my bridesmaids. Desmond's brother Jack, recently returned from five years in a German prison camp and now taking over the running of Glaslough, was our best man.

Desmond had asked his former housemaster at Ampleforth, Father Elread Graham, to marry us at St James' church in Spanish Place. As I walked up the aisle on my father's arm I thought how lucky I was to be marrying a friend—my best friend—and that I could at least be sure that he would never willingly cause me pain.

One of our wedding guests owned a cinecamera and had taken many shots of the VE Day celebrations. With what was left of his 16mm film, he shot us leaving the church. He gave us the entire spool as a wedding present, and Desmond later re-edited it, splicing together the various shots to make it appear as if the VE-day crowds, throwing ticker-tape and shouting and singing, had all assembled on the route to Spanish Place to see us getting married. There were even little boys climbing up lampposts to get a better view of me being helped into the wedding car, and for years our children were convinced that all these scenes of near hysteria were part of their parents' nuptials.

After the ceremony we all went back to South Lodge, the Leslies' London flat, and had champagne and chicken sand-wiches. The sandwiches were all that the royal caterers Searsley Tansley could produce because of rationing. We had already had a family dinner the night before in a private room at Claridges, so that the Leslies and the Bernauers could get acquainted. My father had been very generous, and I am sure he spent his last penny on all this unaccustomed grandeur. He was determined that I should have a send-off fitting to our station in life, even though this had long since been reduced to a whistle-stop by Adolf Hitler.

We spent the wedding night at the Berkeley where Jack and Marjorie were staying. After months of sexual abstinence it should have been sensational, but I was suffering from a nasty bout of cystitis, most probably caused by wedding nerves. This notorious, spoil-sport honeymoon complaint lasted for many miserable months, but it was not our only obstacle. Desmond had decided, as soon as we came back from our visit to Glaslough, that we would have to stop making love. It was essential to our souls' salvation, he said, to enter matrimony in a state of grace. Living in close prox-imity for some time, desiring each other passionately and putting the severest restraint on our need for each other must have done some harm. I am not sure that Desmond ever regained the passionate abandon he had displayed before our engagement. Virtue does not always seem to be its own reward.

To say that our first day of married life was memorable is an understatement. The members of our families were true to form. No sooner had we run a morning bath, and were about to step into it together, than Marjorie rang from her room to ask Desmond to run out and get her some cigarettes. We had just decided to go back to bed when my mother arrived with a large basket full of goodies. She was convinced we were going to starve to death at the Berkeley. Next Jack rang from downstairs and asked if we would like to come and meet him in the bar for a chat, and finally good Sir Shane just walked into the bedroom without knocking to give us a wedding present from one of his many lady friends which he had for-gotten to deliver before. It was as well that neither Anita nor my father made an appearance at the hotel that morning.

We moved into South Lodge after a day or two. Marjorie, who had taken a long lease on one of the larger flats in St John's Wood even before the building was finished, had kept it on when she went to Glaslough during the war. It had been sublet to friends, but was empty at the time. She lent it to us for a three-week honeymoon. As soon as we moved in, I rolled up my sleeves and started to clean up. Marjorie arrived in the middle of it to have tea, and found me up a ladder washing the walls. She sat down and regarded me thoughtfully.

'I can see that you would take good care of this place. I don't think I should re-let it; it will only get filthy again. I'd better give it to you two. All you have to do is pay the rent to the landlord.'

The rent was steep and Desmond was all for turning down the offer. We hadn't two pennies to rub together, but had nowhere to live except Sneath Avenue. I convinced him that even with the high rent, it was a bargain. A fully-furnished, fully-equipped apartment in St John's Wood, containing beautiful antiques, for only the price of the rent? I could take in lodgers to cover that.

Of course, this possibility had never occurred to Desmond or his family, who now regarded it as the London base for all the Leslies and their hangers-on. Whenever my sister-in-law, Anita, came to town, it was like a minor invasion of a major army. She was about to be demobbed and would arrive at South Lodge with kitbags, army boots, horse-blankets and gentlemen whom she referred to as her beaux. Beaux A and B were semi-demobbed by then and, uncertain of their future whereabouts, they too brought their army gear and dumped it with us. Beau C had not yet been released from his submarine duty and did not appear on the scene until much later, with spectacular results. But Beau B often had a teenage son in tow, who left his clothes and socks all over the drawing-room floor. They were mostly grey in colour and made a pleasant change from the khaki we usually had lying around, but it all had to stop when my two gentlemen boarders arrived.

Marjorie was none too pleased when she heard from Anita that I had turned her elegant London base into a boarding-house, but there was really nothing she could do about it. After all we were now paying the rent. Adoring our life in our lovely flat, I cheerfully made the beds and cooked the evening meals for my lodgers.

Every Friday I sat down and did the household accounts. I had a ledger in which I noted down each item against its price and worked out the weekly cost. I could not understand why Desmond always laughed derisively at my efforts. I never had any idea what I had actually paid for individual items and simply wrote down imaginary prices in the space provided, which had to add up to the total I had spent. This fiction made me feel I was keeping house in an orderly fashion.

But before we could settle down to all this domesticity, I had to fulfil my engagement with Montague, the producer of *The Gypsy Baron*. Rehearsals were held in a converted church, within walking distance of our flat, and after a few weeks we set off on the tour that had precipitated our marriage.

Once again I saw a great deal of Crewe Station. This time we went as far afield as Glasgow, a most friendly city, where we had digs in an attic and spent many nights playing 'knock knock who's there' in a gigantic double bed. We paid a brief visit to Edinburgh and saw the amazing camera obscura that projected coloured visions of the surrounding district onto a circular white table.

On opening night in Liverpool the ladies all had flowers handed up onto the stage. I had as many as six bouquets and since I was not the leading lady I felt embarrassed. As it happened, they were all from Desmond, though one of them had a card on it saying it was from the Aghabog Boys' Brass Bugle Band. Desmond never missed a performance, and sometimes he would be in the front of the stalls with some strange woman or other. I discovered to my surprise that these were ladies he had picked up in the street. He never told them that the actress playing the Empress Maria Theresa was his wife, and he got a kick out of it when they applauded me. I don't think that he missed many of my performances over the years, and certainly never failed to bring me home from the theatre after the show. For over twenty years he made my acting career his particular concern, getting much more upset than I did whenever there was a hitch. It was an irony of fate that in the end the biggest hitch was caused by Desmond himself.

Most performing artists will say that there must be a perversity in the constellation that rules their working lives. There may be months, even years when they are out of work and then two or three offers will come at exactly the same time, making it very difficult to choose the right job and turn down the others. I had only ever played bit parts in films, but suddenly, just because I was getting married and was about to go on tour with a musical, the gods arranged for me to have two offers from Hollywood, and a third offer to test for Alexander Korda, which would have fallen in the middle of my honeymoon week. In the end I made a mess of all three and never went to Hollywood or became a movie star. Perhaps it is just as well, though there have been moments in my life when I have regretted it, and have looked with envy at the films of those who did 'make it', but even if I had gone to Hollywood on a starlet's contract, I might never have got any further. Knowing the kind of person I am I feel that I might easily have fallen by the wayside. It is not that I cannot fight, but it depends what I am fighting for and how much it will cost me. And if I had succeeded?—Well I would have missed doing many interesting things, learning many vital lessons, initiating many worthwhile projects and above all I could have jeopardized a marriage that lasted many years and gave me children to bring up away from all the razzmatazz.

The tour over, my film career ended before it had begun, I was now free to settle down to married life and keep house at South Lodge. I felt very odd when people called me Mrs Leslie, but I did a great amount of cooking and began to give parties like other married women. I had always been on affectionate terms with my mother, but now we began to quarrel. She could never credit me with any domestic talents and tried hard to interfere. I yelled that this was my house and that I was in charge. Naturally she took offence.

There were other matters that began to bother me. My father's male influence may have been strong, but my mother's feminine upbringing had left an even bigger mark, and I began to suffer much inner conflict. Feminism was not a word in common use in my youth. The very concept was not then accepted, not even by women. I was a born feminist but did not know it. It took many years before I found out that my feelings were neither shameful nor reprehensible. For a long time I could not admit that marriage and motherhood were not enough for me; I needed a career of my own, not merely to earn money but because I felt incomplete whenever I was not in work.

These 'unnatural longings', as I thought of them then, made me feel freakish and sinful. I blamed my father for having brought me up as a son and giving me what I considered 'masculine' desires. It was a great relief when I reached my thirties and met other women who felt the same, and were not ashamed of it. This may surprise the young 'liberated' women of today. They take it all for granted and may not realize how their mothers struggled to make it better for them. And what about their grandmothers? When I consider my own mother, resolute and spirited as a young girl in an age of Edwardian prudery, and compare her to the difficult, neurotic woman she became—I imagine that she was brought to this state by years of submission and acceptance like most woman of her generation.

The earliest memory of my own feminist leanings goes back to a children's party in Berlin when I was eight. There were games and presents for all the girls. My schoolfriend's older brother was in charge of proceedings. At some point he threw sweets to us as other people throw crumbs to birds. The other girls would try and catch these sweets with squeals of joy, or grub on the carpet and scrape them up. I was almost paralyzed with resentment and would not take part in this game. As I stood there I felt that the big boy, far from doing us a favour, was trying to demean us.

During her trip to London for our wedding, my mother-in-law had decided that we were to be launched into society. By society she meant her own circle of friends, and as a warm-up we were first to meet her Chelsea set. An opportunity arose shortly after the wedding. She got an invitation to a cocktail party given by an antique dealer friend of hers in his house off the King's Road, full of priceless antiques. For some reason we were the last to arrive and the noise that greeted us as we stood in the doorway was ear-splitting. I had on my arm what was called a Dorothy bag, a handbag that protrudes far out on each side of the handle, when I took a step further into the room there was a deafening crash. One of a pair of irreplaceable Ming vases that had flanked the doorway lay shattered on the floor. There was a sudden ominous hush as everyone turned to stare at me. Even now, as I write this, I can still feel the icy chill that went down my spine. It says much for my mother-in-law that she went on introducing me to people after that mortifying incident. She was always warm-hearted, fun-loving and not particularly snobbish for an ambassador's daughter from New England. She also had some fascinating friends, particularly the older female ones. These fell into two categories: the respectable ones and those with a 'past'. The latter were definitely much more fun.

Fortunately our next introductions were less unnerving and we gradually built up a circle of older and wiser friends who gave us much hospitality over the years. There was the Marchioness of Headfort, formerly Rosie Boot, the first English chorus girl ever to marry into the aristocracy. She was a jolly, unpretentious woman in whose heart my own stage ambitions struck a chord. She always gathered a crowd of friends for my opening nights, and even lent us her house in St John's Wood for a scene in a film Desmond produced. And Emily Grisby, who still had flaming red hair when she was well into her eighties, and lived like a recluse in an eighteenth-century house overlooking Hyde Park. We would sit by her bedside and listen to her stories. She had been a great courtesan and one-time mistress of General Kitchener. The story goes that during the Great War, when Kitchener came to her house unexpectedly and found a rival suitor already there, she deliberately broke her string of pearls and kept the peace between the two men by having them crawl all over the floor in a united effort to retrieve them.

Vivienne Woolie Heart, who had many marriages and just as many face-lifts behind her, and who was very proud of both, was another of Marjorie's 'girlfriends' who became a close friend of ours. She looked not a day older than thirty-five when she was really in her seventies, and was quite indefatigable. When we went on a holiday together to Venice she would dance me under the table every night and ring me at eight the next morning asking why in Heaven's name was I not up and why I had kept her waiting to go to the beach. I lost contact with her for a long time and could hardly believe she was still alive after twenty years when I found her again on a visit to New York. I went to her apartment. She was ninety-one and claimed that her doctor, whom she said she fancied, had only confined her to bed because he thought that he would be safer from her if she were there.

Desmond and I spent our first Christmas together at Glaslough. Marjorie put us up in the best and biggest guest-room. There poor Desmond passed some unpleasant days stricken with a viral infection and I had to nurse him and administer some embarrassing treatments. Marjorie, a talented amateur versifier, came up with these lines:

> In the honeymoon bed instead of flirting
> The bride is giving the groom a squirting.

I remember other attempts of hers to encapsulate family history in verse. My father-in-law had a great penchant for clerics and nuns. After he had been to see a cardinal on his deathbed and made a sketch of him, he used the drawing for his Christmas cards. When he was not looking, Marjorie added these words to the cards:

> Here lies the Cardinal on his bier
> Bringing you a wealth of Christmas cheer.

Altogether that first Christmas was probably the best I ever experienced. Being the new bride, I was shown off to the village. A party was given for the estate workers in the old servants' hall in the basement. In the best tradition of country estates, the family mingled with old and young retainers. There was food and music. Anita looked incredibly beautiful in a tea-gown of cream-coloured lace. Uncle Lionel, who had come all the way from the Isle of Mull, entertained everyone with stories of the Loch Ness Monster, in whose existence he firmly believed. Old Wiggins, the gatekeeper, a staunch Protestant, recited a ballad that had eighteen verses, each one of which ended, 'He died for the Queen on Christmas Day.'

The Catholic herdsman replied with, 'The sea, oh the sea—thank heavens lies between England and me.' The implication of all this escaped me at the time as I was quite unaware of the Irish political situation. Fortunately Catholics and Protestants still fought each other with songs alone.

On Boxing Day, known as St Stephen's Day in Ireland, the ancient central heating system came on with much hissing and clanking, and the estate workers and villagers brought their children to see the tree and collect their presents. It seemed to me as if I had strayed into a chapter of an eighteenth-century novel. World War II was supposed to have swept away most of the rituals and formalities our ancestors had observed, but I was fortunate enough to experience the last remnants of a bygone age. Marjorie made it her business to take me around the neighbouring estates where some of the Anglo-Irish 'Ascendancy' were still living. A 'neighbour' could be as much as fifty miles away; people drove through the night to join in the festivities. There were still grand dances and house parties to drive to. You still had your suitcase unpacked and packed again by your hostess's lady's maid, and had your bath run for you while you were changing for dinner.

At Oonagh Guinness's house called 'Luggala', in County Wicklow, the crack was always good. She habitually had a large collection of gifted guests. There you could talk to Brendan Behan, meet Lucien Freud and his wife, Caroline Blackwood, who went on to become a novelist of note and later married the poet Robert Lowell. I always loved to go to Luggala for lunch or dinner, driving down the perilous path that led to the house at the bottom of a steep valley, to stay for a few days.

We made friends with Oonagh's eldest son, Garech Browne, then a fresh-faced youth in Irish tweeds, with the traditional woven *crios* around his waist, surrounded by assorted Irish musicians and painters. Garech had inherited his mother's knack for spotting talent. He cultivated Eddie McGuire and Eddie Delaney, both first-rate artists, launched the Chieftains and later founded Claddagh Records. He even helped finance my first solo evening when it moved to the Duchess Theatre from the Establishment. At the time we met he was living with the daughter of his mother's cook. If Oonagh was scandalized, her attitude was nothing compared to that of her staff, particularly her butler Patrick, a very patrician gentleman. Later Garech married Princess Purna, a dark-haired beauty from India.

None of the family ever knew Marjorie's age. With her blond hair and her stately walk, she could have been in her early sixties when I met her, but she must have been a great deal older. She was longing for grandchildren she could get to know on this side of the great divide, and watched me anxiously for a hopeful sign. The hopeful sign—a dizzy spell—came as I was half-way up a sixty-foot ladder on my way to climb to the clock tower of Glaslough Church. Fortunately Desmond was behind me and caught me.

I had not really planned to have children so soon but Jack was not showing any sign of getting married and I was under some pressure from the Leslie family to produce an heir, so we prolonged our 'state of grace' by not taking precautions. I was pleased enough and thanked my luck that I hardly had any morning sickness and kept healthy and well, as I would do with all my pregnancies. The morning I came home from the doctor, Anita was in the flat. I could not wait to tell her.

'How awful for you my dear,' she said sympathetically, 'don't tell Mummy.' I was taken aback. But she meant well. She was not overly fond of children at that time, especially other people's, and she knew that we could not really afford them. We were living entirely on what our two lodgers brought in, and would now have to let one of them go because we needed the room to make a nursery. Desmond was not earning anything. He was writing his first novel, *Careless Lives*, and I would not be able to work for some time. In the end it was Anita who helped us out. She persuaded her mother to restore Desmond's allowance—which had been stopped when we got married because he was expected to be a responsible husband and maintain his wife himself. But, best of all, she took me to see Dr Grantly Dick Reid.

Relaxation, deep breathing, and above all an understanding of the birth process are today part of any expectant mother's training. It was not so in my day. To popularize and put across his revolutionary method of natural childbirth Dick Reid had written a number of books. This was simply not done. 'Advertising' cried the gentlemen of the medical profession, and advertising was against the medical ethic of the time. To punish Dick Reid for this transgression, and for taking the mystery out of the obstetricians' hands, he was banned from every hospital in the country. His patients found that they had nowhere to go to have their babies except one small nursing home in Woking, his home town, where the matron had stood by him. In the end he was forced to leave the country and start his own clinic abroad. But before that he was able to see me through my pregnancy, though I had to leave London and go to a small hotel in Woking three weeks before the expected date; and since both my boys were three weeks late I saw quite a bit of that small town during two pregnancies. Dick Reid had taken me off cigarettes, tea and red meat to cleanse my system and make the confinement easier. Considering that all my children have been monstrously large at birth, he succeeded very well. I have recently found a letter that Seán, my eldest, wrote to his Granny Marjorie when he was six weeks old, and since I don't think I could improve on it, I will give you the text verbatim:

20 July 1947

Dear Granny,

I imagine that you would like to know all the gory details of my arrival and so I will try to be as explicit as possible. I don't know whether you are informed about Dr Grantly Dick Reid's method of natural childbirth. If not, it will be difficult to make you realize just how much Mummy and I owe to him. Any other doctors confronted with my 'outsize' would have doped Mummy until she would have been unable to 'expel' me herself, and would then have hauled me out with forceps. Instead the whole procedure was a calm and fascinating experience for mummy—and for Daddy who watched me being born.

It seems I have inherited my Daddy's complacency and I really didn't want to make a move at all, in spite of repeated attacks on me with castor oil and rides over bumpy country lanes etc. I know it was naughty of me as the temperature rose, and rose, and rose, and Mummy, who had kept in pretty good shape for the whole of the nine months, began to swell out so much that she could no longer fit into any shoes and her legs were enormous with poison insect bites. She really was a dreadful sight in those three extra weeks, and it was certainly not very tempting for me to be born to such a wreck.

However on 1 June the water in which I had, up to then, been swimming merrily, began to drain away. At one o'clock in the morning Daddy took us to the maternity home but our room had been given away and we were put up in a corridor. The nurses insisted on sending Daddy away, after we had carefully arranged for him to stay with us all the time. We felt rather frightened and lonely when he said goodbye. He whispered into Mummy's ear that he would stay outside in his car, so when no one was looking Mummy slipped out of bed in search of an open window. Daddy spent the night on a ladder talking to Mummy in whispers. Every time a nurse came by he had to climb down a few steps to be out of sight while Mummy rushed to her bed and pretended to be asleep.

In the morning Mummy was moved to a general ward where six women were busy admiring each other's babies. Here, I am ashamed to say Mummy lost her cool for the one and only time. She got out of bed and spent the morning traipsing round the corridors to shake me up a bit. Matron, who saw her, took pity on her and found a private room. We cheered up immediately.

Daddy and Granny Emmy came to visit us and we settled down for some more waiting and a couple of false starts. As it turned out in the end I had the last laugh. Dr Dick Reid had gone to Paris to give some lectures and had I been born that night, he would not have got to us on time. I preferred to make quite sure and on 4 June, at noontime, I decided it was safe to start on my journey properly. Mummy began to feel some pain with her contractions. She had been so well trained however, that she was able to relax completely and so minimized the pain. After twelve hours Mummy began to get a bit fed up, she could no longer relax properly as she was tired and I am sorry to have to tell you that she sought relief in a string of unladylike expressions which you will spare me to record. The doctor, who apparently felt as I did about her language, gave her an injection to make her drowsy, and Daddy massaged her back until his fingers ached.

Eventually he was sent to the hotel to recover.

The second stage of labour finally started at five o'clock in the morning, and I was on my way at last! We were wheeled into the labour ward and the doctor arrived with his assistants. Daddy came back and in his mask and gown he made quite an attractive midwife. He sat down beside our bed and thought that he would be the first to shake hands with me, but he was beaten to it by Mummy after all.

At fourteen minutes to six my head popped out and I could hear Daddy saying that I was 'rather sweet'.

Mummy could only just see me and she was surprised that I had so much hair. Two minutes later the upper part of me was born, and Dr Reid held out my hand to Mummy who shook it gently and with a very sheepish expression on her face said: 'How do you do?' to me. I ask you—what a silly thing to say.

I made one last effort and revealed myself as a MAN. Then I gave a lusty cry. Mummy assured me there was no reason to cry as I had acquired an exceptionally marvellous set of parents. The doctor and Daddy were taken outside, fanned and given a cup of tea to recover from their strenuous labours.

When I was weighed it turned out that I was only a few ounces short of eleven pounds and I looked at least a fortnight old. I have a lovely complexion, large luminous eyes, long lashes and my granny's pretty mouth, and I delight my daddy every day especially when I pee from my cot right out the window, a skill he assures me is inborn and cannot be acquired …'

On my first morning back home at South Lodge, Desmond and I were awakened by a sharp wailing at six a.m. Startled by this unaccustomed sound in our bedroom, it took us a minute or two to adjust to it. Of course it was our baby crying to be fed. We looked at each other and burst out laughing.

Over the next few weeks presents and flowers arrived at the flat. People called to welcome and admire our son. Marjorie sent over a diamond bracelet and Sir Shane stood at the head of Seán's cot and made a pronouncement—'This is a child of beauty and genius'—then vanished again not to come near us for several years.

This did not surprise me. Shane was a man full of contradictions. He was first and foremost a man of letters with many books and poems to his credit, a friend of Tolstoy's and an editor of the *Dublin Review*. After turning Catholic during his student days at Cambridge he further scandalized his Anglo-Irish Protestant parents by standing as the Nationalist candidate in Derry a few years later. The stories his family told me about him were legion. He had never been a conventional husband or father, as poor Marjorie found to her dismay. Handsome and clever, he had swept her off her feet when they were introduced in New York. He had intended to become a priest and on their wedding night he walked around the marriage bed with a censer, wafting incense and chanting purifying litanies before joining his waiting bride. Later he left the running of the household and the bringing up of children entirely to her, never asking how she was managing financially.

Once he met little Desmond in the hall, looked at him with faint surprise, and asked 'And who are you, little boy?' He seldom, if ever, gave his children presents. On our wedding day he handed me a missal. Inside, the name Anita had been carefully crossed out and the name Agnes substituted.

At the same time it was known that he had been most generous to strangers and had put several deserving children through college. If the name 'the good Sir Shane' was often spoken with derision by the Leslies, there were countless others to whom it was the truth.

To me he was always kind and courteous but when asked to help, he did not always know how to go about things. When I came down with a second bout of measles at the age of twenty-one and Desmond phoned him from Taunton Air Base asking him to send me some roses on his behalf, I received a telegram with the cryptic message 'Flowers by Daddy' instead.

To our amazement he came up with the money for our very first car. We found an ancient Austin with a sliding roof that leaked so badly we had to drive it with one hand on the wheel and the other holding a tin can to catch the water. We were very proud of it though, since none of our contemporaries owned cars at the time. I would cheerfully plough through the London traffic, striking terror into the hearts of my passengers by talking to them incessantly, turning my head backwards to emphasize a point.

Now we had a car and a flat in St John's Wood, but we also had one less boarder and another mouth to feed. Desmond was writing novels and had no regular job and I was only working here and there, with the result that we had very little money. Once when I was given an expensive ticket for a charity performance at the Globe Theatre, John Gielgud himself came into the audience to take up a collection. He came to me first because I had an aisle seat in the back row of the circle. All I had in my purse was the sixpenny piece for my fare home. I was deeply embarrassed when I had to look the great man in the face without being able to put anything on his empty plate.

VIII

In 1947, at about the time of Anita's wedding to Commander Bill King, Desmond had just published his second novel and decided we should become film producers. He went into various dubious partnerships. It was obvious to me that film people attached themselves to him for his fund-raising potential. I soon began to recognize the danger signs and whenever he told me: 'You don't understand—he is my best friend', I knew there was trouble ahead.

Since I was the only one in our film company who had actually seen a shooting script, I was sent up to the room we had taken at the Shelbourne Hotel in Dublin, where our first film was to be shot, to try to bring some order into the awful gibberish that passed for the scenario. Seán, in his carry-cot, was howling and had to be banished to the bathroom. The director threw away my carefully amended script when he started to shoot. Our first effort was a short film called *My Hands Are Clay*, about which I would prefer to say very little.

It was during the shooting of *My Hands Are Clay* that I first saw Maureen Aherne, who was to play such a big part in my life. She was then barely two years old, standing in her play-pen, clutching Toto her teddy bear, and gazing at me with azure eyes. Her father Richard, who was appearing in our film, had taken me to his brother's house to meet his little girl when she was three years old. Her mother, Lady Patricia Moore, had fallen from a window at the Shelbourne Hotel during a spell of post-natal depression and Maureen and her elder brother Patrick were being brought up by Richard's family. This left Richard free to adopt a nomadic life. He was now commuting between Ireland, with its bars and racetracks, and California with its film studios and starlets. I was enchanted by little Maureen but did not see her again until she was thirteen, when she came to stay with me at the Shelbourne Hotel and we made some fateful decisions about her future.

The Shelbourne, one of Dublin's top hotels, started life as about three town houses. When Dublin grew in the eighteenth century the building found itself in the middle of the city. The first time Desmond took me there it was still untouched by the hands of the 'improvers' and you had your drinks in the charming Shelbourne Rooms with their Adam blue and white medallions on the walls, subsequently replaced by the Horseshoe Bar. It was the place my mother-in-law always used when she came up to Dublin, and we stayed there ourselves whenever we could afford it and sometimes when we could not.

On some previous occasion Desmond had sent me to Dublin to chat up Harry Clifton, a multimillionaire, to try to get him to invest in our film company. It was my first experience of flying and it was not a pleasant one. In those days aeroplanes flew slowly and at a low altitude, and if there was any turbulence there was no way of escaping it by flying above the clouds. We were buffeted about in the most alarming way. I was feeling sick, but the German in the seat next to me was most comforting. I learnt that he was an industrialist and, guessing that he was not short of cash, I made a date with him for dinner at the Shelbourne, just in case I did not get anywhere with Harry Clifton.

I found Harry in an hotel in Portmarnock. It was my first experience of this great but kind eccentric. He received me in his room, wearing a silken dressing gown, and with his black beard and piercing eyes he looked as I always imagined Rasputin had looked. He informed me that I was the reincarnation of Lucretia Borgia and sent me on my way without buying any shares.

Back in town I made a dinner date with Count de Lalaign, the Belgian ambassador to Dublin, a close friend of Marjorie's, and a charming old worldly gentleman. I realized too late that the date was for the same evening I had agreed

Agnes in Abbazia, aged two,
winning first prize in the summer
parade.

Agnes with an unwanted Christmas
gift.

Agnes with Italian friends Luciana
Petorelli and Agatha Auersberg,
giving the Mussolini salute.

Agnes in a costume copied from her
father's operetta *Princess Caprice*.

Agnes with her maternal grandparents, Franz and Berta Erb, and cousin Rudi, in Wittenberge.

Agnes's parents, Emmy and Rudolf Bernauer, in Abbazia *c.*1925.

Family and friends on the beach at Abbazia *c.*1928. *Left to right*: Agnes, Rudolf, two friends, Emmy, friend, cousin Ilma Gonda, friend, Clary Neuhäusler, uncle Berzi Gonda, aunt Gisela Gonda, cousin Luzie, and lifeguard.

Marlene Dietrich's flat in Berlin, 1930, with her daughter Maria Sieber (*centre*) at her seventh birthday party flanked by Misha Spoliansky's daughters; behind her is Agnes and to her left Conrad Veidt's daughter.

Agnes in her first film role, aged seven, playing a little boy with Jacob Tiedke in *Eine Tolle Ballnacht* .

An early photograph of number one Viktoria-Luise-Platz, Berlin.
The Bernauers occupied the entire first floor of the turreted building.

Agnes in St Mark's Square, Venice,
with grandfather Franz Erb *c.*1930.

Agnes in Austrian national dress at
Bad Ischl, 1935.

Partners Carl Meinhard and Rudolf Bernauer in the early 1920s.

Façade of the Hebbel Theater, Berlin, owned by Meinhard-Bernauer-Büschnen.

Opposing campaign posters in Berlin for the presidential elections of March 1932.

Desmond Leslie in his Spitfire, 1943.

Agnes as 'Vicky' the 'Sailors' Sweetheart' broadcasting to German troops on Radio Atlantik for the OSS in 1943, with Rudolf Bernauer (*left*) and producer Charles Kebbe.

Agnes and Desmond Leslie's wedding, 18 August 1945, at St James's, Spanish Place, London, on the first day of peace in Europe.

Agnes with Joseph O'Connor in *Stranger at My Door*, shot in Dublin, 1949.

Agnes with Marlene Dietrich, Peggy Coster and director Henry Coster, on the set of Nevil Shute's *No Highway*, shot in England, 1951.

to meet the German industrialist. I could not contact him and had not the face to put off the dear old ambassador. I decided I would simply have to meet them both for dinner at the same time. After all there were two separate dining-rooms in the Shelbourne Hotel.

I have a dim recollection of inventing some important long-distance phone calls in order to be able to eat hors d'oeuvre in the main dining-room with the ambassador, and then rush off for melon in the Grill Bar with the German chap. This was followed by minute steak with one of them, another mythical phone call and fish in the Grill Bar with the other. Then a repetition of the routine for dessert. After that, unable to swallow another bite, I introduced my two hosts to one another. 'I have asked a friend to come and join us for coffee,' I told each of them. All three of us ended up most amicably drinking coffee in the lounge. Each of my gentlemen believed that he had been the one with whom I had dined that night.

On another occasion when I was on a flight to Dublin to join Desmond, a man in the seat next to me asked if I would like to do a newspaper advertisement for Pond's cream. He offered me ten pounds. I knew he had recently paid our friend Raffaela, the Duke of Leinster's wife, five hundred pounds for such an ad. Even though I realized I was not in the same league as a duchess, I found the offer insulting and refused. He then handed me his card in case I changed my mind. I pocketed the card and headed for the Shelbourne, wondering why Desmond had not been at the airport to meet me. I found him in the hotel lounge looking somewhat sheepish. We were to travel on to Glaslough but he could not leave the hotel. His suitcase had been impounded. 'Why?' I asked innocently.

'I can't pay my bill,' he said.

'How much is it?'

'Ten pounds,' he said.

I remembered the ad man whose office was on the opposite side of the Green.

'Stay there. Don't move until I come back.'

I took out the card and raced across the square. The ad man had only just arrived at his office himself.

'I'll do the ad if you give me the money straight away,' I panted.

Within half an hour I had had my photograph taken and signed some advertising copy without even glancing at it. We paid the hotel bill and left for Monaghan. For years after that my face appeared in the Irish papers with the caption:

'WHEN HUNTING, SHOOTING OR FISHING, MRS DESMOND LESLIE ALWAYS USES PONDS CREAM.'

I had never been hunting, shooting or even fishing in my life.

Later, a kindly friend sent a copy of Desmond's second novel, *Pardon My Return*, to Kate O'Brien for review. He misguidedly asked her to pay for it. Outraged, she demanded to know why. Our friend told her that my husband was a struggling author, always short of cash. Miss O'Brien produced a cutting of the notorious ad.

'No wonder the young man is struggling,' she snorted, 'just look at his wife's activities.'

Seán was now able to crawl, but when we returned to London on that occasion he was struck down by gastro-enteritis, then a notorious baby killer. We called in doctor after doctor, but since Seán never stopped smiling at them, they did not take his trouble very seriously. I knew how ill he was because it was I who washed his nappies. I carried him around the nursery for hours every night to try and make him forget the pain and discomfort. Finally, in despair, I telephoned Grantly Dick Reid. He came over at once and put Seán on some special medication. Miraculously it worked. But Dick Reid confirmed that it had been a narrow escape and it took Seán some time to recover. Desmond tried his best to be of use, but in those days fathers were not expected to help with the children. To see a man push a pram in the street would have caused a sensation in 1947 and it has taken me some time to get used to the sight, so common these days.

Desmond on the other hand could hardly look after himself, make a cup of tea or boil an egg. He had been looked after by Nanny Weston until he was almost sixteen. Marjorie, who sometimes stayed with us, became aware of my lonely struggle, and when I was offered the lead in Arthur

Schnitzler's play *Liebelei* (*Light of Love*) at the Austrian Centre, she treated me to a few weeks of Desmond's old nanny, who came out of retirement briefly to look after Seán.

Liebelei, which we did in German, is a tragedy. At the end of it I had to rush offstage, ostensibly to kill myself. Now that I was older, and, as I fondly imagined, more experienced, I did not consult my father until the dress rehearsal. He watched patiently and then asked me to come home with him to 'get it right'. He would work with me even if it took all night. I pointed out that my blouse was drenched in tears. 'It is not you who is supposed to cry,' he said, 'it is the audience.'

On the opening night I played the part the way he had taught me. I did not cry, and was convinced I had made a mess of it.

'Not at all,' my father said proudly. 'Look around you. They are still wiping away their tears'.

The Austrian Centre building was very basic in its furnishings. The stairs, the foyer and the stage were just bare boards. Before leaving for the performance I would roll up the oriental rugs in our hall and drag them across to the Centre in Westbourne Terrace. One evening Desmond caught me doing this.

'Where on earth are you taking my mother's precious rugs?' he asked. 'Put them down at once.'

I refused.

'When I act, there will be carpets,' I cried, a statement I have never been allowed to forget.

But it was not carpets alone I wanted at the Austrian Centre. I had written to invite Dame Sybil Thorndike to see the show. On the last night one of the notorious pea-soup fogs that used to plague London descended. All transport was at a standstill and the only people in the audience that night were those who lived close by—all except one, who came from much farther. Sybil Thorndike had walked all the way from Marble Arch in the fog to see an unknown actress play in German, simply because she had written and invited her. The next day she sent me an encouraging letter and told me I could come and visit her in her dressing room any time. We kept in touch for many years and when I moved to

Dublin, her son, the late Christopher Casson, became a neighbour in Sandymount. Once we were even 'married' in an Alan Ayckbourn play.

In 1948, when Seán was little more than one year old, Marjorie took Jack and Anita on a trip to New York. I felt terribly guilty that Desmond was left out only because he had married so young. I suggested he should use the royalties from his second book to buy a one-way ticket to New York. He could turn up at the Hotel Fourteen where his mother was staying. 'Once you are there, she will be pleased to see you and invite you in.'

It turned out just as I had expected, but what I did not anticipate was that Desmond would stay on when the others came home. He was 'making splendid contacts for both of us', he wrote. 'Any minute now' he would 'get a job in New York or Hollywood and bring me over.' There was no mention of baby Seán. His letters were full of the famous people he was meeting and here and there some unknown female names cropped up. I began to get seriously worried, especially because the little money he had left behind was fast running out.

I remembered the time he had 'disappeared' in London when I was breast-feeding Seán. He had rung me at nine p.m. from a party to tell me to start the dinner as he would soon be home. When there was no sign of him at four in the morning I naively rang the police. They laughed at me.

'An accident? If we were to ring all the hospitals each time some husband goes on the razzle ...'

'You don't understand,' I sobbed, 'my husband is not like that. We haven't been married very long.'

But they understood much better than I did. He had met some girl at the party and had forgotten about coming home.

I began to feel abandoned. There was nothing for it but to sublet the flat and move to my mother with Seán. She was delighted. As it happened my father, too, was away in America. After twenty years of marriage, Edith, my brother's wife, had given birth to a daughter, Evelyn Rudie. My father, who had crossed the Atlantic to meet his first grand-daughter, had fallen in love with the little girl. He wrote to tell my mother to pack up the house and join him in Los Angeles. She was needed there.

'Of course I am.' she said. 'They want a Nanny for their child, but I have a child of my own to look after.'

She did not mean me, but her grandson. From the moment we moved in with her she seized the chance to take him over. Moving there was the worst mistake I ever made.

My mother, who had always encouraged me in my work, could never accept that I had other talents. 'Kuche, Kuchen, Kinder' were in her domain, not mine. 'Don't touch that child, you'll kill it,' she would shout at me in front of Seán. She would mash up every morsel of food for him because he was 'delicate', and made him feel he would not survive in my care without her ministrations. Once when I came home from a day's work in Denham Studios, I found Seán in bed in a darkened room. He had fallen off a chair and bitten his tongue, and the doctor had been called. When I rushed to his bedside to comfort him, he screamed with terror.

I went into a deep depression and sat for hours in my room just staring at the wall. Unfortunately I was too young and ignorant to understand the danger to my son. Until the age of three, a child identifies with its mother. If the mother has been branded 'no good', so has the child, and its confidence is undermined.

I should have gathered Seán up and moved to the nearest YWCA. Instead all I did was to engage a French au pair girl and make her a kind of buffer between me and my mother. She was efficient and did provide temporary relief for me. I was now able to join Theatre 48, a promising young company attached to an art gallery in St John's Wood, which today would be called 'alternative'. I was particularly pleased when I was given the lead in their second production. David Tutaev, the director, was a third-generation Russian, small of stature but with an irresistible magnetism. He cast me as Yolande, the unfaithful wife, in Armand Salacrou's play *The Unknown Woman of Arras*. It was a fitting role for me at that time because I had fallen in love with Tutaev. But unlike Yolande, who flaunted her infidelity and drove her husband to suicide, I was in a turmoil of anguish and guilt. What if Desmond should return after all these months?

As usual, I was very bad at rehearsals. In those days, I had a great fear of 'miscarrying' a part and gave little indication of how I was going to play the character eventually, sometimes not before the dress rehearsal, when there was no longer a director to stop me in full flight. David was getting impatient. The company had been founded and financed by two large lesbian ladies, whom we nicknamed the Fairies. The Fairies had taken a great dislike to me. For one, they believed that I was responsible for their nickname, and getting to know my husband's family background, they were suspicious of my 'dedication'. To make matters worse, they disapproved when I became what they termed 'inordinately' concerned about my costumes. I have always considered that an actress's wardrobe in a play is an integral part of her characterization. I went to some length to design my Yolande clothes and had them made by Irene, my own dressmaker. The Fairies thought my attitude superficial and declared that I was not serious about my work. They also disapproved of my relationship with David, their 'white-headed boy'. David's several discarded lady friends, whom he had involved in our production in various ways, watched me with gimlet eyes. None of these tensions made me blossom in the part.

The one person with whom I could relax was a girl of my own age, also from Berlin, Renée Goddard. She had arrived in England with a children's transport after her father had been executed by the Nazis for alleged complicity in the Reichstag Fire. She had been interned and spent most of her teens in Holloway prison during the war. She was now playing Yette in *The Unknown Woman of Arras*. A young actor of Greek parentage, Michael Cacoyannis, later famous as Michael Yannis the film director, played my husband.

Close—too close as it turned out—to the opening night, I finally came to grips with Yolande and I believe I played her reasonably well. I was waiting for David to tell me so after the opening night, but he had been too nervous to watch and had spent the time pacing the adjoining art gallery.

The following morning the Fairies called a meeting. After the great success of the night before, they had received an offer to transfer the play to a theatre in the Strand. But they had decided to replace one of the cast—me.

Outraged, Renée Goddard stood up. She called on the company to strike. To my amazement they agreed, but I could not accept such a sacrifice. I was convinced the Fairies would have no trouble replacing all of us and the play would move into the West End regardless. Eventually I persuaded the cast to stay with the production. David, who had not seen my performance, remained silent throughout these discussions. When I got back to Sneath Avenue, I went straight to bed, drew the curtains, and did not get up for days. I believed that I would never work again.

The following Sunday there was one more performance of *The Unknown Woman of Arras* at the Gallery. How I got through it I cannot now imagine, but I remember a stranger coming to my dressing-room afterwards. He was a youngish man, dark-haired with a moustache, and spoke with an American accent. He congratulated me on my portrayal of Yolande. He told me he would like to come again when we were playing in the West End. Embarrassed I told the stranger that I would not be in it then. 'I'll be abroad', I lied hastily, 'making a film.'

The stranger gave me his card. 'Tennessee Williams USA,' I read.

This was the first but by no means last time that I invented a job to get me out of an embarrassing situation, only to have the job materialize. In less than six months I was offered a part in a Dutch/English co-production *Niete Verhebst* (*But Not in Vain*) which was to be filmed in Amsterdam.

Meanwhile a girl who worked in our box office was rehearsing Yolande. I kept away from everyone at Theatre 48 but Renée rang me to say that she had got me tickets for the West End opening. I told her I could not possibly come, but she insisted.

'It's like falling off a horse,' she said, 'if you don't get up at once you'll never ride again.'

I thought I had done my 'getting on again' at the second performance, but to please Renée I decided to take her up on her suggestion, though not quite in the way she had expected.

The opening scene of *The Unknown Woman* had some very effective strobe lighting, and to emphasize the effect I had worn a black and white striped dress. I took the dress out of my theatrical trunk, and, flanked by two faithful admirers, arrived at the theatre 'in costume'. David Tutaev nearly fainted when he saw me. His ex-lady friends rushed to his side. I threw them a dazzling smile even though I was inwardly shaking and we took up our seats in the front row. The first thing the unfortunate leading lady saw when she made her entrance were my stripes. Since the audience that night were the usual first-nighters who had attended the first night in St John's Wood, they also recognized both me and my stripes. The whole thing became a *cause célèbre*. The buzz started in the interval, in the front row: 'Was that the professional actress, watching the amateur who had supplanted her making a fool of herself ...'. Of course I am sure I had never been as 'wonderful' as I was now made out to be, but that is the way a myth will grow. Far from being finished, I had at last started to 'arrive'.

David and I eventually forgave each other.

When the time came to leave for the filming in Holland, I was told that the English partners had no money to pay the cast a salary. We were to be on shares of the profits, but the daily allowance the Dutch partners would pay us was so large that we should be able to save a substantial sum of money. Indeed five pounds per day did seem a great deal of money in 1949, but how were we going to bring it back to England under Dutch currency regulations? We made extravagant plans. Perhaps we could club together to buy a car and drive it home, or smuggle some diamonds, sell them in London and share the cash. In the end none of these plans were realized.

I checked into the hotel in Amsterdam together with my film husband, Martin Benson, with whom I had travelled. The hotel porter promptly mistook him for my real husband since we did everything together. We drove together to the studio at Duivendrecht each morning and dined together each night. Not surprisingly, the porter's eyebrows shot up when David Tutaev arrived, moved into the hotel, and occupied all my free moments instead of Martin.

In the film I was playing a pregnant Jewish girl on the run from the Nazis. I actually had to give birth in a stable in the final scene with much groaning and moaning. A large pillow stuffed into my knickers represented the baby. I thought that if this film had come along a year or so earlier when I was carrying Seán I could have been in work all through my pregnancy. I do not recall whether the film made much impact when it was shown in England. None of us ever got the promised percentage of profit anyway, and the 'large' subsistence did not go as far as we had expected. The hotel was expensive and there were too many temptations in post-war Amsterdam for people like us who had grown up during a time of austerity. Free of the miseries of Golders Green for seven glorious weeks in this charming old city, with its Indonesian eating places and satirical cabarets, I became a little reckless with my money whenever I was not working in the studio.

During my days off I managed to find Ilma, my cousin, who had survived so many years in Belsen. She was now married to an old friend who had avoided the camps all through the war hidden in an attic in Amsterdam by his courageous landlady. They now had a small son, Ronnie, who was born when they were both well over forty. I was pleased to find Ilma comfortably settled, and not traumatized by her horrendous experiences, but I was unnerved by the normality of her bourgeois household—her everyday concerns with shopping, cooking, dressmakers' appointments and baby care amazed me. I had imagined that survivors of the Holocaust would bear the marks visibly and forever. Perhaps my cousin was just one of a few fortunate ones who managed to forget.

My enthusiastic accounts of life in Amsterdam had stimulated Desmond into taking the boat back to Europe and joining in the fun. At the hotel the head porter's eyebrows had already been raised to their upper limits, so all he could do now was to wink at me knowingly when David Tutaev went back to London and Desmond arrived in his stead.

Desmond had brought me a suitcase full of American clothes and underwear the like of which we had not seen in Europe since before the war, if ever. Things I had never before possessed were strewn all over the hotel room floor and I had a marvellous time modelling them for Desmond. As it turned out it was lucky he had brought them to Amsterdam.

On our last day I found that the hotel bill was larger than my allowance permitted. While a taxi waited outside the door to take us to the airport I was engaged in frantic negotiations with the barman inside. How much for this jacket? How much for this skirt? The price he paid me for each garment was never quite enough to cover the bill as I raced back and forth between his till and that of the receptionist. The suitcase was opened and shut a number of times until all was paid. We had now missed the plane we were booked on and the porter told us we would be fined at the airport before we could board another one. The barter started all over again. I was now down to my undies and had to squat under the bar counter and remove a lacy bra and satin slip and hand them up to my friend the barman until the last guilder was raised and we were on our way.

When we got home there were a number of issues to be dealt with. Top of the list was the return to South Lodge. Since my tenant's lease was up anyway, this we could do fairly quickly.

The other important matter was my infatuation with David Tutaev. Since Desmond had been frank about his involvement with some of the ladies he had mentioned in his letters, and since one of them had even followed him to London, or at least arrived for a 'brief' visit, as she claimed when we met, I did not lie to him. After pouring a bottle of milk over my head, Desmond faced the situation with a degree of tolerance. Not so David Tutaev, who could not accept that things were different now that Desmond had come back. I had been brought up to believe that marriage was forever, 'for better or for worse', and that infidelity was the 'worse' one had to put up with and forgive and that anyhow I could never be the one to break up our home. In the end David brought about a solution by getting engaged to an American girl and following her to New York.

In spite of, or perhaps because of, *My Hands Are Clay*, Desmond did not give up his ambition to be a film producer. Once more he set about trying to raise finances and found a Mrs Wolverton, who lived in a large, ugly house in Wimbledon with her daughter, and who agreed to take up most of the shares in our company. I don't really know how he ever came across her. At the beginning I did not question her involvement. The film had a very good part for me in it, at least it should have been a very good part, if only our script-writer had made up his mind whether I was to be a heroine or a villainess before we started shooting. Since I could not get any definite directive from anybody, I had to play the part throughout with a deadpan expression, to leave the way open for last-minute character revelations. My two leading men in the film, which we called *Stranger at My Door*, were Valentine Dyall and a new young man, Joseph O'Connor, whom I had found in the pages of the Spotlight casting directory and who was perfect in the Irish part.

The crew was assembled by Paul King, the co-producer, and we now only lacked an editor. We interviewed a young man during lunch at our local Austrian restaurant in St John's Wood. He ordered boiled fish and boiled potatoes while we were tucking into the delicious Viennese dishes which were the speciality of the house. Asked if he was perhaps suffering from a stomach complaint he assured us he was 'quite all right, thank you'.

I told Desmond afterwards that in my opinion this chap would never be able to edit a film. 'He hasn't the necessary imagination.' Desmond said I was being quite absurd and gave the man the job. He had to be replaced after little more than a week. Since the new editor could not possibly know which shots were the right ones, I was put into the cutting room with her to help look for them. In this way I learnt a great deal about editing and realized that it is one of the most vital aspects of film-making and that, although I prefer the stage, I would not have minded being a film editor, having the control over timing and dramatic effect that you cannot have as an actor in a film.

We had hardly gone into the second week of shooting when a crisis nearly ended the entire project. Desmond had raised the bridging money from some of Marjorie's friends, but we now needed Mrs Wolverton's investment to continue shooting. She claimed that her own partner, a big financier, was going to come up with the money any minute.

I had harboured serious doubts about her for some time

and began to get alarmed when, at Christmas, she sent me a couple of turkeys—normally unobtainable without meat coupons under Sir Stafford Cripps's post-war austerity regime—which smelled to high heaven. Before throwing them into the dustbin, I made a phone call to the police station in the country town in which Mrs Wolverton's financial partner was supposed to be living. They told me no one of that name was known in the district. I rang Mrs Wolverton's house, where Desmond had just arrived to sign over our shares, and warned him that there was something very wrong and begged him not to sign anything. He said I was making a silly fuss over some smelly turkeys and went ahead with the deal. It soon emerged that the mysterious money man was none other than her local butcher, he of the rotten turkeys and father of the whey-faced youth supposedly courting her daughter who was always hanging about her house when we came for a business meeting. The truth was that his father had sent him to be present whenever the shares in our film company were being discussed. Mrs Wolverton, who had pocketed the money, was not only cheating us, but also her butcher, who believed he now owned our company.

The butcher ended up without money or shares, Mrs Wolverton ended up in jail and we ended up without finance to finish the film and with no Christmas dinner.

Desmond somehow managed to complete the film with nothing but the bridging money, but when it was all shot and edited there was no cash left for any music. Desmond then bought some reels of music track from music libraries and locked himself into the cutting room for many days and nights. He emerged with a very effective sound-track for *Stranger at My Door,* which he had made by playing some of these tracks backwards or re-recording them on top of one another until he had achieved the desired effect. The music turned out to be almost the best thing in the film and Desmond's experience in the cutting room was the beginning of his career in what was then known as *musique concrète.*

When *Stranger at My Door* was finished, Monarch Films took over the distribution. The film was shown in several countries, even in the United States. My brother Emmerich, now called more simply Emery, who had not seen me since I was thirteen, wrote in great excitement that a girl who looked just as he imagined I now looked had appeared on his television screen, and the titles at the end had confirmed that he had indeed been watching his little sister.

To our surprise we were now invited for a weekend at Blenheim Castle by the Duke and Duchess of Marlborough. We had once stayed there during a large house party, but had had very little contact after that with our hosts, who were Desmond's distant cousins.

Unfortunately it was a complicated and embarrassing visit. The Duke had accepted an offer from some Wardour Street tout to let him make a documentary film at Blenheim, and the Duchess, who had not taken to the man, told us that she thought we should make the film instead. The Duke was determined to keep to his arrangement and there was constant bickering between the two which started at the breakfast table and continued late into the night as the Duchess tried to push her chosen protégés—us—at the unwilling Duke. We did not know how to tell the Duchess that it required more than good intentions to make a film and that we simply did not have the finance or facilities to take on this project even if we had been welcomed by her husband.

We were taken into corners by the warring pair and given separate talkings-to, so we were most relieved when the weekend came to an end and we were able to leave, carrying a large polar bear skin from the gallery floor away with us—a bribe from the Duke for us to disappear and not bring up the subject again.

To the dismay of successive nannies, the ducal polar bear ended up on the nursery floor, where the unfortunate ladies would stumble and trip over its bulky head, usually when carrying trays. Eventually it was banished to the basement of South Lodge and devoured by moths.

Desmond went on experimenting with sound tapes at home. He found a brilliant sound engineer, Rupert Neave, who built him a console with which he could mix any sounds. I am told that Rupert Neave has since become the guru of sound engineering. His name is spoken with hushed reverence by people in the business and the console he built for Desmond, one of the first of its kind, is now priceless. I hope it is still safe in the old kitchen at Glaslough, where it was put in 1963 when we moved to Ireland.

When we realized the potential of the sounds Desmond was creating, we turned our spare room into a studio where he amassed hundreds of tapes containing thousands of sounds: bees humming, cars hooting, babies crying. He used these sounds as a painter would use the colours on his palette to create sound 'pictures' and ended up with whole symphonies. He was, I believe, one of the first to work this way. Others followed, but hardly anyone had his combination of self-taught technical know-how and ability to compose. If only he had continued with his unique work after 1963 he would today be at the very top.

We soon found that the combination of our respective talents turned out extremely well. Involved in theatre, film and television, I was able to invite my directors home for a drink and Desmond would lure them into the studio and play them his compositions. Hardly any of them ever left our flat without ordering a piece of incidental music or a sound-track for their next production. Of course it took some time before we reached this point, and after *Stranger at My Door* we were as broke as ever.

Unfortunately, none of our efforts to get rich quickly ever met with success. Nobody bought the hand-made leprechauns Desmond had once acquired in Dublin in vast numbers, or ordered the Bibles we advertised as the 'scandalous book no one can afford to miss'. The friend who had briefly lodged with us thought he would embarrass us by paying the much-needed rent. When I declined the bottle of whiskey he offered instead, on the grounds that we were teetotallers, he sent us a basket of unripe pears from Fortnum and Mason. The Swiss watchmaker I had picked up in Paris, who promised we could make a fortune selling his watches in England, had been carted off to jail by the time we arrived in Lausanne and we had to bail him out.

There was now a polio epidemic in London and I fled to Brighton in a panic with little Seán. We stayed in the Hotel Desmond.

At weekends Desmond would come down from London like all the other husbands. He joined in the general merry-making at the bar but could never afford to buy a round. Back in London he sent me twenty-five pounds via the hotel manager. I went to the office to collect it and was told it would be kept there against our bill.

'I get the impression', the manager said, 'that this is the only money you possess.' Unfortunately, it was. Humiliated and angry as I felt, I could not now sweep out of the hotel.

Polio epidemic or not, I had to take Seán home the following week, just in time for the annual Film Ball at the Albert Hall. At ten pounds per head, we could not afford to buy tickets, but on the night of the Ball we dressed ourselves up, Desmond in his brother's dinner jacket and I in my mother's white fox furs. We hired a Rolls and gave the driver five pounds to pick us up at the back of the Albert Hall and take us half-way round to the front entrance. As we stepped out of the Rolls and swept inside in all our finery nobody dared ask us to show our tickets.

We quickly located some friends in one of the boxes. Champagne was flowing, we were introduced all round and in no time at all I was offered a job.

I went to Manchester to play the lead in a terrible B-movie. The company, called Mancunian, was a family business owned by a man and his two sons, one of whom directed the films, but none of them had really made the transition from the sausage factory they had been running before. It would be impossible to describe the contortions we often had to go through, twisting our bodies and heads backwards if we were to look into the camera. The dialogue was reminiscent of *My Hands Are Clay*. My most vivid recollection of the several films I made for this company was an episode set in a Paris bistro. The comic duo Jewell and Warris were playing sailors who had strayed into the place by mistake and got embroiled in a brawl. I was the Apache girl with a heart of gold who wanted to rescue them.

For this scene we had rather a good little set. Some of the chairs had been made of balsa wood and most of the bottles of wax. This was to enable the extras to hurl them at each other in safety. A large contingent of wrestlers from the Manchester Stadium had been engaged to give the brawl a look of authenticity. No one realized how much the wrestlers really hated each other. As soon as the director shouted 'Action', they set upon each other with genuine ferocity. They hurled not just the balsa wood chairs and wax bottles, but everything movable, at each other. Bodies crashed to the floor, blood was flowing. I was to pull my two comics right through the middle of all this mayhem, but I was terrified.

'Go on! Go on!' yelled the floor manager and pushed me into the middle of the heaving mass. He pushed the comics after me. Glass flew past our ears, wood crashed by our elbows as we made our way through the wrestlers as fast as we could. We reached the far end just as the bistro wall collapsed. We could hear the ambulance sirens wailing in the distance. The cameraman was still rolling his camera. It was all he could do because there was now no possibility of reshooting the scene. The set was almost completely demolished. I imagine this was the best scene our company ever produced.

IX

In 1951 a message came from Glaslough that Marjorie was seriously ill and was not expected to live through the night. Papa Shane, Jack and Desmond had to hire a special plane to take them to Ireland because the doctor had not telephoned until mid-afternoon, by which time the last scheduled flight had already left. I could not go with them because little Seán was in the throes of mastoiditis, a recurring problem. The pain was so severe that late that night I had to take him into my bed and read stories to distract him.

When the hall clock struck five a.m. there was a sudden noise at the front door. A strong gust of air swept along our corridor towards my bedroom door at the other end of the passage. The door flew open and the temperature dropped. Little Seán sat up very straight in my bed, put his hand on the affected ear and exclaimed 'Mummy—my pain has all gone'. Then the icy blast was sucked out of the room and retreated down the hall towards the front door again. After that there was total silence. I lifted Seán out of my bed, carried him back to his nursery and settled him on his pillows. 'We can both go to sleep now,' I told him, 'Granny is no longer ill and she wants us to rest.'

Early next morning Desmond telephoned. They had been too late getting into Glaslough. Marjorie had died in her sleep before they arrived.

'At five o'clock this morning?'

'Yes. How did you know?'

'She came here to tell us.'

Some days later I was at Glaslough hosting Marjorie's

funeral. A lunch was given for the mourners who came from both sides of the Irish Sea. The guest of honour was Seán T. O'Kelly, President of the Republic.

Years before Marjorie had made her own arrangements regarding her place of burial. As the first member of the Leslie family who had died in the Roman Catholic faith, she was not laid to rest in the vault of the Protestant church within the grounds but in the small enclosure she had made at the churchyard wall by a path that leads to the lake.

With Marjorie's death we could afford a nanny for Seán, which would make it easier for me to work. After a lengthy search we came across an Irish hospital nurse, Rita Flannery, who was looking for a temporary place in a private house. She agreed to come and look after Seán for six months.

Since she now had only one 'patient' in her 'ward', Rita was very concerned over his health, and whenever anyone enquired after him she would answer 'he is sinking'. In time we got used to her ways; the six months turned into six years and she left only when she got married. The wedding was held at South Lodge.

Desmond suddenly decided to write a 'potboiler'. He searched through the libraries for a suitable subject that might interest the general public and would make a good documentary. He got interested in various esoteric movements and philosophies and finally developed a passion for the recent phenomenon of flying saucers, spending long hours on interviewing people who claimed to have had sightings and sometimes even encounters with the alleged interplanetary travellers. He was pleased when he found a publisher for the result of his investigations but doubtful when the publisher suggested that he share the book with one Adamski, an eccentric American guru, who had entrapped in plaster the footprint of the Venusian he claimed to have met in the desert. To help him make up his mind, Desmond prepared once more to travel to the US to meet Adamski.

This time he had little encouragement from me. He had promised me a potboiler, and now he was writing a crazy book that no one would buy. I could not have been more mistaken. At that time, flying saucers had hardly touched the public's consciousness. Few books had been written about them, certainly none that treated the subject impersonally and unemotionally. Desmond never claimed to have had an encounter himself, but he explored the probability of their existence with meticulous care. The public was ready for his book. If George Adamski's soon-to-become-famous photograph of a flying saucer was a faked-up lampshade, as was suggested many times, no one has been able to disprove or discredit it. Desmond was asked to appear on television to be grilled by someone who would try to expose the flying saucer cult as an enormous fraud. Desmond himself suggested a suitable opponent. He had met a young man, a protégé of Air Marshal 'Stuffy' Dowding's, who was a schoolteacher and an amateur astronomer. The BBC accepted Desmond's suggestion and in 1953 he and Patrick Moore had an amicable slanging match on the box. Patrick never looked back. He was put under contract by the BBC there and then and became England's most famous television astronomer.

I was very much shaken when a young man in a shabby raincoat arrived on our doorstep one night out of nowhere and showed us how it could be proved that two objects photographed thousands of miles apart in different countries were of identical dimensions. The young man, a Mr Crump, had used a method called orthographic projection, nowadays widely used to measure different shapes, and he certainly managed to convince me scientifically of the identical dimensions of the saucers photographed by George Adamski in California and by Steven Derbyshire in the Lake District. If both these people had been able to take pictures of identical objects, there must be such objects, whatever they may be or wherever they come from. The Crump incident changed my attitude to flying saucers, and I have waited many decades to have the mystery of these apparitions officially solved.

It was while Desmond was staying with George Adamski in America that my brother-in-law Jack Leslie called on me in our London flat. Jack, the eldest of Marjorie and Shane's three children, and the heir to both Glaslough and the baronetcy, had valiantly struggled all alone at Glaslough after his release from a prisoner-of-war camp in Germany. He had been incarcerated there for four long years. His erstwhile fiancée had married someone else and he had decided to move to Rome and give the estate to his older sister Anita. He told me this over lunch. I was taken aback as I had not expected him to abandon the family estate and certainly not to ignore Desmond, the next male in line.

When Desmond took too long to return home to take up this matter with Jack, I sent out letters in all directions to Jack and other family members, singing Desmond's praise and expressing my dismay that he had been left out. Obviously I was blinded by love and could not see Desmond as clearly as his family did.

In the end I won half the battle: Jack divided the estate between Desmond and Anita and a company was formed. Anita, her husband Bill King, Desmond and I were made directors, though Anita's fifty-one shares gave her the final say. Anita and Bill began to divide their time between Glaslough and their medieval castle at Oranmore, outside Galway. Bill took over the running of the farm and Jack went to live in Rome.

Desmond seemed content with this arrangement and was much taken up with the publication of *Flying Saucers Have Landed*, which he had agreed to share with Adamski.

This book, with the Adamski photographs, was one of the first of its genre and was translated into almost every modern language. Desmond now became a household name with the lunatic fringe, and we received letters and phone calls from the strangest of people, including ladies who wanted Desmond to father their children, to create the perfect man. Mediums with messages from Mars were not uncommon. Invitations for Desmond to lecture arrived in large numbers.

Since Desmond was now very much involved with lecture tours in the United States, I thought it a good time to take up one of Jack's many invitations. Leaving Seán in Nanny Flannery's care, I visited him in Rome in his miniature palazzo in Trastevere, an old part of the city. I knew he was knowledgeable about architecture and paintings and expected he would be a fine guide.

I was not to be disappointed. There was little in Rome Jack did not know about, and he devoted many hours to taking me around the city and the Vatican. It intrigued me too that my father, who had studied architectural history, had seen the excavations done in Mussolini's time. The post-war era, which turned most of Europe's capital cities into something resembling Bedlam, was only in its infancy the first time I went to stay with Jack, and it was still possible to steer the little Beetle he allowed me to drive through empty streets, park it easily, stop and admire a façade or a statue and return to the palazetto in a leisurely fashion. When I went back there in 1964, I found I could not stand the overcrowding, dust and noise of Rome for more than a day or two, and I was glad that I had had this early experience.

On that first visit in the early fifties I also formed a new friendship. I met Farouk Fuad, who was the ex-King of Egypt, living in exile in Italy and getting a very bad press everywhere. I was introduced to him, much against my will, by Keith, someone I had met in Rome who worked for the British Council. I had been brainwashed by the world press, so that when Keith first suggested I should accompany him to some bar and meet ex-King Farouk in person, I tried to refuse.

'Don't be silly,' said Keith, 'you'll like him enormously. He is a splendid fellow!'

'A splendid fellow! That gluttonous, gross, extravagant …'

'Oh shut up', said Keith, 'and come along.'

Within five minutes of meeting Farouk I discovered a number of things about him that astonished me. He didn't drink—it was against his religion—and he ate very little. His enormous bulk was caused by glandular trouble. Above all, he had perfect manners.

We spent a pleasant evening, oblivious of our surroundings, discussing literature, science and the British school system, of which he was a product.

All through the blazing Roman summer, Farouk was a generous and entertaining host, taking me to places I might never had known, such as the Chinese restaurant which was

143

run and staffed entirely by the ex-Chinese Ambassador and his family. 'They are the lucky ones,' Farouk would say of his fellow exiles. 'I wish I had the know-how to carve out a niche like that for myself! A man without work is a sorry thing. All that people ever want me for is the ballyhoo. I've been asked to manage football teams, run variety shows, open night-clubs. Never anything that could make use of my education and experience'.

If Farouk the host was colourful, Farouk the guest was exemplary. My brother-in-law Jack asked me to invite Farouk for a lunch party. I bought some grilling steaks for the occasion. In my excitement I miscalculated and bought one fewer steak than we needed. I cut one piece of meat in half, trusting that Jack and I would be the last to be served. Farouk declared that Egyptian custom demanded for the guest to do the honours, took the dish from me and 'buttled'. When his turn finally came, there was only one miserable and truly 'minute' steak left. I could swear that I saw him wink at me wickedly as he sat down to eat it.

On my last day in Rome Desmond arrived to take me home and we gave a small farewell party for all who had entertained us. I invited Farouk. He was to join us at the Hotel Excelsior. He declined, explaining that there were people in Rome, especially among the English community, who might object to being seen with him in public. 'But I'll pick you up afterwards and take you both to dinner.'

True to his word he turned up at the appointed time and had to stand for almost an hour by the revolving doors while our guests took protracted leave. Embarrassed, I finally persuaded him to join the stragglers in the lounge.

Farouk noticed my brooch. It was a Leslie heirloom, shaped like a bow with an antique pearl in the centre. Some great aunt or other must have been in financial difficulties for the spaces where diamonds had once glittered were empty. I joked that I planned to have a host of gentlemen friends. Each would replace one of the missing stones, so that I would have a great many stories to tell my grandchildren about the brooch.

'I will save you the trouble,' said Farouk. 'Give me the

brooch. There will be only one story and it will be about me!'

'You must not say such things in public unless you really mean them, your majesty,' I told him, handing him my brooch.

Many weeks later in London, some gossip reached me from a Roman acquaintance: '… and do you know what that awful Farouk lives on these days? … English women. Would you believe it? These poor creatures hand over their jewellery and he sells or pawns it.' I could guess where that story had originated. When I told her, my Roman friend was horrified. 'You'll never see that antique pearl again.'

A few days later the telephone rang.

'This is your Egyptian friend,' a distant voice said. It did not register immediately.

'Who?'

'Old Farouk, of course, you nitwit,' my husband said on the extension. 'How are you, you old so-and-so?'

'Your wife's brooch is ready for collection,' said the old so-and-so on the line from Rome.

The following week the brooch was in my hands. All the stones had been replaced and the brooch was delivered by special courier to London in a diplomatic pouch.

Farouk and I became regular correspondents, though he never signed his name in ink. This was because of some deep-seated Eastern superstition.

My parents had often talked about their marvellous holidays on the French Riviera. Monte Carlo became a magic word. I had always been fascinated by the idea of holidaying on the Riviera, and in 1951 I finally persuaded Desmond to take me there. My mother insisted that we leave four-year-old Seán behind with Nanny Flannery at some 'beneficial seaside place on the cool and healthy coast of England' while we set off for the south of France in our rickety little car.

After a hazardous and thrilling drive over the Alps we arrived on the autobahn behind Cannes. Since we had shed our clothes bit by bit while the temperature rose on the descent from the mountains, the car was full of socks, vests and cardigans and looked more like a laundry basket than a respectable motor vehicle presented by a baronet to his children. As we drove along what could have been the Kingston bypass, looking for somewhere glamorous or even just pleasant to stop, I was so disappointed that I burst into tears. We changed course and instead of continuing towards St Tropez we went east towards Monaco. As soon as we got on to the coast road and arrived in Monte Carlo, things began to improve. We stopped for a moment outside the Hôtel de Paris. A porter in a white suit, wearing white gloves, eyed us suspiciously in our 'laundry basket'. The Casino on the other side of the road, palm-enclosed and turreted, beckoned to us. This was it! I wiped my tears and begged Desmond to stay— at the Hôtel de Paris if possible. 'We can't afford it on our twenty-five pound allowance,' he said sagely. In those currency-starved post-war years, British travellers were allowed to take only twenty-five pounds out of the country. 'But if you like, we'll book in for one night and then look for some cheap B&B tomorrow.'

We mounted the grand stairs to the entrance and went to the reception desk in the sumptuous hall. The place seemed almost deserted, and the receptionist gave us a huge room in the annexe and had the porter drive our offending vehicle to some hiding place behind the hotel.

Once in the room with the huge double bed and every mod con one could imagine, we quickly forgot the last part of our journey. The receptionist had pointed out a lift in the foyer that took guests of the Hôtel de Paris straight down to the now-famous Beach Club, which even then cost ordinary mortals a small fortune to get into. We unpacked our bathing suits, put on the luxurious towelling coats the hotel provided and, taking advantage of the lift, arrived by the swimming pool. To our surprise there was only a small number of people sitting under the umbrellas and most of them were people we knew from home. We spent a wonderful afternoon there. We were asked where we were staying.

'At the Hôtel de Paris,' we answered proudly.

'That will set you back a pretty penny,' someone said.

We hastily gathered up our bathing things, shot up in the

lift and went straight to reception.

'Alas,' said Desmond, putting his hand in one pocket as if to bring out an imaginary telegram. 'We've just had news that makes it imperative to return home immediately. Can you give us our bill.'

'Certainly,' said the receptionist. Did I detect a twinge of regret in his voice? 'Here it is.'

Desmond looked at the bill. It was incredibly low. He put his hand into the other pocket of the towelling coat as if to bring out another imaginary telegram.

'Er … I have just had news that we can stay on for another week or so.'

'That is good, monsieur,' the receptionist said with a pleasant smile.

We went back to our grand room in a daze. Sitting round the pool with some of our pals the next morning we worked out the reason for this small miracle. Nineteen-fifty-one was the year just before Onassis took over the management and financing of Monte Carlo as a summer resort to compete with the more popular places such as Cannes, Nice, and St Tropez. This season the Hôtel de Paris was still empty and glad of any customers. We had not fooled them. They could guess that we had very little money and had decided that, young and not unattractive, we could only be an asset in these bad days. And an asset we certainly managed to be, sweeping down the stairs in our best evening clothes, on our way to the weekly gala at the Grand Hotel, ticketless, and making sure we were late enough to have missed dinner. This way we would not be charged, but were allowed onto the terrace to join our friends for a drink and the cabaret. It was the Film Ball at the Albert Hall all over again, but this time we did not even need a Rolls to take part in the expensive jollities without paying. We spent a wonderful and glamorous holiday, earmarked a pleasant and affordable hotel for our next visit and decided to make Monte Carlo our holiday playground for years to come.

When we got home, we found that poor little Seán had spent his 'healthy' holiday being sick with earaches and sore throats because the winds on the coast had been cold and cruel. Despite my mother's protestations, we did not leave him behind next time but exposed him to the heat-wave on the Riviera rather than to the cold spells at Hastings. From then on we rarely took a holiday without our children and to my mother's amazement they blossomed.

X

But life was not all holidays. I was usually either looking for work, or, if I was lucky, actually working. Planning ahead has been stressful for me to this day. I was delighted when I got my first West End engagement immediately after we returned from our trip abroad. It was in James Elroy Flecker's *Hassan,* which was to be directed by Basil Dean at the Cambridge theatre. I was to understudy both female leads and had two lines in the production. One of them would bring the house down every night. It had to—it was the last line of the play.

To save some money I was not called for the first week of rehearsal. I arrived at the Cambridge theatre full of excitement and apprehension. As I walked through the auditorium towards the stage, Basil Dean was taking the company through the tone poem that ends the play. Lusty male voices rang out, 'We take the Golden Road to Samarkand!' By the time I reached the footlights, my own line was due. Anxious not to be outdone by the powerful sounds of the chorus, I raised my voice. 'They have their dreams and do not think of us!' I bellowed.

There was a moment of silence, broken by Basil Dean's quaking voice, 'Miss Bernelle, we want quality—not noise!'

It did not seem a very auspicious start. Dean was a notorious bully and famous for picking on the weakest and least important member of any cast. In this instance it was me.

Each day when we came to the poem he corrected the emphasis of the words.

'No, no, Miss Bernelle. Not "They have their dreams and do not think of us", but "*they* have their dreams ...", he said on Monday. On Tuesday it was 'They *have* their dreams ...', on Wednesday 'They have *their* dreams', on Thursday 'They have their *dreams*'—and so forth. By Saturday morning he had exhausted all possibilities. I sat down in the middle of the vast stage and giggled.

'What is so funny, Miss Bernelle?' Basil Dean enquired.

'Well, Mr Dean, you have now made me emphasize every single word in my sentence differently on different days. What are you going to do next Monday?'

The entire company, which included Laurence Harvey and Arthur Lowe, all seventy-eight of them, actors, singers, dancers, started to laugh.

Basil Dean was speechless. The worm had turned.

I expected dismissal. I had not yet realized that the only way to deal with a bully is to stand up to him.

Far from sacking me, Basil Dean took me to his heart in a spectacular way. He decided I should play the leading part before the run was over. He came to every understudy rehearsal and coached me himself instead of leaving the job to the stage director, as is the custom.

He had another costume made for me in case the leading lady's would not fit me. On several nights, when Hilda Simms, who was playing Pervaneh, was late arriving at the theatre, he had me dress and stand by to go on. It was nerve-racking, particularly since Hilda was suffering from pernicious anaemia and was more often than not very late, but she always managed to get to her dressing-room in time, which disappointed me and apparently enraged Basil Dean!

The production, though opulent and very beautiful to watch, came off after a month. Though I never got to play the part of Pervaneh, I learnt a great deal during that time at understudy rehearsal and have always been grateful to Basil Dean, that grand old man of the theatre.

Seán's first experience of travelling to Spain came in 1952 when my Aunt Martha Hausdorff, who had emigrated there with her husband Kurt, invited us to stay with them in Barcelona. My uncle, who was a generous and indefatigable host, showed us not only the daytime tourist attractions but also the nightlife of that city. One evening in a club on the Ramblas de Flores I was recognized by a Spanish agent who had seen me in either *Not in Vain* or *Stranger at My Door* or even perhaps in one of the dreadful Manchester B-movies. He asked my uncle if I would consider singing in this night-club and introduced us to the owner, Señor Martinez, an ex-bandleader and a terrific, if rascally, character. This man offered what seemed to me a small fortune if I would appear in his club. Made a little reckless by the amount of Spanish wine we had drunk, I agreed to come to the club in the morning to sort out my 'repertoire'.

I woke up the next day sober, but in a cold sweat. I didn't have any repertoire. On my way to the club I stopped off at a music shop and bought a lot of sheet music. Songs that were so familiar that I could probably sing the words without having to learn them first. I plonked my 'repertoire' on the piano and went over to the microphone. I had never in my life sung through a microphone, and when I heard my voice reverberate in the room I was greatly encouraged. I sang my way through 'They Say that Falling in Love Is Wonderful', 'Hits from Oklahoma', 'The Irish Lullaby' and other such gems. The night-club owner seemed satisfied with my vocal talent but asked if I always sang straight through each song.

I dared not tell him that I had never performed any of these songs before and he gave me some good advice about starting with the chorus and then going back to the verse, and suggested several other small refinements. When he told me he would pass my music on to his band I became terri-fied. I insisted that I would have to come and rehearse with his pianist every morning. He must have thought it all a little odd since the agent had represented me as 'La artista mas estimada parta acta sociedad inglese' (the most famous cabaret performer in the English-speaking world), a sentence now repeated on all the ads. The pianist, who could not speak any English, always misunderstood my instructions during rehearsal and never played the song I was actually singing. This was a good thing because I learnt not to depend on the accompaniment and even if the band had played 'God Save the Queen' I would have been able to sing 'The Irish Lullaby' without losing the tune. When the open-ing night came, I waited anxiously in my little dressing room behind the stage, while variety act after variety act appeared to do the so-called 'warm up'. This was unnecessary since it was not just warm in the club, but sweltering hot. Señor Martinez had invited the upper crust of Barcelona society for the debut of his 'great star', and, a little the worse for drink, he staggered on to the stage between each preceding act to go into eulogies about the wonderful artiste—me!—who was to follow. Eventually the audience, hot and bored by his bragging, began to barrack him. My Spanish was limited, but even I could understand what they were shouting: 'Well, let's have this paragon and see what she can do.'

After two hours of Andalusian warbling and shaking of castanets, it was not a very auspicious moment for me to make an entrance.

I had ordered a deep green satin dress to be made by the best couturier of Barcelona, and someone had taken me to the top hairdresser of the city who had given me a bright green streak in my dark hair, which matched the dress. This streak would not be all that extraordinary these days, but in 1952 it caused a sensation when I finally stepped on to the stage. The audience burst into a loud discussion of my dress and hair and went on talking at the top of their voices all the way through my performance. I was too inexperienced to know how to get them to keep quiet. Tense as I was anyway, I launched into my 'repertoire', trying to drown them and pulling dreadful faces in the process. The evening was disappointing and Señor Martinez said afterwards that he would only keep me on if I accepted half the agreed salary. I could not very well argue, and started on what was to become one of the most instructive weeks of my working life. I discovered that to get the audience to stop talking I only had to stop singing, if necessary in the middle of a word, and look at them as if the next line would be some great and unexpected revelation. They would instantly fall silent and I could continue with my song. Quite quickly I developed a 'style'.

The club began to do well in spite of the opening night fiasco, and when a well known Spanish grandee, who fancied himself as the 'double' of King Edward VII and always dressed exactly like him, became a fan of mine and sat at a corner table almost every night to watch my show, the place was soon full to capacity. One night after the performance

Señor Martinez pushed a strange man into my dressing room. A waiter appeared with a magnum of champagne, put it on the table and locked the door behind him when he left. Martinez had told me that this night-club owner from Madrid wanted to engage me. Compared to tough and worldly Señor Martinez the man with whom I was locked into my dressing-room did not look to me in the least like a Spanish night-club owner. I realized that this was just a wealthy customer to whom Martinez had 'sold' me—as was the custom with the other females who appeared at his club. He had often enough announced me as a 'great English lady who was not for sale'.

I turned to the embarrassed stranger and asked him how much he had had to pay Martinez for the champagne. He named an exorbitant price. This confirmed my suspicions.

'Well then,' I said, 'since you have paid for it, we might as well drink the champagne and afterwards go our different ways.'

He seemed relieved at this suggestion. Martinez had obviously bullied him into an adventure he had not really sought. When we had finished the champagne, I knocked at the door and Martinez released me.

'Aniez,' he cried in dismay 'so quickly?'

'But of course,' I said with a radiant smile. 'It did not take long to arrange. I leave for Madrid tomorrow morning.'

Martinez now fell for his own lies.

'But you are under contract to me,' he shouted.

'I know,' I said, 'but since it was you who arranged it I didn't think you would mind'.

He rushed me to his office, pulled out the drawers of his desk and flung all his papers in the air. Eventually he found my contract and held it up to me.

'All right,' I said. 'Calm down, I'll stay, but don't you ever dare to sell me to anybody again.'

The rest of my engagement passed without incident. I had learnt how to perform in a noisy cabaret and had managed to save enough money to take Desmond and Seán to Palma di Majorca for what I expected would be a lovely break. We never saw anything of the island except the Grand Hotel. Ants invaded our room and were all over the walls and in the toothpaste; rain clattered on to the terrace floor. Of course the sun came out the day we left, but I didn't care. I was too glad to get home and felt like kissing the ground at Heathrow when we landed.

I soon found out the reason for my nausea. I was not ill. I was pregnant.

Egon Larsen and his English partner had written a revue in English, mainly for those refugees who had decided to stay in England. Desmond contributed some hilarious songs and sketches. An unknown English comic joined the company; his name was Ronnie Corbett. The whole thing, reminiscent of the shows we had done at the Free German League, was a huge success. It had been scheduled to run for three weeks, but went on for five months. This caused me problems about my costumes. Pregnant as I was, I continued to expand and ended up doing all my pieces in a yellow Chinese jacket that was wide enough to hide the bulge.

Desmond now confessed that one of his girlfriends was also expecting. Naturally I was deeply upset but relieved that at least he had told me himself and had spared me the humiliation of finding out from a stranger. I agreed that we should take the child and bring it up like a twin sibling to our new baby. Unfortunately, or perhaps fortunately, the girl found a childless couple who were only too ready to adopt her daughter as soon as she was born.

That same summer Desmond and I had been invited to a friend's wedding in Genoa, and since there is a perfectly good rail connection from Monaco along the coast to Genoa I persuaded Desmond to take me there. Seán stayed in Monte Carlo with Nanny. When we reached the Italian frontier, an official came to inspect our passports and we found that I had taken Seán's passport instead of my own from the drawer. At first the official was very difficult. He could not, he said, let me into Italy without identification, 'I don't know who you are. You could be wanted by Interpol.'

'I am Agnes Leslie, the wife of the gentleman whose British passport you have just examined.'

'Can you prove it?'

I remembered that I had been photographed at the airport when we left London. I searched my handbag and produced the newspaper clipping.

'There,' I said proudly. 'Now you see.'

'Oh yes,' said the official with a knowing leer, 'I see you are Agnes Leslie, the wife of the English gentleman beside you. Then who is Agnes Bernelle, the Hungarian actress, leaving for the South of France?'

Fooled by my clever outfit, he was now convinced that he had come across an illicit couple on a dirty weekend. 'Va bene,' he said, handing me back Seán's passport. 'I hope you have a pleasant time in Italy.' He was Italian after all. I can't remember how we got back into Monaco, but back we went after a couple of days.

At the Beach Club an elderly but attractive man had taken up a permanent position on a stack of lilos just outside the ladies' lavatory. He had one of the first instant cameras and could take pictures of any female on her way to the loo. He would then develop the photograph rapidly and present it to the astonished subject on her return. This way he was able to meet any woman he fancied without moving from the spot. This was how I got to know Victor Sassoon, cousin of the poet Siegfried, and our summer acquaintance blossomed into a lifelong friendship. Victor had fallen out of an aeroplane when he was thirty-eight years old and had spent the rest of his life in a wheelchair, though he was able to hobble about on two sticks. He was enormously wealthy and very generous. When he left for his home in the Bahamas that year and was giving out his customary parting gifts to summer favourites, he handed Desmond an envelope with enough foreign currency to enable us to stay another fortnight.

These extra fourteen days advanced my 'delicate condition' too far for me to be driven back over the Alps, and it was decided to send me and Seán home by aeroplane. When Desmond went to book, there were no seats and we had to go on the waiting list. Desmond gathered up Nanny and set off for home in the car. He said he had left enough money at the hotel to cover our bill and give us some extra cash. When I found I could not manage the hilly streets of Monte Carlo in the heat without a car, I decided to take the little train to Cannes where the ground was flat. Unfortunately Desmond had forgotten the money he had borrowed from the hotel and there was nothing left after I had paid our bill. I had just enough for our train fares.

We went straight to the Hotel Martinez. When I booked in with Seán, I felt like some international confidence trickster, as I had no idea how I was going to pay our bill. I could not write out any cheques since the currency regulations still applied. None of my English friends would be able to lend me money for the same reason and Desmond was by now somewhere in the Massif Central with Nanny and could not be contacted.

I put Seán to bed and slowly descended the stairs that led down to the reception desk. Who would bail me out in my condition? Luck, and the clever outfit that concealed my pregnancy, came to my aid. Norman Donniger, an old pal from Manchester filming days, suddenly appeared in the foyer. He seemed delighted to see me and invited me to join him and a bevy of beauties for dinner. During dinner the beauties, who were not fooled by my outfit, made all kinds of snide remarks which fortunately Norman missed. He abandoned the beauties and took me to the Casino instead. He gave me a chip to amuse myself with and for the one and only time in my life I won at the table just when I most needed to. I was able to go back to the Martinez and pay a week in advance. So far so good, but I still needed cash to feed myself and Seán. I asked Norman, who was going home early the next morning, to leave all his unspent cash for me with the porter at the Grand Hotel where he was staying. Norman promised he would and I went to bed reassured, when suddenly the door opened and someone tiptoed in and put something on the bedside table. Then I could hear the same person taking off their clothes and putting them on a chair. The cad, I thought, It's Norman coming to extract payment in kind for the money he has left for me. After all these years of friendship, how dare he?

I switched on the bedside lamp and sat up. So did Seán, who had been woken by the light. We were confronted by a strange nude man, who seemed as astonished to see us as we were to see him. It was the man from next door who had mistaken the room and was trying to go to bed without waking up his wife. Norman's money was waiting for me the next day.

Eventually we were able to get on a plane to London and my second son was born just before Christmas. Desmond was waiting to drive to Woking to be with me again, but since it was very foggy I did not telephone him from the nursing home until Mark, a twelve-pounder, was lying in the cot beside me.

When we brought him home, Seán was quite put out to have to wait some years for this helpless creature to grow into the playmate he had been promised. He carried out some interesting experiments on the survival capacity of a human baby. A plan to see if Mark could bounce if he fell out of the window was fortunately abandoned and eventually the boys grew so fond of each other that Mark became quite ill when Seán went off to board at Ashfold school, and Seán arranged with the headmaster to have him follow there without consulting us. Unfortunately they never had enough years to share the same activities and Seán inevitably moved on to other interests. I would not recommend a five-year gap on purpose; it was just that I was not particularly fertile. After Mark it took eleven years for me to have another child.

One of Desmond's most durable ladies was a young American actress. Since she was frequently out of work, just like me, I often had a certain amount of sympathy for her, especially as Desmond did not always treat her well and I had to send her flowers or telegrams in his name when she had an opening night. On his thirty-first birthday we were giving a party and invited her to it. She rang to say that she could not come because she had nothing to wear. I felt guilty to think that my wardrobe was bursting with clothes, as we were doing well at that time, and Desmond was always generous where clothes were concerned. I told her to come to the flat and pick something, which she did. Before she left I gave her some money and made her promise to spend it all at the hairdresser, which she also did, but which had dire consequences. She changed the colour of her hair and when she arrived late Desmond answered the door but did not recognize her. 'Come in, come in,' he cooed to this glamorous stranger and added 'Where have you been all my life?' That was the end of the affair.

In 1953 my father died of a brain haemorrhage after some terrible days when his mind had failed. I did not cry actual tears; I was too traumatized by the loss and the cruelty of fate which had robbed him of his last, modest dream. Incapacitated by an earlier stroke my father had valiantly taught himself to read and write again at the age of seventy one in order to finish writing his book *Das Theater Meines Lebens*.

It was a document that looked at life from the calm and resignation of old age in exile and it was also a piece of German theatre history. My father did not live to see it published. When he had gone, I carried him around inside myself for a long, long time. He had been Svengali to my Trilby since my early teens. I never worked on any part without him drilling me and he began to worry about me as the years went by. 'Whatever will you do when I am gone?' he would mutter.

I cannot say exactly how long it took me to be truly free of my father but I did remember the first time I discovered what it is to 'act'. In 1954 we were doing two plays by the Indian author Rabindranath Tagore in a small theatre off Leicester Square. I had a part in *Sacrifice*. After the interval came *The Post Office*, also a one-act play, with an all-male cast, in which the Angel of Death appears to a dying boy. One night when I arrived at the theatre, I was told that the leading actor in *The Post Office* had fallen ill. There were no understudies and so everyone had been 'moved up' one part, except of course the boy. Only the part of the Angel was left over. Angels are not supposed to have a gender so I was to play that part. In frantic haste I tried to learn the lines while I changed my costume in the interval. When I went on stage there was nothing between me and the audience except a yawning void. The words had to come from deep inside my being—and they came! They reached out to the audience and I could feel their emotion coming back to me from the void. It was a most exquisite moment which I try to live again each time I stand on stage. When I came off that night, I was trembling but exalted. The actor who had been the Angel until then said 'you know, of course, that I can never play that part again!' and I took over for the run, happy, but ashamed, that I had called myself an actress for so long and had only now found what it was all about and only just in time.

One of the most important roles of my career came up just months after my father died. It was the part of Salomé in Oscar Wilde's play of that name and one night when I lay soaking in my bath and worried who would teach me to say my lines I heard my father's voice speaking the words inside my head.

In the summer of 1956, Frank Thring, the Australian actor-manager, decided to come to England in the hope of getting into the West End. He began by leasing the Q Theatre, five miles from the centre of London, to put on a season of new plays he had brought over from Melbourne. He was convinced that at least one of these plays would attract attention and transfer to a West End theatre. Frank was an actor of some power and his most spectacular role had always been that of King Herod in *Salomé*. For this reason he had included *Salomé* in his Q repertoire, although he did not expect the play to be among the winners.

Salomé had, indeed, been very seldom performed. Sarah Bernhardt, for whom the title part was written, rehearsed it in Paris, but never played it on the stage. Hilton Edwards and Mícheál MacLiammóir put it on in Dublin, and London had only had one, semi-professional, production in Swiss Cottage with Bernice Rubens, the writer, as Salomé.

What Frank Thring, being Australian, could not have known was that July/August was a 'silly season' at the Q when no self-respecting theatre-goer would be seen dead inside the building. The summer of 1956 was no exception. The sun was blazing down and the customers stayed away throughout most of Frank's season. Most—but not all. *Salomé*, the Cinderella amongst the world premieres, packed them in! I had gained the part of Salomé at an audition and needed all my confidence to tackle it virtually alone with an indifferent director and a host of problems which went beyond just saying lines.

First there was the dance of the seven veils. The ballerina who had been engaged to teach it to me discovered soon enough that I could not follow her balletic steps and allowed me to improvise a kind of temple dance to the sound of bells and African drums played on stage. As soon as I was free of the Royal Ballet discipline I was able to produce a passable version of my own. It was this dance which taught me an important lesson: never take too much to heart what the critics say. No two people will react the same way, particularly no two critics. While one reviewer claimed that my dance was so intoxicating that it justified my demand for the head of John the Baptist, another said that 'I clumped about the stage like an elephant about to jump into a hot bath'. I realized that neither of them could be right.

Then there was the problem of the final speech, which I knew I was not getting right during the first weeks of rehearsal. I pushed my voice deeper and deeper into my diaphragm but it seemed to me to be less and less effective for the chilling finale. By chance someone lent me a book which described Sarah Bernhardt rehearsing the part in Paris; a sentence struck me. It mentioned the 'flute-like quality of her voice'. I decided to try a flute-like tone, rising ever higher towards the climax, 'I have kissed thy lips Jokanaan.' It was the answer to my problem. The audience's reaction each night confirmed me in my decision and so did the eminent critic Harold Hobson of the *Sunday Times*, who put Frank and me on television to play a scene and demonstrate how the play should be done.

The worst problem was the leotard which had been made so that I would be decent on stage after I had discarded the last veil. After the dress rehearsal the director told me I could not possibly wear it. It was made of net material and wrinkled every time I moved. 'You look like a dried prune,' he told me. It was now too late to make another and in my usual first-night panic, I simply left it off and became the first 'non-stationary nude' on the English stage. We were expecting to be closed down by the censor and attacked by the public but the censor ignored us and the only letters I received were letters of praise.

After the success at the Q theatre, the St Martin's Theatre offered to have *Salomé* transferred for a limited season. But Frank had spent all his money. There were frantic telegrams to his mother in Melbourne, phone calls to financiers in Sydney, endless meetings with cautious bank managers in London. A sizeable sum was hastily scratched together, but try as he would, Frank was just five hundred pounds short. He needed another backer and time was running out. The management at the St Martin's had to have a definite commitment within the week. Wednesday came and there was still no sign of the money. I was getting desperately anxious. The West End transfer seemed to me the chance of a lifetime, the big breakthrough every actor and actress dreams about—and I was going to miss it for want of five hundred pounds.

I could not sleep and walked through Hyde Park in the early hours of the morning to calm myself. I ended up in an all-night coffee bar at Hyde Park Corner owned by Peter Cosmo, an old pal of mine from the Herz Cabaret days.

Peter treated me to a hot chocolate and asked me why I was looking so upset. I told him my problem.

'Wait a moment,' he said, 'I'll introduce you to someone who could help.'

He came back with a small, swarthy American who said his name was Max and he would have the money by Saturday morning. I looked at Max's careworn face, his shabby suit and thanked him politely. I finished my hot chocolate, made my farewells, went home to bed and forgot all about the incident.

Saturday morning Frank was on the phone.

'Do you know a chap called Max something or other?'

'No, I can't say I do'.

'Well he says he's a friend of yours and has just put down five hundred pounds on my desk—in crumpled fivers—for you to play at the St Martin's Theatre'.

We started rehearsals at once, made a few minor changes and had a better costume designed for me. Max turned up from time to time to watch rehearsals or to supervise costume fittings and press interviews.

I was unnerved. What had he in mind for me? But he asked little in return for being an 'angel'. It seemed that all he wanted was to book the entire theatre on the second night for the boys of the Bushy Heath American Air Force Base. A chosen few of them were to take me out to dinner after the show. Apart from this all Max did was to wave to me cheerfully before disappearing down the Leicester Square underground.

The opening night brought the hoped-for success. Max was there, self-effacing and quiet as usual. Before the curtain rose on the second night, I had one of my rare flashes of insight. I turned to the company.

'Boys and girls, we've got to be specially good tonight—the backers are in.'

We had a great reception that evening and the dinner afterwards was delicious.

It later transpired that Max was paymaster general at the air base. On the Friday before our deadline he had handed each airman his pay—less a fiver. 'You're backing a show, son,' he told each of them, 'you're gonna be an angel.'

The airmen so enjoyed the experience that they formed a syndicate that backed another show, and another. The Pentagon eventually found out and sent frantic orders to put a stop to their angelic activities, but by then it was much too late; the Air Chief Marshal himself was now up to his neck in theatre promotion.

I had enjoyed starring in the West End enormously and was sad it was all coming to an end, but I was full of hope that this was only the beginning, and that there would now be many more jobs for me on the London stage. Not so, as I would discover to my dismay.

For several years I had great difficulty in finding any work at all, particularly in comedies or musicals. 'This is the girl who cut off the prophet's head. She can only play high drama,' the managements must have thought and often did not even allow me to audition.

One man who did let me come and sing for him was Noël Coward. Having failed a previous audition for him by singing an Ivor Novello song for a revue he was casting, this time I was even more stupid and chose to do a satirical cabaret number from one of the German revues which had been translated into English for a musical. After the customary 'Thank you, we'll be in touch,' I left by the stage door. I had not got more than a few yards from the theatre when the stage manager came running after me.

'Mr Coward has asked me to thank you for doing the audition. He wants you to know that he was fascinated by your choice of song and your style of delivery. Unfortunately he is looking for straight singers.'

I might have done better in England had I remained a pathetic refugee and not become Mrs Desmond Leslie. I remember once standing in front of the St Martin's Theatre and looking at our *Salomé* photographs when the strange man who was standing beside me began to discuss the actress who was playing Salomé. He had obviously not recognized me because he said: 'And did you know that her husband bought the show for her to get into the West End?'

During the next few years, with little or no work, I kept myself busy with singing lessons and learnt to ride in Hyde Park. I was studying singing under Margaret Philipsky, an Austrian soprano, later married to Ernest Possony, another Austrian refugee who had been an eminent singing teacher in Vienna. My father had suggested that I take singing lessons to strengthen my speaking voice but he was quite dismayed when, encouraged by my teachers, I began to take the idea of an opera career seriously. He did not think I really had the voice for it. I was lucky enough with Margaret and Ernest, two generous people, who were giving me free tuition.

They were teaching me the 'Schtau Methode', which worked on the presumption that anyone who can speak can be taught to sing. Whether the sound was pleasant or not was another matter. By this method we were required to practise for hours on end, exercizing our diaphragms by producing the most horrendous sounds which came from the depths of our stomachs. Margaret, whose English was less than perfect, would terrify the English students by shouting at them 'Bugger, bugger!' when she wanted them to 'dig deep' into their innards.

My father, when he had heard me doing my own 'buggering' had been shocked and felt I was wasting my time. He always said, 'You'll never sing.' Consequently I developed a psychological blockage and got into all kinds of difficulties when I had to sing properly on stage. I would do well at auditions, get singing roles, rehearse them easily and then be scared to death on opening night. It was the old

Svengali/Trilby complex at work. For many years I fought against my father's 'voice' whispering to me on stage 'you'll never sing' when I least expected it. I even went to a hypnotist to rid myself of this complex. Once I had a dream and this dream was prophetic.

I dreamt I was standing at Speaker's Corner in Hyde Park. Ernest Possony, whom I much respected, was standing on a box and pointing to a large notice-board with a long stick. 'On this side, ladies and gentlemen,' he was saying, 'I have written the names of all those singers who will make careers in opera. On this side,' he pointed his stick to one name only, 'you see the name of one of my pupils who will branch out in a totally different direction but will succeed.' I strained to read the name of this singular pupil. It was my own. And it is true that I had to unlearn a great deal of what Margaret and Ernest had taught me. Putting over the kind of songs I now sing requires a different technique altogether, especially where vowel sounds are concerned, but I also know that I should no longer be able to produce any sounds at my age if I had not learnt the basis of voice production from Margaret and Ernest.

The riding lessons were truly bizarre. Lilo Blum, whose stables and riding establishment were just off Hyde Park, was employing a retired Polish cavalry officer to instruct her clients. He would lead a 'posse' of pupils into the park right through the heaviest traffic at Hyde Park Corner, shouting 'Don't worry—horses have right of way.' Of course the buses, taxis, and even the horses themselves did not know that, and we usually had to cling to our terrified animals' necks while they reared up and snorted as the traffic bore down on them. The Colonel had a girlfriend in Chelsea and more often than not led us from the comparative safety of Rotten Row into Sloane Street and beyond on horseback, to deliver a billet-doux of chocolates to his lady love.

When Rita Flannery married, I advertised for another nanny and found Marie, a pretty redhead, born in the Midlands of Irish parents. She too was a great success and she stayed with us until her fiancé bought a farm in Ireland and they were married.

This left us with Irena, who came from a tiny village in Italy to help in the house. She was a small, lovely and unspoilt, but bright enough to learn to speak English quickly and to put up with our city ways.

After a year Irena went home to marry Giuseppe, her childhood sweetheart. I baked her wedding cake myself, taking the recipe from Mrs Beeton's renowned Edwardian cookbook. Since this required lavish amounts of every ingredient used, my mixing bowl soon overflowed, and I think I must have used every vessel I had in the kitchen before the cake was put in the oven. Irena staggered to the airport carrying the result, a mammoth confection consisting of four enormous layers. I told her to put away the top for a christening, but she told me later that the entire village had lived on it for days.

We were astonished when Irena and Giuseppe returned almost immediately. Irena seemed very distressed. I finally persuaded her to tell me why. In her village it was still the custom after a wedding night to hang out the bed linen for all to see. As there had been no tell-tale bloodstains on her sheet there had been a scandal. Fortunately Giuseppe, less bigoted than his relations, had understood that this did not necessarily mean Irena had already lost her virginity; not every girl goes through adolescence keeping her hymen intact. I could hardly believe that this monstrous tradition had survived into the twentieth century anywhere in Europe, but remember Irena and Giuseppe being vastly amused a year later to see white flags with a large red circle in the middle lining the Mall when the Emperor of Japan was in London on a state visit.

Giuseppe was looking for work in London, but for a while he helped Irena—who was now pregnant—and we found ourselves in the privileged position of having a 'houseman' of our own. He was sharing Irena's little room and I had difficulty in rearranging her tiny space to accommodate him and the baby that arrived nine months later. I bought a collapsible bed and somehow they managed to squeeze together. Irena, who always claimed that she came of noble stock, had a more 'aristocratic' pregnancy than I had ever experienced: she was sick almost all the time and after the baby was born we all had to tiptoe around the flat and speak in whispers in order not to wake the child. Our friends often teased us because, they claimed, the entire household revolved around little Angelina, but it was well worth it for the loyalty and affection we received in return.

Desmond and I were invited by Victor Sassoon's sister-in-law, the Princess Giulia Ottoboni, who lived in a splendid house on a hilltop above Monte Carlo beach, to stay. We would have had a wonderful time that season, if Giulia had not put one of her cars at our disposal. It was one that her butler also drove to do the shopping.

During one of his drives down the precipitous hill, the butler must have had some accident, for he put the car in to be repaired and presented Giulia with the bill, claiming that we had done the damage. Giulia was big-hearted enough not to mind paying for the repair, but she could not, at first, forgive us for not telling her about it. There was no point in blaming her ever-faithful butler, and the whole affair spoilt our holiday. It confirmed the opinion I had formed after the unfortunate weekend at Blenheim Castle that you should not frequent the houses of the rich and powerful if you yourself are poor and insignificant. I have never changed this opinion and have often avoided personal relationships with people far out of my social, financial or even artistic class, unless I could return their hospitality in equal measure. I may have missed many a useful contact that way, but I knew the pitfalls only too well.

Fortunately Victor now decided to take us off to Siena to see the Palio. After a drive along the coast of France and Italy, during which I was constantly car-sick because of the smooth, swinging motion of Victor's car, and after racing through Florence despite my protestations that we ought to stop and see its famous sights, we halted long enough outside the town to buy a toy for the boys at home from a street vendor. It was a plastic rocket, activated by tap water, and Victor and Desmond could not wait to get to Siena to play with it.

When we arrived in the enchanting ancient city, it was bustling with people dressed in medieval clothes and carrying large banners in preparation for the many open-air displays and processions the following day. We installed ourselves in the only modern hotel in Siena and went to visit the Italian family Victor knew, from whose balcony overlooking the famous square we were to watch the race the next morning.

In the equestrian world it would be hard to find a more bizarre event than this annual competition, dating back to the Middle Ages, in which the entire population of the town is engaged with a fervour that borders on the hysterical.

Victor explained that the Palio, in which each district of the city runs a horse, is held in the town's oval-shaped central square, with the racecourse as its perimeter, and the spectators squashed into the centre. All around are the houses of the most privileged citizens, whose wooden balconies groan with family members and their friends on the day of the race. Everyone gets so excited that you would think their lives, or at least their livelihoods, depended on the race, whereas in fact no money changes hands. For weeks before the race the participating horses are locked up to prevent rival owners from doping, stealing or harming them. The riders are often offered enormous bribes to lose and anything underhand is allowed during the race. The year we were there we saw jockeys attacking their rivals with whips as they were about to overtake them, and the horse that came in first lost its rider but was still declared a winner. Nothing could match the elation of our hosts and their guests when their riderless horse won. I thought the balcony would collapse beneath us with all the shouting, embracing and jumping up and down.

If our hosts went wild, the winners below went even wilder. That night the festivities were momentous. Few people remained sober. Victor had barrels of wine positioned at the street corners from which cups of chianti were dispensed. The celebration dinner was held in the street at long trestle tables. The mayor hosted the meal for local dignitaries, and also for us, the guests of honour, who were placed at the head of the table—next to the victorious horse.

The following day when Victor, Desmond and the chauffeur were sleeping off their hangovers I crept out of the hotel and made for the railway station. I had no intention of passing the day launching the water-rocket from our hotel window as my travelling companions were planning to do. I had better things on my mind. I was taking myself to Florence for an orgy of cultural delights.

Nobody had told me that this particular day was a rare public holiday in Florence. Every church, every public building, every gallery was closed. I managed to get a glimpse of Michelangelo's *David* (which I was later told was only a copy) in an open courtyard, saw the famous bronze doors of the Baptistery and looked down upon the Ponte Vecchio from a hillside I had climbed in the heat of the day. But as far as paintings, churches and other treasures were concerned, I might as well have spent the day playing with plastic toys. When I returned to the hotel in Siena I told my party that they had missed a great deal.

Back in Monte Carlo Desmond was pursued by a beautiful blonde. She was a German princess and her husband considered it his princely duty to reciprocate by pursuing me. Flattered as I was I did not fancy him: I had come across someone far more interesting. I had met Claus von Bülow on a raft which was anchored off the Beach Club and we became firm friends that summer. Back in London, where he then lived, he proved himself to be a marvellous companion.

Desmond was going through what can only be described as an 'esoteric orgy' with more and more UFO nuts and mediums occupying his time. After a transfiguration medium turned himself into a 'Chinaman' on our living-room carpet, I felt a need to distance myself from these goings-on. I became lonely and felt isolated and Claus was around a great deal to cheer me up and to take my cultural education in hand. He brought me the latest books to read and took me to concerts and art exhibitions. We spent many hours in the flat listening to classical records, and when the German princess who had followed Desmond to London, telephoned to complain that Desmond was deceiving both of us with some Scandinavian beauty queen who had sent him a return ticket to Copenhagen, Claus took the receiver and dealt with her. I began to depend on him more and more.

Claus, who was then only twenty-eight, had achieved a law degree and then silk at an incredibly early age, and a brilliant career was predicted for him. He was at that time accredited to a law firm in the City as a junior counsel.

I was anxious to repay him a little for all the time and care he had lavished on me and when I was given tickets for a lunchtime wine tasting at the Mermaid Theatre, I invited Claus. Unfortunately I was delayed and rather late getting there. By the time I arrived, Claus had been 'tasting' every wine without bothering to spit out the sample. He was now well into his cups and muttered something about a case he was supposed to conduct in the law courts at two o'clock that day.

I did my best to get him there, but he could not remember the number of his court and dragged me from trial to trial, interrupting the proceedings with much clattering and many irreverent remarks about the 'idiot' judge, delivered at the top of his voice, without ever finding the court in which he was expected. It was the end of his legal career in England, though he never admitted it. Shortly afterwards he became private legal adviser to Paul Getty and left for the United States. We never saw each other again though I had news of his doings occasionally through mutual friends—his marriage to Sunny Auersperg, the birth of his daughter Cosima and his eventual arrest for the attempted murder of his wife. I followed his two separate trials avidly in the international press and on television, and was relieved when he was finally acquitted.

XI

In 1953 Renée Goddard introduced me to Philip Saville, the television director, and his wife Jane Arden, who were running one of the earliest improvisation classes. Meeting these two talented people was a revelation. Jane, a brilliant writer, far in advance of her time, was a feminist and an altogether extraordinary person. She certainly loved having power over people and could be dangerous and even destructive, but the positive side of her character made a relationship with her worthwhile. Progressive and liberal, she opened my eyes to a great many things I had never dared to admit to myself and gave me the confidence to follow my career without guilt.

I did a great many plays and sketches at Bush House for the German service and once landed a leading part in a series based on *The Third Man* opposite Orson Welles, who also directed. Orson was a charming and courteous man to work with and his method of directing radio plays was ingenious. When we were all assembled in the studio to rehearse the episode we would record later that day, Orson handed us each a script, but we were not given the parts we were going to play. Everyone had someone else's part to work on. It can be difficult to do justice to a part in such a short time and it is always easier to notice where other actors go wrong in rehearsal. By the time six o'clock came and we were told to take back our proper parts each of us had found out exactly how not to play them.

When the Orson Welles series was over I was called to Paris to be interviewed for a sizeable part in a French film. I made friends with the director and his crew and they invited me to join them for the Bastille Day celebrations. My pals, the crew of the film company, who were decidedly left-wing, joined up with some like-minded companions and, with me in tow, went on a wild rampage through bars and bistros of the sixth *arrondissement*, and later joined forces with some more official party-members on the Place de la Concorde.

A huge crowd had collected there. At one end there was a stage with a microphone, through which some politicians of the Left were addressing the populace. Somehow I found myself next to the temporary stage. My pals shouted something to me, which I could not understand, and, before I knew what was happening, I was lifted on to the platform and heard one of the officials announce to the crowd that they were looking at an English actress, who had come to deliver a message from their comrades across the Channel.

I looked down the enormous square. I suppose I should have been terrified. Whether it was the effect of the *vin ordinaire* I had indulged in earlier or the feeling of absolute power up there on that platform that encouraged me, I cannot tell. I thought: this is what Mussolini and Hitler must have felt! I took a deep breath, picked up the microphone and made my speech, in French! A language which, under more sober circumstances, I speak only moderately well. I cannot remember exactly what I said—something about solidarity and brotherhood I suppose—but the moment was one of intoxication and surprise as I heard the roar of the crowd that greeted my message. Perhaps I had missed my vocation, I thought. I did not, in the end, get a part in the film. Evidently when I was sober, my French was not good enough.

When I was back in London Jane Arden telephoned and asked me to come away for a weekend with her and Charles Laughton and his manager. She had written a beautiful play called *The Party* and Oscar Loewenstein was going to produce it in the West End. Apart from Laughton, who was starring, the cast was to include his wife, Elsa Lanchester and two young unknowns, Ann Lynn and Albert Finney. Laughton, whom we were to call Charlie, wanted Jane to make some small revisions to the script and had invited her to a quiet country hotel to work. He had agreed that she could bring a friend.

For anonymity's sake we were lodged in the hotel annexe. The woman who was looking after us there was convinced that Jane and I were two floozies the men had brought along for their pleasure. She would refer to Charles Laughton and his agent as 'the boys' and was put out to discover that one of the 'floozies' had actually written the play they were working on.

Desmond and I flew to Edinburgh for the out-of-town opening of *The Party*. The production was as magical as Jane's script demanded and was very successful when it arrived in the West End.

Jane began to make a great deal of money. She bought herself a beautiful white sports car, too small to be used as family transport, as she would tell you with a wicked grin. She bought very expensive clothes and tried hard to interest me in exciting new designers such as Mary Quant who were taking London by storm, to join her on her shopping sprees; but I was not a successful West End author and could afford only the odd garment out of the end-of-season couture sales.

Living in London in the fifties was very stimulating—new ideas, new opportunities, new buildings everywhere. The Royal Festival Hall, the Film Institute and later the National Theatre were built on the South Bank site. The Royal Court Theatre reopened its doors to new, exciting playwrights such as Osborne, Wesker, Pinter and Frisch.

Desmond and I made the most of what was going on. I had been pregnant with Seán when I went to my first ball and perhaps, as I had missed much of what makes growing up pleasurable, it took me a long time to mature.

Fritz and Dorothea Gotfurt invited us to the Chelsea Arts Ball. It was to be fancy dress and Desmond decided to go as a Martian, painted silver from head to toe. I became irritated by his endlessly trying out the bulbs and batteries for the flashing eyelids he had designed for himself, and on the night itself I was even more irked when I found myself more or less abandoned in my mundane Cleopatra outfit while my Martian spouse was constantly being chased by females who could later be identified by the silver on their cheeks and noses.

When we were invited to a private dance for New Year's Eve I took my revenge. I commandeered Desmond's flashing bulbs and attached them to the metallic bodice of my Salomé costume, exactly at the spot where only pink netting was covering my nipples. The batteries I placed under the arm, as Desmond had done, and when he took me on the dance floor I pressed my arm against the metal top from time to time. Immediately the bulbs responded and I could 'flash' my tits whenever I chose. At first the other guests thought they had imagined it, but when they realized my flashing tits were real, it became the sensation of the evening and we were driven around London from party to party so I could 'flash'. Desmond, outdone by his own invention, took it all in good part.

At a dance we were invited to about this time I met a distinguished-looking silver-haired man with whom I spent most of the evening sitting and chatting behind an aspidistra. I liked his sense of humour and agreed with most of what he said. I was dying to know who he was, so when it was time to leave I asked him straight out. In his romantic black cloak he gave the impression of being an artist or at least an actor manager in the old tradition. 'Not at all,' he said apologetically, 'I am merely the headmaster at Ashfold, a boys' prep school in Buckinghamshire.' I took down his address 'just in case', though at the time Desmond and I had no intention of sending our sons away to board before they were to leave home to go to Ampleforth, Desmond's own public school.

In the 1950s, at the height of the Cold War, a small ray of hope foreshadowed the peace that did not come for so many years: Khrushchev paid a visit to America. Instead of encouraging him and helping him to thaw the political ice, the media in the West was sceptical and sometimes even hostile. We telephoned the Russian Embassy in London and expressed our dismay at Khrushchev's reception, and instantly received an invitation to have tea with Mr Malik, the Soviet ambassador. Over the teacups, Malik told us of the hill somewhere in Russia where his grandfather and, in the next war, his father had been killed.

'I do not want my son to be killed there,' he said.

We found there were quite a few issues on which we could

agree with him and he was astonished when he found that one of his 'British' visitors was a Hungarian whose countrymen's revolt had so recently and so ruthlessly been suppressed by his own countrymen. He gave me a rose from his garden when we said goodbye.

The dark clouds that had been gathering were made more ominous by the development of atomic weapons. We went on marches and sit-down demos, and even helped to organize an anti-bomb pirate radio station run by Bertrand Russell and Vanessa Redgrave from our roof at South Lodge. Needless to say this was without the knowledge of the Norwich Union, our head landlords, and we had to smuggle these valiant people up to the roof by the backstairs. Finally we joined the biggest ever anti-nuclear demonstration in Trafalgar Square. The police turned out in vast numbers and surrounded us. Word spread that anyone arrested while sitting down in the Square would have to pay a fine of one hundred pounds. It took six policemen to lift Desmond into the Black Maria. Once he was inside I jumped to my feet. Ever mindful of our finances I felt that at that price one arrest in the family was all we could afford. Besides we had left the boys at home and one of us had to get back to them. They were watching the demonstration on the television and were quite worried when they saw their daddy being manhandled and arrested by the police. They were relieved when I arrived back unscathed, if a little dishevelled.

Of course Desmond, being Desmond, managed to have a great night in prison. He shared a cell with George Melly, Shelagh Delaney and Vanessa Redgrave. I was envious when he returned the next morning, having paid only a paltry fine.

Desmond now embarked upon a series of love affairs of which he made no secret. He would take me to his rendezvous in some club where we were known and go off on his date, leaving me behind in the sure knowledge that I would be picked up and taken out by someone else. Once when he was spotted by John Mills, the owner of the club restaurant Les Ambassadeurs, on a flight from Paris with a female companion, he insisted I go with him and his friend to the Ambassadeurs bar to demonstrate my approval of the trip and save the lady's reputation. These situations left me open to many advances, most of which I fended off, but if I occasionally succumbed it was mainly to give myself the guilt I needed to accept Desmond's behaviour. I would never humiliate Desmond in public or in private, nor did I drop revealing photographs on the living-room floor, as he often did, whether by accident or on purpose it was hard to know.

I suppose today ours would have been accepted as an 'open' marriage.

One of Desmond's conquests I never actually met. He had acquired her on the telephone and I had listened in on the other line when I picked up the receiver to make a call and inadvertently heard him speak to someone on a crossed line. 'You have a lovely voice,' he cooed and made a date for lunch.

I noted time and place and rang the restaurant on the appointed day. 'You have a Mr Leslie lunching there,' I told the waiter. 'Would you please tell him that Mrs Leslie would like to speak to him.' In a moment the waiter returned: 'Your son says he will call you later, madam,' he said. I could not help but admire Desmond's ingenuity.

That year I finally managed to get arrested with our friend Ollie Moxon, an ex-Spitfire pilot, when we were pasting anti-bomb posters on public buildings. I thought I had at last 'made it' to jail. I was indignant however, when the officer at Bow Street asked if we were the 'Anti-Queer Brigade', or members of 'Keep Britain White', and was even more put out when the sergeant in charge sent Ollie down to the cells and sent me home. It had not occurred to me that he would mistake me for a tart in my short skirt and black fishnet stockings.

Compared to my usual demonstrating gear the fishnet was not up to standard. There was the old mink coat in my closet of which it could truly be said that it had seen better days. It had started life in Germany over half a century ago, a birthday gift from my father to my mother. The story goes that it was already past its prime when I was born, so that my mother put it in my playpen for me to sit and dribble on. After featuring in the tube shelter episode during the London Blitz, it passed to me in my mother's lifetime and I always took immense delight in wearing it to anti-nuclear demonstrations to confound the media who loved to label us demonstrators 'scruffy' and 'unwashed'.

At the time of the Cuban missile crisis in 1962, when the Americans had their rocket launchers trained on Russian targets and were ready to let them off, ten thousand marchers were converging on the American Embassy in Grosvenor Square to hand in a letter of protest. We were stopped from entering the square by a large contingent of mounted police and were forced to sit down on the roadway. It was then that the mink proved particularly useful. There was a building site at the corner of Duke Street and Grosvenor Square where the original houses had been demolished but the new blocks had not yet been put up. Together with Eileen, Oscar Loewenstein's wife, I laboriously climbed to the top of the heap of rubble. I had to take off my mink as I got hotter and hotter and Eileen and I threw it to each other in turn as we scrambled upwards. At the top we found ourselves perched on a large hoarding. Down below stood a Black Maria. A policeman was looking up at us, his arms outstretched, ready to grab us as we jumped down from the hoarding into the square. 'Catch' I shouted and threw the mink down on top of him. Before he could disentangle himself we jumped, snatched the coat from off his head and sprinted towards the Embassy to hand in the letter. And while the other demonstrators were still patiently sitting down, we hailed a taxi and drove away with the mink.

Since Desmond was being forever pursued by golden-haired Scandinavian and German ladies, I now decided to become a blonde.

My transformation worked well to begin with. I think every woman should change the colour of her hair at least once in her life. It gives the opportunity to meet a totally different set of people. Apart from our milkman, who began to whistle at me, my most useful success was at an audition for the Palladium pantomime *Aladdin*. I was cast in the part of Scheherazade. It was the most expensive and lavish production I have ever been associated with. The cast included my former co-star Valentine Dyall as the villain, Sonny Hale as Aladdin's mother, and a host of others, with Norman

Wisdom in the leading role. The sets were unbelievably luscious, with one backdrop, which was only seen for a few moments, made entirely of emerald-green velvet. The moving track on which Scheherezade's golden couch rested was peopled with Nubian slaves, who waved large ostrich feather fans over my head, and it took the best part of ten minutes for this exotic platform to move me down to the footlights, to the strains of the famous Scheherazade music by Rimsky-Korsakov. There were seven male dancers with shaved heads, painted green all over, who surrounded me at almost every step, known as the 'Yul Boys' after Yul Brynner. I was blissful in this large company of actors, singers and dancers. I rehearsed my big opening song for many weeks in the rehearsal room with a pianist and had no difficulties with it. Unfortunately, Norman Wisdom resented anyone on stage who might take the limelight away from him. He had the other comedian's lines drastically reduced, and a female comic's one and only scene cut out before opening night.

In the second act of *Aladdin* I had no song but a scene that I had to play facing the stage strapped to a huge swan that was illuminated from within. As the entire company on stage fell to their knees I shot out from a stage box on my swan to hover spectacularly over the auditorium. To reach this box, I had to slip through a pass door in the dark and go though the ante-room where Val Parnell, the impresario and manager of the Palladium, had his private bar. He would wait for me every night and hand me a small glass of whiskey to help me 'face the perilous ride'.

Once, during a matinée when my sons were in the audience, Mark's voice rang out. 'Look' he cried excitedly, pointing at the shimmering vision on the 'swan's back', 'that's my Mummy', thus shattering the other children's illusion.

Working at the Palladium was much like being on board an ocean liner. There were many useful services available including dancing classes and a masseur who brought his collapsible table into our dressing-rooms. Most of the stage hands worked in the Covent Garden markets in the mornings and you could give them your shopping list the night before. There was hardly anything they could not get for you: fruit and groceries, meat, vegetables, candy-striped sheets and crockery at reasonable prices. Wednesday was Nanny Marie's day off and I would bring the boys with me to the theatre. The stage director was not to know, and to escape his watchful eye they were passed behind the scenes from department to department during the performance. If I had left them in Wardrobe before I went on for my first scene they could end up in the plasterer's shop backstage by the time I came off, or I might see their little faces peering down at me during my song from the very top of the proscenium arch from where the backdrops were lowered. The stage director never caught up with them as they were passed from hand to hand. 'It's Wednesday,' he would say to me, 'I know they're here somewhere.'

Robert Nesbitt, the director, was nicknamed the Prince of Darkness because of his stern, almost forbidding ways, but also for his dark good looks. On Valentine's Day I sent him an anonymous card—a picture of Cleopatra on her throne surrounded by Nubian slaves, which left little doubt as to the sender.

'Was it you who sent me the Valentine Card?' he called after me the following day. When I said it was he gave me a delighted smile and from that moment on never stopped smiling at me whenever we bumped into each other. Although the kiss he once bestowed on me was very chaste I can truly claim that he carried on a 'love affair' with me entirely by way of our lighting-board. From time to time an interesting new spotlight would appear on my face during the performance. Even the rest of the company would notice it. 'He was in front last night,' they would say, 'he's put another light on you.'

Having appeared in pantomime at the London Palladium I had no difficulty getting the part of principal boy in *Robinson Crusoe* at the Gaiety Theatre in Dublin the winter of 1957.

The Gaiety's owner, Louis Elliman, came to London for the auditions. He had no idea of my Irish connection but he cast me in the part and it suited me quite well to be working in Dublin over Christmas because the children could go to Glaslough with Desmond and we could see each other at weekends.

I went ahead to Dublin to start rehearsals. Jimmy O'Dea, the popular Irish comedian, starred as usual, and the company included Maureen Potter, Ursula Doyle, Hal Roach and Danny Cummins.

I crossed over in a raging storm and arrived more dead than alive in the early hours of the morning to be scooped up at the dockside by the stage director and rushed to a pub in the dockland area, where Jimmy O'Dea awaited me with five Irish coffees arranged on the counter in a row, to 'give me courage' as he said. And though I do not like either coffee or whiskey and try to keep away from cream, I found the combination irresistible, even at that ungodly hour, and downed the lot. They certainly gave me enough 'courage' to rehearse.

The company fell into two groups, the comics and the straight people, and they rehearsed separately in the upstairs bars at the Gaiety and managed to maintain as little contact as possible. The director did not appear until the dress rehearsal! For three weeks we managed to stagger along under the capable leadership of the stage director.

I was handed some songs and told to learn them for the first run-through, which was held in a large studio under the supervision of Alice Delgarno, the ballet mistress and principal dancer.

In the absence of any real authority, I decided to substitute some songs I fancied for some of the ones I had been given and did not much like. During the first run-through, whenever my music cue arrived, Alice was more and more bewildered.

'Why are you singing 'Volare' when it says 'Roaming in the Gloaming' in my script?'

'It has been decided to change it, Miss Delgarno,' I said without batting an eyelash.

From that day on the expression '*it has been decided*' entered into our family 'language' and is used, even now, whenever anyone takes the law into their own hands and is trying to cover up.

Alice Delgarno's bewilderment was nothing to Jimmy O'Dea's whenever I opened my mouth to speak my lines at the first run-through. As far as he was concerned the only worthwhile moments of the pantomime were the comic turns he had been rehearsing with Hal Roach and Danny Cummins.

'What are they doing?' he would ask, aggrieved, pointing at me and the principal girl. After fifty years in the business, Jimmy would not concede that there was a storyline in these shows in which his character, the Widow Twanky, was not always involved. Once the show was running, Jimmy could be the very devil on stage, making personal remarks about people he knew in the audience and trying to make the other players laugh.

His Irish company was well used to him after years of pantomime, but the principal girl, another import from London, and I were easy targets—or so he thought. The girl had a particularly pungent English accent. It fell to her to hand Jimmy a map on stage, which I had previously given to her with the simple words 'Here is the map!' which she repeated to Jimmy.

'The ma-ap, oh the ma-ap,' echoed Jimmy gleefully imitating her way of speaking.

The following night I thought I would fox him by calling it a chart.

'The chort—oh the chort!' cried Jimmy delightedly.

Next time I came up with 'ordnance survey', which nearly stopped him in his tracks.

I much enjoyed these little moments and searched through dictionaries for more and more outlandish names for our humble map. The entire company would wait with bated breath every time the map scene came around, to see, or rather to hear, what I would say and what effect it would have on Jimmy O'Dea. One night I did manage to 'corpse' him with the words 'cartographic representation'.

Apart from the sheer pleasure of working with Jimmy O'Dea and Maureen Potter, who was the Crown Princess to his King, I remember *Robinson Crusoe* for other reasons: Jimmy's twenty-first anniversary at the Gaiety, which we celebrated on stage after the show; the time Hilton Edwards and Mícheál MacLiammóir came up and joined us on stage; or Brendan Behan on a backstage visit discussing my 'concept' of playing principal boy as earnestly as if I were playing Lady Macbeth; the wonderful simulated storm that shipwrecked our stage schooner which heaved and rolled dangerously, the like of which we have not seen on the Gaiety stage for many years. It seemed a miracle that I escaped being hit by the mast as it crashed on to the deck each night.

But above all it was the priests I remember from that production. Back in the 1950s the Catholic clergy were not allowed to go to the theatre, but there was no rule to forbid them from being backstage. In some of the provincial theatres in England I had worked in, priests used to hire themselves out as stage-hands and scene-shifters in order to catch a glimpse of the shows they wanted to see. In Dublin they did not need to work so hard to achieve the same end. All they had to do was to come to the stage door and ask to hear confession. After that they could stay and watch from the wings.

Imagine my amazement when I first arrived at the Gaiety and was confronted by the bizarre spectacle of the chorus line in their exotic costumes, queuing up on the iron staircase to confess their sins, while the orchestra struck up the overture; or later during the blackout after the shipwreck scene when I would regularly fall into a gaggle of stage-struck clerics huddled together in the prompt corner, amongst whom I would thrash about in the pitch dark until I had disentangled my arms and legs.

Halfway through the pantomime season I caught a chill and lost my voice. It was agony to sing through what appeared to me to be a mass of cotton wool in my sinuses. I thought of all the times I had messed up my work when my voice was clear and resonant and I swore I would never again let neurosis stop me from using it properly once it was restored to me. To my amazement I found that my 'Dublin chill' achieved what no teacher and no hypnotist had achieved before: it freed me from my father's curse.

During the last week of *Robinson Crusoe* Desmond came up to Dublin. We had lunch with Richard Aherne, whom I had not seen since he appeared in *My Hands Are Clay*, and his teenage children Maureen and Patrick. They were staying with Oonagh Oranmore (formerly Guinness) at Luggala and Oonagh had invited us over. She told me that Maureen's aunt and uncle, who had brought up the motherless children, had died within six months of each other. Richard had been summoned from California and had been trailing the children around Dublin not knowing what to do with them. Oonagh, with her usual kindness, was now giving them a temporary home at Luggala.

I had not seen Maureen for many years and could hardly believe that the gauche creature with the wire-rimmed glasses sitting across the table was the same child I had so admired when I had seen her in her playpen a decade or so before. She was pale and sad, her stringy hair was tied back severely and her budding breasts were squashed flat by a washed-out garment of uncertain colour. When she spoke, and she spoke seldom, it was in a nasal whisper.

After lunch she asked timidly if I would come upstairs so that she could show me her 'treasure'. We climbed to the top of the house, and there, in the little room under the eaves she picked up a small box. Inside, a pair of false eyelashes lay on a bed of cotton wool. There was something strangely touching in the way she held her 'treasure' out to me. I took a closer look at the child to whom these lashes meant so much. Here is an ugly duckling just waiting to emerge as a beautiful swan, I thought. I invited Maureen to the pantomime and to spend a few days with me at the Shelbourne Hotel. She was delivered there by Oonagh's chauffeur the very next day. I had already spoken to Jojo O'Reilly on the telephone.

'Please come over and help. There is rescue work to be done.'

I knew she could be relied upon to take a hand.

Jojo picked us up at the hotel and we set out to work the transformation we both believed we could achieve. The first thing that went were the awful glasses.

'You don't need them at your age. Train your eye muscles to do without them.'

Next we went to a city store and bought some decent teenage clothes. After that came a visit to the hairdresser. Maureen emerged with golden hair in soft waves, and, as I had suspected, she was beautiful.

When we came back from the pantomime that evening we sat up in bed and talked for hours. I discovered that Maureen's dream was to be a ballet dancer but that her father could not see any way to make this possible. I was astonished. I knew that her maternal uncle, Lord Garret Moore, was the director of Covent Garden Opera House. It seemed to me incomprehensible that this connection could not be called upon in some way, if only to advise, but Maureen assured me that her father hated all her mother's relations, particularly her granny, Lady Drogheda.

For a worthwhile ballet training, I was told, one had to be accepted at White Lodge, the school outside London where potential ballerinas received their all-round education before joining the Royal Ballet as trainee members.

Richard, who I knew was spending his late wife's inheritance on horses and drink, claimed he could not afford to take Maureen to London for an audition and all that this implied. Besides, he said, the life of a ballet dancer is a strenuous one, not fit for his daughter, who should grow up to be a lady.

I decided to take a hand in Maureen's future and I often wonder what would have happened to her if I had not done so. Might she still be alive today?

After some time and a great deal of persuasion Richard brought Maureen to us at South Lodge. There was one memorable afternoon when Karsavina, the Russian dancer who had once been one of the most famous ballerinas in the world, and was now a delicate octogenarian, came to tea and Maureen danced for her in our sitting-room. Karsavina was very encouraging and promised to arrange a meeting with Dame Ninette de Valois.

Richard and I took Maureen to audition with Dame Ninette. She told us that Maureen was certainly talented enough to train with the Royal Ballet, but that the stoop she had acquired would have to be treated by their own osteopath before they could make a definite decision. She wanted to see Maureen again in six months' time.

Richard was none too pleased. He was longing to get back to Hollywood where he had his cronies and probably also a lady friend or two. I told him he could leave Maureen at South Lodge while she was having treatment.

Maureen settled wonderfully into our household and the boys showed no sign of jealousy when they came home from boarding-school in the holidays. Family life was obviously what she had been missing and she began to blossom. Richard went back to Hollywood and we heard not a word from him. This left us with all the decision-making. We found a private tutor for Maureen to bring her up to White Lodge standards in case she was accepted there. Maureen worked hard and learnt to speak French in no time at all.

One night when I was reading in bed, there was a gentle knock on my door. It was Maureen in her nightie wanting to cuddle up to me.

'Agi,' she asked timidly, 'would you mind if I called you Mummy?'

There is nothing that would please me more, I thought, but this was too serious a matter to make a hasty decision.

'I'll tell you tomorrow when I have spoken to Desmond.'

As I expected Desmond was very understanding.

'If she calls me Mummy then I will have to be her Mother in every way from now on. This imposes responsibilities which would involve you as well,' I told him. 'Are you pre-pared to take them on?' He said he was if it made me happy. And so it was agreed.

'From now on,' I told Maureen, 'you must always think of me as your mother, and you must come to me first if you get into any kind of trouble, whatever it may be.'

With the exception of her years of adolescence, when we were separated, and the last week of her life, when I was in America, Maureen always did just that.

The years of separation were forced on us in the most unexpected way, and I cannot make up my mind to this day how far I was to blame. Maureen's grandmother was living in London. She had not seen Maureen since she was a tiny child. She had lost her own daughter in such tragic circum-stances and was delighted to find a beautiful granddaughter living so close by. I invited Cathleen Drogheda to lunch.

The lunch was a great success and what I had hoped for came to pass. Lady Drogheda began to take an active interest in Maureen. She bought her clothes and presents, took her to Covent Garden when the Royal Ballet was performing and to her uncle's country house for weekends. That was as I felt it ought to be. Richard was not around to make any trouble, but trouble came nevertheless.

At the end of six months Maureen's back was straightened out sufficiently for her to be accepted at White Lodge. Full of joy and excitement she went off to be a weekly boarder and came home to South Lodge every weekend. Desmond and I would pick her up from the station on Friday afternoons and took her back there to catch the train for Richmond on Sunday nights.

One Friday when Maureen got off the train I noticed that she was deathly pale.

'I can't speak to you, Mummy,' she whispered when she joined me on the platform. 'Daddy came to the school and made me swear on the Bible that I would never see you and Desmond again.'

I could hardly take in what she was saying. 'But where are you going now?' I asked.

'Granny is sending a car to pick me up here,' she said and burst into tears.

Within her short life Maureen had already lost two mothers. Now she was to lose a third.

'Don't worry, darling,' I said hastily, 'There must be some sort of misunderstanding. We shall sort it out—I promise. Just don't get too upset. By next weekend you will be home again.' But I was over-optimistic.

Somehow I found Richard in London and he came to the flat. 'I have been told that Maureen is calling Agnes "Mummy" and that you are trying to take her away from me altogether.'

'How can we?' Desmond asked him, 'You are her father, we are only fostering her at the moment and have no legal rights whatsoever.' Tactfully we did not dwell on the fact that he had gone off to America for almost a year without sending as much as a postcard to ask how she was getting on or to give us his address.

'People are saying I abandoned her,' Richard said peevishly.

Does that surprise you? I was tempted to ask, but for Maureen's sake I held my peace.

We knew that Richard had neither the means nor the intention of leaving California to make a steady home for

Maureen and her brother in London, and we were confident we could work something out amicably. Maureen aged thirteen was reaching puberty, a time any girl would need a mother to turn to. Surely Richard's love for her would overcome the resentment he felt towards us? But to my utter dismay nothing we said could persuade him to lift the cruel ban.

Many years later, when we came across him again in Ireland, he claimed that he had been forced into this action by Cathleen Drogheda who, he insisted, had been the one who was jealous and who had suspected my motives as lesbian. Cathleen Drogheda was dead by that time and could not defend herself against such accusations.

I could not keep in touch with Maureen once she was living with her grandmother. Causing her to break her vow would have put her under tremendous strain. I had to accept the situation, but the sudden and unexpected loss of her caused me a great deal of pain for a long time to come.

Agnes as Salomé (*top left*) at St Martin's Theatre, London, July 1954 (photographed by Angus McBean); Agnes in the musical *One Girl a Day* at the Palace Theatre, Manchester, April 1959 (*top right*); Agnes as Principal Boy in *Robinson Crusoe* at the Gaiety Theatre, Dublin, December 1958 (*above left*); and a poster for Agnes's solo show in the second Dublin Theatre Festival, 1961.

Michael Dress,
composer.

Maureen Aherne,
aged twelve.

Anges and Seán in
Brighton, 1949.

Leonie Leslie King's christening at the Brompton Oratory, London, in 1951,
with (*left to right*) Sir Shane Leslie, Anita Leslie King, Commander Bill King,
her godmother Winnie Carlton Paget, Mary Churchill, unknown, and
(*second row*) Jack Leslie, Agnes, Mrs King, Desmond Leslie, unknown, Diana
Daly and Roger Frewin.

XII

I had been blonde for several years now and I was getting tired of the kind of people I never met as a brunette. I had come to an agreement with the Wella Farben Hair Studio and they used to colour my hair a soft silver blonde once a month. All I had to do in return was model for them if the occasion arose. The occasion did eventually arise and I presented myself at the Wella Farben stand at Earls Court for the annual Hairdressing Fair. I was hoisted up on to a platform. The girl who began to bleach my roots was not my usual one. This did not bother me. I had seen her occasionally at the hair studio. She appeared a little nervous and overawed by the vast crowd of spectators which had gathered around the platform.

I shut my eyes and thought of higher things as she rinsed the bleaching agent out of my hair and began to comb it. A gasp went up from the crowd. I opened my eyes and to my horror I saw that most of my hair had come off my head and was now firmly wedged between the teeth of my young lady's comb. She became frantic and combed me even more vigorously than before. More handfuls of my silver locks became detached from me. I was in imminent danger of turning bald.

The girl was in tears. I saw the funny side of the situation.

'Ah well,' I said to her, 'I've been a blonde long enough. Tomorrow you'd better cut my hair very short and give it a brown rinse. Then I can go home and lead a normal life once more, and meet the kind of people I really like.' Then I waved to the crowd and stepped off the platform.

A most unexpected letter reached me one day from Yugoslavia in the late fifties. It came from a retired official of the municipal administration at Opatia, formerly Abbazia. He wrote that I should make a claim for the Villa Belvedere as it had never been officially sold, merely requisitioned by the Yugoslav government.

The next time we were in Italy, Desmond and I and the boys went to Istria across the Adriatic on a hydrofoil and succeeded in getting an instant visa after giving an undertaking not to write any defamatory articles about the Tito regime.

I had never before returned to any place after many years without finding it so utterly unchanged in a physical sense. Abbazia/Opatia looked to me at first glance exactly as I remembered it. I could show it all to the children. The lido beach, the Victorian Badeanstalt, my little park with the bandstand, the hotels with their large terraces, the promenade and the shops all seemed unchanged. Excitedly I walked my family from end to end of my childhood paradise, but was it really the same? The people in the streets were shabby and sad-eyed, there was little one could buy in the shops, the beach was deserted. The spirit of wayward but enchanting Abbazia was missing in sombre Opatia.

When we got to the Villa Belvedere, it had ceased to live up to its name—beautiful view. Tito had built a villa for his mistress just below it and all one could see now were her dustbins.

There were a large number of people billeted in our house. A professor from Zagreb University and his wife were living in my nursery. A family of peasants occupied my father's bedroom and another family my mother's. They were all very excited when I introduced myself. 'Ah yes,' they said in broken Italian, 'La figlia del Tedesco, il patron.' The daughter of the German. The owner! They offered us tea and took us on a tour of the house. They begged us to settle a dispute they had over the size of their share of our balcony.

I found a pair of lions' heads still screwed to the wall on the staircase. They had rings through their noses which had once held a silken cord. 'Take them, take them,' cried the peasant father and he tore them off the wall. It is all I have left now of the Villa Belvedere because I could not bring myself to make a claim and displace all those people. They needed the house more than I did.

The first real blow to my marriage fell in the summer of 1957 by the pool of my beloved Monte Carlo Beach Club. The sun was blazing down on us from a clear blue sky when Desmond announced that he had fallen seriously in love with a girl called Susie and was going back to Paris the next day, where she was waiting for him. If I wanted to divorce him he would quite understand.

It all seemed totally unreal, especially in that setting, but off he went and I was left to 'sit out' the children's holidays in a state of shock. I could and would not accept the idea of divorce.Our relationship was for ever and could not be broken just like that. It just didn't make sense to me. I prayed he would get it all out of his system in Paris.

Once again I found myself stranded on the Riviera. The currency restrictions were going to make it very difficult to pay what we owed on rent or allow us to buy tickets to travel home. Desmond had taken the car to Paris and I did not know where he was staying. Someone introduced me to a very smooth Russian, who was reputed to make his living in shady money deals on the international market. He was attractive in an unattractive sort of way and started taking me out for meals, which I hoped would lead to a financial inter-change. Unfortunately he was after my virtue and dangled the possibility of a small currency exchange in front of me as bait.

Another person who was around that summer was Leonard Urry, a London theatrical agent. His job in Monte Carlo was to report all the goings-on, scandalous and other-wise, to his present boss, my 'Rasputin' of old, Harry Clifton, who was staying at the Hôtel de Paris but was too ill to show his face.

One afternoon, embarrassed and uncomfortable, I was having tea with my Russian in the lounge of the Hôtel de Paris. Thinking he would 'land' me at last as I was getting more and more anxious to get home, he was being particu-larly exasperating. At that moment a small page-boy came down the stairs in full view of everyone carefully balancing a silver tray which was piled high with banknotes. Slowly he picked his way across the polished floor until he reached our table. All eyes were upon us as he handed me the tray, and announced in ringing tones that 'Meester Arry Clifton sends his compliments to Mademoiselle Bernelle and wishes 'er to leave the Monsieur, her escort, this very minute, and never to speak to 'im again!' Gratefully I gathered up the money— about a hundred pounds in French notes—and walked away from the table leaving my astonished 'escort' behind.

I went straight to the desk and asked for a double room. Then I telephoned the airport and booked three seats on the midday flight the next day.

I went in a taxi to the little house we had rented and brought back the boys and our luggage.

That evening we sat snugly in the huge bed in a room at the hotel, consuming the vast quantities of spaghetti bolognese room service had brought up to us and toasting Harry Clifton in mineral water. My attempts to thank him by telephone had failed. Evidently he was still too ill to speak to anyone.

The months that followed were not happy ones. Desmond eventually returned from Paris, as I had hoped, but he began to vacillate between me and his new 'love' in a most irritating and unnerving way. One minute it was off and then it was on again. I had some tearful discussions with him. The one I still remember took place just after we had come back from the holiday and he from his assignation in Paris. To have an excuse to have stayed there so long he had used a business scheme involving, of all things, carrots. He had brought back with him a carrot as a sample and during our row I had been frantically nibbling it and finally had demolished it altogether. 'Now you have eaten my sample carrot and ruined my business prospects!' Desmond shouted suddenly. We both saw the joke, burst out laughing and had to call a temporary truce.

It was decided that this Susie was to be invited to lunch to meet me. I agreed to this as I hoped she was a nice girl and would be put off Desmond when she saw our family home and the children.

On the day of the lunch Desmond went to pick her up. The lunch went surprisingly well. She was a nice girl and I instinctively liked her and she me. I was rather put out, though, when at the end of the meal Desmond took her off again and parted at the door from me like a son who had brought his intended home to mother. I did not know until much later, when she told me herself, that poor Susie had no idea that Desmond was actually living with us at South Lodge. He had told her we had separated years ago, so all my plans of making her feel guilty came to nothing.

Shortly before this unhappiness entered our lives Desmond had formed an association with the writer Simon Harcourt Smith. He was the sort of flawed character to whom Desmond was always fatally attracted. His diplomatic career had foundered, we heard, on some scandal involving plagiarism. Had we taken more notice of these rumours we should have been better prepared for what was to follow.

Simon, who had developed an interest in electronic sound and had good connections in the advertising world, flattered Desmond into forming a partnership. The Nieve console and other expensive equipment we now had was moved into Simon's house. Simon took over the running of the business side, and, alas, the running of our lives as well. His wife once told me that Simon had broken up a number of marriages deliberately and I found something sinister in the way he introduced Desmond to all kinds of diversions, mainly of the sexual kind, to build a power base for himself. My barely concealed suspicion was a danger to Simon and he used Desmond's infatuation with Susie to separate him from me. In no time I found myself sucked into a vortex of intrigue.

Desmond had told me that he had finally broken with Susie but Simon rang me up to say that this was not true and that Desmond still saw her regularly. 'Why are you telling me this?' I asked him. 'Are you not supposed to be Desmond's friend?'

We had a row on the phone and I hung up on him, glad that now I would not have him around any more. The very next day I had a letter from him complaining about my bad manners.

'Why are you taking it out on me,' the letter said, 'that Desmond has gone back to Susie because of my machinations.' But the word 'my' had been crossed out and the word 'his' written above it—a neat little Freudian slip Simon had not bothered to conceal. It confirmed all my suspicions.

Once again I begged Desmond to give up Susie. He got angry when I threatened to leave, and called my bluff. I have a painful memory of leaving the flat, egged on by Jane Arden, holding Mark, just home from a children's party, with one hand and a red balloon with the other. I arrived at Jane and Renée's house still clutching both and was promptly put to bed with a fever.

Next day I went back to South Lodge to pick up Seán. Desmond offered to let us stay there and took himself off to Chelsea to set up house with Susie.

I now went through a breakdown. Apart from taking the boys off my hands some afternoons, my mother was not much help to me at that time. She claimed it was all my fault because I had 'shouted' at Desmond. Renée on the other hand came and stayed nights with me and I cannot imagine what I would have done without Seán, now eleven years old, who took over the responsibility for Mark whenever I could not cope. I thought he was far too young for such a burden and telephoned Mr Harrison, the glamorous headmaster of Ashfold School, and persuaded him to take Seán as a boarder the following term, even though he had not been 'put down' for the school at birth.

Desmond kept in touch by telephone, and one day when I had a fierce migraine he came to the flat and drove me to a house in St Mary Abbott's Place where neither of us had ever been before. It was the London base of the White Eagle Lodge, which Desmond had heard about on a radio programme, and which had, and still has, a great reputation for spiritual healing. A tall, handsome woman with amazing blue-green eyes opened the door. 'My name is Leslie,' Desmond began. 'I am bringing my wife because …'

'Don't worry about your wife,' said the woman, whose name was Joan Hodgson. 'We have been waiting for *you* for quite some time.'

Before he could protest, Desmond was taken into the lodge.

Having deposited Desmond with her mother, Grace Cook, who was at that time the principal healer at the Lodge, Joan took me into a small quiet room and let me pour out my heart. She then sat with me without speaking for quite a while. She must have passed some healing rays to me because when I left again with Desmond I felt much refreshed, both physically and spiritually.

From then on I returned regularly to the Lodge.

On Renée's advice I was also seeing her mother-in-law, Eva Mellinger, who was a psychoanalyst. Although I began to gain some insight into other people's behaviour and felt at times that they were made of glass and I could see right through them, I did not get much insight into myself. Yet, I had only to sit quietly beside Joan and I would suddenly understand what Eva had been trying to tell me.

But there was more than understanding that passed between Joan Hodgson and me, as I would soon discover.

Jane Arden had just given birth to Dominic, her second son. Weeks after her confinement she was still in hospital and was not even allowed visitors. An exception was eventually made for me and I went and sat by her bedside. She was pale and shaking all over. The baby was nowhere to be seen. Suddenly a strong urge came over me. I wanted to make her better. I pictured her with little Dominic in her arms. The image of colours blue, white and gold came into my head. I passed the image through my finger-tips and directed the colours towards Jane. I had no idea what made me do this but suspected I had picked it up from Joan Hodgson. After only a few minutes, Jane stopped shaking, her breathing became normal and she fell asleep.

When the nurse came with her tray of drugs and tranquillizers, I sent her away. 'She won't need them tonight,' I heard myself say to the astonished nurse.

Next morning Jane was on the telephone.

'Whatever did you do to me?'

'I'm not at all sure,' I told her.

'Well come and do it again please.'

Four days later Jane was discharged from hospital.

When Desmond came to take out the boys, he explained that the method I had used instinctively is called 'colour-healing'. A number of books had been written about it. I had never seen any of these books nor had anyone ever told me about this therapy.

Since that time I have known other moments when I felt an 'urge' to help someone in pain or distress, and when I follow these urges they always work. I began to consider seriously whether I should try to develop this gift further, but felt that I was not spiritual enough. I enjoyed smoking, drinking, making love and acting too much to become a real healer. Perhaps I set myself too high a standard and squandered a gift from God, and so have not been able to relieve anything but the most minor of ailments. At least I never refuse to follow my urges when they come.

While Desmond and I were apart, he worked hard in the studio Simon had now set up in his house, making tapes for J. Walter Thompson and other advertising firms. From time to time Simon would telephone me and complain about Desmond, accusing him of being lazy and dishonest. I knew he enjoyed causing trouble between us, but was there more behind it? I resolved to find out.

I had met a rather dissolute but otherwise amiable character, whom I shall call Harry, who was quite willing to play any part I would devise for him. I told Simon that I had met a big financier who was interested in putting some money into the firm. 'As you are so dissatisfied with Desmond why not dump him and go into partnership with my friend Harry?'

Simon swallowed the bait and arranged for me to bring Harry, my 'financier', to his house at a time he was able to send Desmond out on some errand. He agreed to let Harry have the run of the studio for a time to see how they would get on. He gave Desmond a fortnight's holiday—without pay, of course.

Harry now had access to correspondence, invoices and receipts. It emerged that Simon had simply used Desmond to produce the tapes he was selling, passing Desmond off as his 'young assistant', and sending him out for cigarettes whenever a client was due at the studio. He had pocketed the cheques these clients had paid.

I now had Simon where I wanted him and only needed the occasion to confront the ever-gullible Desmond with the evidence.

The occasion arose when my sister-in-law Anita invited us to Glaslough for the children's Easter holidays. The old blue room worked its magic and Desmond asked me to take him back. I said that I would, but only if he gave up Simon as well as Susie.

'But you don't understand, he is my best friend,' he said as expected, but when I showed my proof he was furious at Simon's betrayal and swore he would get his own back—but by stealth and without a confrontation. This was not what I had planned and I did not really approve, but had no choice but to play my part. Harry and I were to meet Simon for dinner while Desmond was to remove his equipment from the house. It was a tense situation and I refused to let Simon buy me as much as a drink.

'I can't be your guest because I don't like or trust you,' I told him truthfully. 'And don't you trust Desmond too much either,' I added in spite of myself.

'I've left him alone in the studio,' Simon said, puzzled by my behaviour. 'He gave my wife a fiver to take herself to the flicks. Perhaps I had better telephone home.'

Harry and I looked at each other in alarm. The evening seemed more and more like a scene from a bad thriller. Simon came back from the phone satisfied.

'He's there all right,' he announced smugly and allowed Harry to carry him off to some all-night party in Shepherds Bush.

I went home and sat, for what seemed hours, in the dark. Desmond arrived a little after midnight, the equipment safely in the lift.

An hour later Simon was on the phone. He had, of course, no idea that Desmond had just returned to me. He went into a paroxysm of rage about Desmond's 'cowardly deception'.

'Of course it was never his idea to leave me,' he said, 'someone else has put him up to it, and I think I know just who it is.'

I did not bother to disillusion him.

In spite of my expectations the weeks that followed our reconciliation were not easy. It was a period of slow and sometimes painful readjustment, but one incident still makes me laugh when I remember it.

Desmond, true to form, had been running a second mistress all the time. She was a Swedish fashion model and her name was Helena Sieuer. As the girl Susie's second name was Drane I had coined the phrase 'Oh yes, out of the drain into the sewer' on which Desmond had been dining out all through our separation.

Soon after he came back home, we had to spend an evening at separate functions. I arrived back late and found Jane Arden in our bed. We were putting her up for the night and I had made a bed for her in the studio. I had left the door open and the light on, but Jane being Jane she had gone to our bedroom instead. She woke briefly to tell me that Desmond had come in earlier but had left again in a towering rage, muttering something about not being master in his own house any more and never coming back again. I became hysterical and rushed downstairs where the family Morris was parked and drove as fast as I could across town to SW7. I vaguely knew that Susie had moved to a house on the Chelsea Embankment.

I searched up and down the deserted street for my elderly but still conspicuous Jaguar. I feared Desmond had gone back to Susie on this flimsy excuse, and was determined to find him and explain. The Jaguar was nowhere to be seen. Puzzled, I turned to drive home but on the way when I passed through Sloane Square and saw the Jaguar parked outside the Royal Court Theatre. Aha, I thought, this explains it. He has gone to spend the night with Helena Sieuer instead, she has a flat beside the theatre. I pressed the bell. A female voice came over the intercom. It sounded elderly and not a bit like Helena's. I asked who it was. 'This is Helena's modder from Sveden. And who is zat?' I did not know what to say. I could not tell the old lady that I was looking for my husband in her daughter's bedroom in the early hours of the morning. I mumbled something about being an old friend of her daughter's and having locked myself out of my own apartment. The buzzer went, the door was opened. I could not go back on my story and meekly climbed the stairs. The reason for the mother's presence became clear. Helena was in bed with a badly broken leg. She was alone, her shattered limb encased in plaster. There was no sign of Desmond and having told her mother that I was locked out of my flat, I ended up sharing a bed with Helena.

Next morning we telephoned around town, but could not find anyone who had put Desmond up. The only place we did not think of was the Royal Court Hotel across the square, where he had actually spent the night. When I got home that morning, he was already there before me.

Much less amusing was the incident that nearly wrecked our marriage for the second time.

One evening Desmond came home and announced that he wanted to drive my Jag to Monte Carlo the next day because he had been given an assignment to do a special recording. I wanted very much to go along and have a second honeymoon in the place where we had spent so many happy times.

'But what about the children?' Desmond asked. We had no nanny at the time. I rang my mother and she agreed to come over and look after the boys for a few days. We started to pack and Desmond, who always took an interest in my clothes, spent all evening picking out what he wanted me to take. I was thrilled.

Early next morning I woke up with a start. I had forgotten to pack my passport. I went to the little drawer in my desk where I always kept it. The drawer was empty. I shook Desmond awake. 'Don't worry,' he said, 'in any case we can't leave till the afternoon. I have an appointment. You have plenty of time to look for it.'

'I won't find it today if it isn't where it belongs. It could take ages.'

'Then you'd better go to the passport office immediately and get another. I'll ring them up and ask what you need to bring with you.' He lifted up the telephone. 'They say you don't need anything. Just go along, but go along quickly.'

I dressed in a hurry. When I reached the front door I stopped dead in my tracks. Surely, I thought, it isn't possible to get a new passport without documentation. And then I knew. 'You took it, didn't you?' I asked Desmond. He reached into his dressing-gown pocket and drew out the passport. Susie was in Monte Carlo and thinking of getting engaged. He simply had to go and see her, perhaps for the last time. I felt numb. It wasn't so much Susie but the knowledge that he would have let me go to the passport office in vain. I went to the medicine cupboard. 'Watch me,' I said, 'I am going to take these five sleeping pills. Don't worry. They're only to put me to sleep. Now off you go to your appointment.'

When he had left, I went back to bed but try as I would I could not go to sleep. I took a large suitcase and put my toothbrush into it. Then I went across to the garage where we kept the Jaguar. I started to drive. I drove and drove all day and all night in a kind of daze neither eating, drinking nor sleeping. I could not feel anything except the urge to drive.

I picked up a hitchhiker somewhere and had to fight off his advances on a lonely country road. In some big city a chap in army uniform took me to the pictures, but I did not register the film or the chap. I booked into a small hotel and remember being glad I had taken a toothbrush. The rest of the drive remains a blur. I had visions of a trench in which I was to lie and look up at the sky. The trench would be some-where by the seashore and I had to drive until I found it. Eventually I reached the sea.

I got out of the car and lay down on the beach. I knew it was important to touch the earth with my belly. And then I heard the voice.

'Get up. You must go back and carry on,' it said, 'I can't!' I shouted, but still I obeyed.

I got back into the car and drove for a couple of miles. I reached a village. It was, as I learnt later, called St David's and was in Wales. Outside a grand-looking hotel I parked the car and went in. I had not emptied my bladder since leaving home. I paced up and down in the lounge, feeling as if my brain would explode, until the manager, alarmed by my odd behaviour took me by the arm. He asked who I was and what I was doing. I could not tell him what was impossible to tell.

'I can't pee,' was all I said over and over again.

The manager suggested that we telephone my home—my husband?

'He won't be there, he's gone to France,' I told him, but of course he might not have wanted to leave without the Jag.

The manager was kind and efficient. He contacted Desmond, gave him the train times to Fishguard, and made him promise to come and fetch me. Then he took me to the doctor.

'I can't pee,' was all I could say to him too. The doctor gave me an injection which worked, and the manager took me to a small guest-house in the town. 'Your husband will be here in the morning,' he said and put me to bed.

Next day, when I heard Desmond's voice downstairs, I was seized by a strange panic. I had so much hoped he would come and fetch me home but now all I wanted was to get away from him. Desmond tried his best to be kind to me. Before I was even dressed, the doctor arrived. He examined me and told Desmond I was fit to be driven home but that he thought I needed long-term help. He suggested some clinic in Hampstead.

We set off on the long drive home in the open car. The sun which had been blazing all week had disappeared, the beautiful landscape was dull and depressing. From time to time I tried to jump out of the car. Exasperated, Desmond stopped by a public phone box and called our flat. Seán, who had not gone to school that day, answered the phone.

'Are you coming home now, Mummy?' he asked anxiously.

That settled it. We continued the drive without incident. We drove through Oxford where we had spent part of our honeymoon and had a friendly dinner at the Randolph Hotel where we had stayed thirteen years before. Once home Desmond seemed not to bear me any grudge for having spoiled his plans, but neither did he arrange to get help for me. I fooled myself into thinking he had abandoned his trip to France.

A few days later at the breakfast table, I suggested we go to a friend's opening night.

'Fine, I'll ring and order tickets,' Desmond said. 'Surely you will find someone to go with you. I'll be on my way to France.'

For a moment I feared for my mind but then I became very calm.

'You don't really want to go, you want me to stop you,' I said. 'But I won't. I'm going to have my hair done and then take the boys for an outing. I can't say now if we will be here if you decide to come home.'

Desmond left in the Jaguar while we were at Greenwich clambering all over the *Cutty Sark*. Over the next ten days I refused to accept Desmond's phone calls from Monaco and returned his letters and telegrams unopened. He came back three weeks later with Harry by his side for 'protection'. I ignored him completely.

My mother now telephoned us from a German spa where she was on holiday to say that she had almost died there from a heart attack. She was a little better now and wanted to see me and the boys once more before she departed this life. She sent us plane tickets and we met her in Munich. From there we all flew to Venice.

Our hotel was the Grand Hotel which looked out on to the Grand Canal. We spent a lovely fortnight taking the motoscafi across the lagoon to the Lido Beach every day. My 'dying' mother accompanied us everywhere.

I enjoyed swimming far out into the Mediterranean and was often followed at a discreet distance by a very handsome, black-eyed young man. One day he caught up with me in the water and asked me in Italian where I disappeared to every evening when the sun went down. I answered as best I could that we were not staying on the Lido but in Venice proper, at the Grand Hotel. He continued to talk to me very rapidly in true Italian style. I could not understand a word he was saying but nodded politely, smiled at him and swam back to the shore.

That night when we were having dinner on the terrace the porter called me to reception. I was taken aback to see my black-eyed Italian standing there complete with his very expensive luggage. When I asked what he was doing in our hotel he cried, 'But you agreed that I should come here tonight and make love to you!' I was appalled, and since my Italian was obviously not adequate to tangle with my determined suitor the only way I could prevent him from making an embarrassing scene was to give in to him. He obviously considered himself a classic Italian lover but since he asked to be confirmed on this point at every turn, the night became a frightful bore and I was relieved the next morning when I managed, with the aid of a dictionary, to persuade him to go back to the Lido, baggage and all. I ushered him into the lift before my family had come out of the dining-room.

We were offered a lift to Rome in someone's car, put my 'dying' mother on her plane to London, where she survived another eleven years, and set off to stay with my brother-in-law Jack in his miniature palazzo.

I gave the boys as good a tour of Rome as I could, and on our second day Farouk telephoned.

'I heard that you are in town. I am in Formia, on the West Coast in a small hotel. You must come and join us.'

'But I have my children with me ...'

'That's just why you must! My girls and little Fuad will be delighted to have them!'

When I packed our bags there was consternation all round.

'You cannot possibly want to go and stay with that man,' said my friends.

A little gingerly I stepped off the train at Formia, clasping the boys' hands tightly. A comfortable old lady was waiting for us on the platform.

'I'm Nanny', she said, 'and I am to take you to His Majesty.'

On the drive to the hotel we learned that Nanny had been with King Farouk for nearly sixteen years. Throughout all this time, which encompassed splendour, turbulence, exile and tribulation, she had never been more than a stone's throw away from him and his children.

'You must be the only person so loyal to him.'

'Oh no, Madame. There are several of us: his private secretary, his bodyguards, his major-domo and, of course Mademoiselle. She has been with His Majesty even longer than I have!'

I noticed that her voice took on a special lyrical tone whenever she referred to Farouk, and I tried to imagine some of the debaucheries ascribed to him in the newspapers with Nanny and Mademoiselle smiling serene approval. It was too absurd.

We spent a happy day on the beach with the King and his household. His relationship with his three daughters and the little boy King Fuad was that of an ordinary affectionate parent. We sunbathed on the sands, went for rides in a small speedboat and splashed about in the sea. The children insisted that Farouk should play 'Walrus', a role for which he was eminently suited because of his bulk and his moustache. Again and again he submerged himself and re-emerged from the water, sputtering and snorting, to topple the children over and to catch them again. My boys and little Fuad squealed with delight.

That night we all dined together al fresco under the branches of an olive tree. How different an image he presented to us there from the one projected of him by the media. He must have sensed my thoughts, because he turned to me and said, 'You realize that you are perhaps the only European who has ever shared in our intimate life and seen us as we really are.'

Later that night, when I was putting the boys to bed, I received a formal invitation to join the King on the terrace. I went—with some trepidation.

He was alone, his vast bulk enveloped in a long white robe, which lent him an unaccustomed dignity. I thought of the photographs I had seen of him as a handsome crown prince before he became gross and physically distorted when he was struck down by a glandular disease. He held out his hands. I wondered what was expected of me but Farouk put me to shame.

'You came to Rome alone this time, with only your children. Are you unhappy?'

I lowered my eyes.

'Are you free?'

'Your Majesty, I am a Catholic.'

'Ah yes, I forgot. It is a pity for me. We get on so well together and our children like each other. If ever you are free, remember I shall be waiting. Wherever you are, I shall always be there for you. I did not intend to marry again ... but if you should ... by chance ... consider.'

'Your Majesty,' I said, 'I can never be free.'

The days that followed passed quickly. Farouk did not speak again of marriage. But how we talked!

He was much concerned with the future of his two elder daughters. It was not so much their financial situation that bothered him, although he was, at that time, beset by money troubles. Contrary to popular belief he had not brought a vast fortune out of Egypt. His attempt at land development around Formia had run into difficulties. It was the girls' personal fulfilment that obsessed him.

'They are women with women's needs. As Moslems in a Catholic country what chance have they of finding husbands?'

He spoke of his royal past with detachment—'I don't think I was a very good king'—and of his heritage with good-humoured irony—'The last of the Pharaohs they have called me. What nonsense. My father was a brigand and my mother was French.'

I recalled his modesty years later when my friend Ivor Powell, an expert on Egyptian affairs, explained the historical facts surrounding Farouk's reign and abdication. Ivor claims that his departure was not greeted with unreserved joy, as most of us have been led to believe. True, a need for progress could not be denied, but Farouk, once he had sown his wild oats, had seriously attempted reforms. The manipulations of British diplomacy and the pressures brought on him by warring western nations had thwarted him at every turn. The end of the monarchy in 1952 was a personal disaster for a great many Egyptian people.

When we said goodbye in Formia, I never dreamt that I should not see him again. A poignant moment came when I returned to Rome and had lunch at the house of one of Jack's friends. Proudly he showed us Farouk's collection of precious stones, acquired by him from the Egyptian government for a song only that morning.

In 1965 news reached us of the death of King Farouk in Paris. When I switched on the television a panel of 'experts' were discussing someone 'gluttonous … gross … extravagant …' We had heard it all before, these descriptions of the last ruling King of Egypt. The panellists went on and on. By their own admission none of them had ever as much as shaken his hand. Now he was dead and only those of us who had known him well were mourning him, but while Britain was still reviling him, his country had reclaimed her exiled son. Forty members of the house of Mehemet Ali were waiting to say prayers by his tomb when he was laid to rest in Cairo.

Goodbye old friend, I thought, I'm glad that at last you're home again.

When we were back in Rome Desmond telephoned. He had tracked us down to Jack's house and suggested we should meet him in Brussels, where he could take me and the boys to the World's Fair. There he behaved as if nothing had happened and gave us a wonderful time. He was so disarming and the boys were so thrilled that we were all together that I had not the heart to spoil it. I made it up with him without further discussion. The 'worse' slowly turned to the 'better'. It was the start of the best years of our marriage. Susie married her new man—I saw their wedding picture in some magazine at the dentist's. Helena went back to Sweden. There were no more ladies as far as I could tell.

XIII

Desmond was now working for the World Record Club, which sold LPs by subscription, providing the background music for a series of potted Shakespeare plays. Peter O'Toole, who was then young and 'emerging', was recording *The Taming of the Shrew* with his wife Sian Phillips. *Lawrence of Arabia*, his first film, had not yet been released and few people knew his face.

'If you'd like to see Peter O'Toole, why don't you come across to the studio,' Desmond said to me one lunchtime. From behind the glass partition of the control box I watched the two principals rehearse a scene in front of the microphone.

'Well, what do you think?' Desmond asked when they had finished.

'I think she is delightful,' I replied, 'but as for your Peter O'Toole—that young technician over there, twiddling with the knobs of the mixer, has more oomph in his little finger.'

'Good God,' Desmond cried. 'How did you know? That *is* Peter O'Toole. He is in the control box to monitor his wife rehearsing their scene with a stand-in.'

With Desmond's salary from the World Record Club we were able to take a holiday with the Club Méditerranée on Corfu, together with the Savilles and including our four boys. At the last minute Philip could not come and Ann Lynn, who had been the juvenile lead in *The Party*, Jane's play, took his place. The camp on Corfu was a wonderful change from ordinary vacations. Everyone lived in well-designed straw huts and ate in the open air. The food was French and excellent and the wine flowed freely. The spirit of the camp was one of gaiety and *laissez-faire*. When Ann complained to the management about the strange goings-on in a neighbouring hut occupied by a lady plying her nightly trade, she was told, 'Mais c'est normal, Madame!'

It was on Corfu that I had my second healing experience. Outside one of the huts I came across a man clutching his forehead in obvious pain. The minute he had passed me and was going down some stone steps I felt that I had to do something about him. I told him '*asseyez vous*' guessing he was French, and he obeyed without turning round. Standing above and behind him I put my hands over his head, I thought of blue. Within a few seconds he rose and turned to me. His pain had obviously gone. '*Vous êtes une sorcière*' (you are a witch), he said and after that I could not pass him anywhere in the camp without being pointed at and called a witch. I often wish I was able to help my children in times of disease but the urge never comes when I am too close to someone.

By the time we returned home, we owed a great many people hospitality and our friend Helen Strong, who knew someone with a sizeable garden in Chelsea, suggested that we should borrow his house to give a joint party—a Roman orgy. She would make the decorations and design the invitations.

Helen was a large, handsome girl who had somehow become an integral part of our lives. She had a habit of losing prospective suitors to younger women and each time one of her beaux married someone else she would come and cry on my shoulder. The result was that we took her on our annual visits to Glaslough and other trips to divert her. Helen was very different from my other female friends such as Renée and Jane. Her general outlook on life set her apart in our set; at the same time she seemed a little more sex-obsessed than we were. I was not quite sure how we had acquired her. She seemed to have come out of nowhere and was the butt of much derision from my own cronies. This, of course, made me fiercely protective of her.

I also felt slightly embarrassed and even guilty when Desmond took me on little pleasure jaunts and we stayed in comfortable hotels while Helen would trail along after us complete with tent and sleeping bag. I had an uneasy feeling that this situation would end badly—and so it did, but I never guessed how badly. Fortunately she is not Desmond's type at all, I told myself. His ladies were always svelte, sophisticated and sometimes very rich. Most unlike this gallumphing, naive Walkyrie.

Helen had recently helped me give a big party at Glaslough and I was glad to accept her cooperation with the 'orgy'. We sent out invitations on vellum to make them look like ancient scrolls.

A taxidermist provided a splendid lion and when I drove him away, his head, which was attached to his torso by a spring and was sticking out of my car window, would bob up and down and frighten people waiting at bus stops. I was offered large sums of money for him by passers-by and eventually installed him in the coal cellar our guests would have to pass on their way out to the garden. There was a notice saying CHRISTIANS THIS WAY and the lion, with some large bones my butcher had given me, was illuminated by an eerie red light.

A large crowd of Christians and Romans arrived, dressed in togas made of sheets and bedspreads, with wreaths on their heads. It is astonishing how handsome even the least attractive men and women can look in these simple costumes.

We had spread some tiger skins on the lawn and our guests reclined gracefully on the ground eating with their fingers in true Roman fashion, and drinking from goblets we had borrowed from a film studio, together with a set of papier mâché columns. Bunches of grapes hung suspended from branches above, and on top of each column were bowls of sand soaked in methylated spirit which gave a mellow flame. The wine—cheap plonk—was flowing freely and music from an old gramophone came wafting from the bushes. Everyone appeared to be having a marvellous time.

On the other side of the garden wall the reporters were clamouring to be let in to take pictures, but we had decided to ban the press on this private occasion. The frustrated murmurs from the other side of the wall were the only sounds that did not blend with the music.

One of our guests had leaned too heavily against a pillar. It toppled over and spilled the burning contents of the bowl on to the tiger skins, which burst into flame. Fortunately, since it was all out of doors on the lawn, the fire was extinguished in record time, but not before some hysterical guest had telephoned the fire brigade, the ambulance service and the police. They arrived with sirens screaming and brought the band of reporters with them in their wake. In an instant the garden was black with policemen, ambulancemen, firemen and journalists.

One of the guests, a young engineer home on leave from a job in Africa, had valiantly but foolishly tried to stamp on the burning skins with his feet. Since he was wearing only flimsy sandals, his feet and shins did not come out of it too well. We submerged him in a bath tub full of cold tea, recommended by a guest who was a doctor, until we were able to get him to the hospital.

The next day our Roman orgy was splashed all over the front pages of the London papers. ROME BURNS IN SW7! One of them screamed. Another quoted Desmond as saying, 'Ah yes, we burn Christians in Chelsea.' It sounded facetious and I was upset.

I rushed to the hospital to visit the young man, hoping he was all right and wondering if he was going to sue us.

I found him sitting up in bed surrounded by several beautiful women. His picture had also appeared on the front page and he had had a steady stream of visitors. He was beaming at me. 'Sue you? Good heavens, no! I wouldn't dream of it,' he said, popping strawberries and liqueur chocolates into his mouth.

'Someone who saw my face in the paper and remembered me from before I went away has offered me a job right here in London. I don't have to go back to Africa next week and I can take some of these lovely ladies to dinner when I get out of here.'

One Girl a Day may not have been the most memorable musical I have appeared in from an artistic point of view, but it did leave me with some absurd memories. It was lavish with seven glamorous actresses representing the seven wives of an Eastern potentate. Each was associated with a day of the week and each was of a different European nationality. I was Wednesday and Italian, dressed in a folksy costume with Ruritanian overtones. I had to sing a song and then storm off-stage screaming blue murder in a jealous rage in Italian.

The script-writer apparently did not speak that language, and had left a large blank in the script for my exit speech, expecting me to provide my own dialogue. He was lucky. Irena, our Italian maid, came from the hills above Naples and was not at a loss for some juicy Neapolitan swear-words, which she provided willingly. I was able to sound off in what must have been a hair-raising harangue to any Italian-speaker, but was merely an incomprehensible exit speech to the British theatre-going public.

We set off on a tour of the provinces and had a jolly time. Seven youthful actresses together in one show, sharing dressing-rooms and digs, was more like a school trip than a theatrical tour. The cast included a pair of straight singers, baritone and soprano, who played the star-crossed lovers and had a mushy duet in the romantic setting of the Blue Grotto in Capri.

Halfway through the tour, in Manchester, there was no one to look after the children, so I had to take them with me. I went ahead to check on the accommodation and took a taxi from the station. The taxi-driver gave me a curious look when I told him the name of the street.

No wonder! Our destination turned out to be the notorious red-light district. We stopped outside an appalling slum. The front door had been ripped off its hinges, bits of newspaper and other flotsam and jetsam were blowing about in the front garden. Upstairs, the apartment was full of dust and grime. I turned to the landlord, a terrifying troglodyte straight out of a Charles Addams cartoon, and told him I had made some mistake and we could not, after all, rent his apartment. He began to growl ominously, and I scuttled down the stairs and jumped into the taxi I had cautiously asked to wait, the troglodyte in hot pursuit, shaking his fist after me and roaring loudly. 'Drive on,' I urged the taxi-driver. For some reason we could not find a single bed anywhere in Manchester that evening. It was time to be in the theatre and get ready for the show. I would have to sleep in the dressing-room that night. As I approached the stage door I saw,

209

through the glass panel, a welcoming light from inside. Relieved to have reached safety at last, I pushed open the stage door. There in the booth to receive me was the stage-door keeper—my troglodyte!

By the time the children arrived next day I had found rooms in a small hotel. Mark insisted on coming with me to the theatre. This meant the boys would have to miss the evening meal. By pure chance I came across a gas cooker underneath the vast stage of the Hippodrome. It was connected up and I made my arrangements. I bought two plates, two knives and forks, a frying pan and a great deal of cooking oil. I had a nice long wait during the love duet in the Blue Grotto so, dressed in my silken frills and ribbons, I would sneak down below stage with the boys and cook their supper. Steak and onions was their favourite and steak and onions it usually was.

The fumes that rose innocently from my frying pan made their way upwards, wafted between the boards of the stage and floated cheerfully into the Blue Grotto, straight into the nostrils of the star-crossed lovers. If they had been tearful before, they were much more so now. They complained bitterly to the stage director. He made a tour of inspection and reached the lower regions of the Hippodrome just as I was ladling the food to my boys, who were holding up their plates like so many Oliver Twists.

'I don't believe it,' the stage director cried. 'This can't be happening!' I expected my notice at the end of the week but it did not come. Evidently actresses who can swear in Neapolitan are hard to come by in Manchester.

The tour of *One Girl a Day* was long and lucrative. When it ended, I had saved enough to take my family to Italy. Irena the Neapolitan maid came with us to visit her parents. Before setting off for home we went to Naples to pick up Irena. On the way to the platform for the Naples/Rome express I was approached by a railway porter who offered to carry my suit-case. He swiftly disappeared into the crowd with my precious case placed jauntily on one shoulder. He never reappeared. Desmond, Irena and the boys had climbed aboard the waiting train which was getting up steam. The guard put his whistle to his lips. I refused to get on without my suitcase.

The carriages began to move. I did not, and was left on the platform without my suitcase, without money or tickets.

There was only one thing left for me to do. I still remembered my Neapolitan exit speech. I launched into it and, fired by a raging fury, swearing loudly in Neapolitan, I paced up and down the now deserted platform. The platform did not remain deserted for long. Soon a large crowd collected. I did not stop swearing.

Suddenly the crowd parted, like the Red Sea, and a smartly dressed *carabiniere* walked towards me with my suitcase in his hand. By the cast of his features he could have been my porter's twin.

'Signora,' he said admiringly, 'any English lady who can swear so beautifully in Neapolitan deserves to have her suitcase back.'

I had barely settled back into London when I found myself flying to Berlin. Even after more than twenty years I had never thought of going back. Unless something specific reminded me of my past in Germany I never thought further back than my schooling at Holmwood. I clung to my Englishness and did not want to have it questioned in Berlin. But Jane Arden persuaded me otherwise.

She was going over for the opening night of *The Party* at the Residenz Theater. Renée, whose husband Michael was working at the Berliner Ensemble at the time, was already in East Berlin. I called at Jane's, with a present for her to deliver to Renée.

'Why don't you come with me tomorrow and give it to her yourself,' Jane said. 'I am sure we can get another seat on the plane.'

'I can't up and leave just like that. What would Desmond say?'

Jane did not think that was important. 'It's the best chance you will ever have,' she said, 'going on the spur of the moment, with me there to give you support.'

I met her at the airport at seven o'clock the next morning.

We landed at Tempelhof and went straight through passport control—two young Englishwomen in fox fur and leather coats, two smart NATO allies who did not need visas.

In no time at all we were driven away in a smooth Mercedes by Sigmund Hammer of the Residenz Theater. Here and there I thought I recognised a district, a landmark, something familiar. Memories rose and burst like bubbles as we sped through the city towards Jane's hotel.

I wrote down my experiences in Berlin when I was still under their spell. After more than forty years I would find it difficult to recapture the mood, so I have included part of this account here as it appeared in the *Cornhill Magazine*:

On our first dizzy day in West Berlin Jane and I spend all our time at the theatre where her play has reached dress-rehearsal stage. After the rehearsal we meet the actors in their dressing rooms and I mediate between them and Jane. We talk shop. I am amongst my own. They are all artists, non-political animals. I might be back home in London. But as soon as we're on our way to the hotel, a few minutes' walk through the darkening street, I am assailed by fears, doubts and apprehension again and also a longing—for what—for whom?

Back in our room Jane says wearily, 'I've promised to dine with my German agent. He has plans for the play, and wants to talk. I suppose I had better meet him alone. Would you mind?'

Mind? By now I cannot wait for her to go! I want to fly out into the city, to see, to touch, to find ...

I am out in the street in my white leather coat, among the evening crowds milling round the Gedaechtskirche, picking my way over rough stretches where the road is up, navigating wooden pavements on stiletto heels, temporary wooden pavements that lead to the Taunzienstrasse where all is neon and opulence. In my white leather coat, past the shops that look at first glance as thought they were still the same. This is Salamander where they always bought my shoes, the shop with the X-ray machine, fascinating, mysterious, thin black bones, my skeleton feet, like those of a bird, wriggling in a pool of green ... 'Not enough room for play in that shoe, Miss. Bring a larger size please!' ... But no! The name of this shop is unfamiliar, they are all unfamiliar these shops, new names, new owners. Only the pavement is the same!

The funny pavement has large stones with a slate-coloured mosaic boarder on either side. Not even the block-busters have ruined the pavement! I used to walk along it gingerly in my new shoes ... walk along it without stepping on the lines ... Can I keep it up? Yes ... yes ... no! Mustn't step on the grey mosaic. Only people in a hurry do that, grown-up people, in a hurry ... but today I'm in a hurry myself. A girl in a white leather coat, a grown-up stepping on the grey mosaic! Wish I could stop and linger ... I'd like to stop for twenty years on each stone, at each corner ... But there isn't time!

I am going home now and must go quickly.

There is a commotion outside the Kaufhaus des Westens. Two chauffeurs argue and a crowd collects. I let myself become part of the crowd. I stand and gape—like any Berliner, but the anonymous instant passes. I hurry on!

I could turn to the right now, Motzstrasse. Intimate route of childhood, paved with Nanny's small diversions to be savoured slowly, gently. Better hurry on … take the next road, a main road. Cinemas, hat-shops, teenage memories. 'What kind of hat would Moddom care for?' 'Moddom,' thirteen years old, will never forget that exquisite moment. Cinemas and hat-shops, but there seems to be no street at all here! The whole corner is one vast excavation with a narrow path of planks to bridge it.

'Excuse me,' says someone. 'Is this the way to the Martin Luther Strasse?' I lean against the wooden hand-rail and look at the man and his plump, placid wife.

'Yes, this is the way to the Martin Luther Strasse. To be exact you are in the Martin Luther Strasse already. Over there, on that heap of rubble was a hairdresser's shop. A very elegant place it was too, and sometimes my mother would take me with her to have my hair done.'

'We're not Berliners', says the woman, embarrassed. 'We find it difficult to find our way around. There's so little indication.' Her fat hands take in the scene of desolation with a sweeping movement.

'It's easy when you really know. I haven't been here for over twenty years, but I find it easy, very easy!'

They give me a curious look and pass by me precariously on the plank …

I've reached the spot where the Scala Theatre used to be, but there is no sign of it now. The buildings are mostly new, and I look at them with unseeing eyes. I can't take them in at all, even though I am no longer hurrying. I walk slowly now, hesitant, apprehensive, but it is just around the corner now … just around the corner …

My mother has told me that the house has gone, the square razed to the ground, and very little left of the street leading to it … but there *is* something there … I know there is *something* … a few hundred yards containing *me* …

And all at once I'm in that street … an eerie jumble of devastation, dark ghostly ruins outlined against the sky. A wind is tearing through the empty spaces. I shiver in that white leather skin I have wrapped around me … something inside me bursts … I cry … I didn't know … I couldn't know it would be like this.

They shouldn't have done it. They shouldn't have done it to me! As I run towards the square I think of the bombers low-flying over my city, my square. I used to cheer them on their way. Now I am weeping.

My mother has told me the square is destroyed, yet there is the square, solid and still in the moonlight. It is all around me, complete except for one gap, one hideous black hole that once was the house where I lived.

I am climbing about now on rubble and stones, over splinters and earth, over fragments of tiles ... white and black marble tiles with grass pushing through .. the floor of a hall ... a cool marble hall that used to resound to my feet.

I kneel on the bombed site and touch the tiles with my fingers ... cool tiles ... marble tiles ... orderly tiles. Fragment of order in a chaos of rubble. All that remains of my childhood, all I can find of myself ...

I cannot tell how long I've been kneeling here till at last I find calm. The houses in the square reveal their prosaic truth; they are new, nearly all of them reconstructions. Impersonal concrete where once stood the familiar houses of my friends. I lift my head to where the night air fills the void above me. At least there is nothing there—only the sky.

Slowly, leisurely, I wander over to the centre of the square. Poor little moonlit gardens—how sparse and ragged you've become! They must have blown your trees to pieces, those bombs; those great big bombs I sent you. I wonder did you ever miss me up there on the empty window ledge? And did you know that once you were my world? My universe, pulsating here below my window. Expanding, reaching out, like me up there, hot cheeks flushed against the window pane.

Now you are silent in the moonlight. When did your spirit die?

Not in the war. Nor on the Night of the big raid. Not even when you let the jackboots march across you, unprotesting. But on that day long ago, when I climbed down from off my window-ledge and looked on you no more. Little square of my childhood, lively square, many-splendoured square. What happened to you when the bright eyes of this child no longer held your image?

Can it be possible that I never spoke about you? Not to my husband, to my children? But how could I have described you in a new tongue, in a new land? How could I have made them see you, these new people who only know the formal elegance of squares locked within railings. True squares. 'Square' squares. When you, my little square, are round!

Round and open you were then too. Vulnerable and gay, a meeting place, classless, undiscriminating. A city's life in miniature.

Who would believe your absurdities? A lover's bench; a paper kiosk; a children's pond; a nurse's pram and suddenly a yawning abyss, the entrance to the Untergrund!

And here I stand by that entrance again, by the blue glass sign that arches the stairs and the ground beneath me vibrates again with the muffled rumblings of the little train—the little train that would carry me to school. There is a picture of a small girl in an album, a girl with a frightened smile on her first day of school, on this spot, on this square, by this Untergrund.

If they took it again this picture right here and now, it would all seem the same, the girl and the square and the Untergrund, but the girl is a woman now and the smile on her face hides a different fear, for tomorrow will bring confrontation.

They are passive now, most of them sleeping, those people I dread, those who like me were born in this town. Tomorrow this spot will be humming with people but tonight the square is all safety and moonlight. Magical moonlight. For what other than magic could have brought Cafe Wilko from the Bayrische Strasse right here to my square where the cinema used to be?

Eagerly I walk across towards the dim glow of neon, when an old man stops me. 'Zehn Pfennig!'—Can you spare me some pennies? I had not noticed him in the shadows, a shabby old beggar on a rusty old bench.

My hand automatically goes to my purse. But, of course, I haven't had time to change any money. 'Klein Kleingeld,' I tell him. 'No change! But I'm going to get some over there in the cafe.' The man shuffles back to the bench.

Inside, Wilko's is not in the least like the one I remember—the most marvellous ice-cream parlour in all the world! This one is merely a cafe—but it does sell ice-cream! Not the thirty glorious varieties of pre-war days—just three: vanilla, chocolate and strawberry, but my hand trembles slightly as the girl behind the counter hands me the familiar shell-shaped wafer! A shell-shaped wafer, to be found nowhere else except in Berlin.

'You are the Wilko from the Bayrische Strasse?' I ask the girl as I hand her my note. 'I used to come in every day on my way from school! You sold lime and banana and pistachio with nuts.'

You? What am I saying to the teenage girl behind the counter who pushes my change across with a shrug of her shoulder. Post-war generation, of course! What can she possibly know of lime and banana and the unsurpassed rapture of pistachio with nuts!

The flavour of strawberry sorbet give me nostalgic comfort. I return to the gardens where the old man awaits me. I know I can't leave until we have spoken. It is very important, though I cannot say why. And so we sit together—the old man and I—with the sighs of the square all around us.

'I lived here, you know, a long time ago,' I tell him at last.

'So did I! Always loved the place. I still come every day. Can't get away from it!'

' ... and over there, where that gap is now, that was our house.' I want him to look, to understand; but he follows his own train of thought.

'... There used to be girls, scores of 'em ... girls in blue, always crossing the square.'

I remember them too, those girls in blue, coming daily to the Lettehaus to learn to cook. Good little Haus-fraus in the making.

'... blue they wore ... blue overalls ... always crossing the square and laughing! Always came here at midday to see them have lunch in the square ... always laughing they were ...'

I remember.

'Always laughing!'

Suddenly his mood changes. 'How old do you think I am?'

I turn to him. He becomes real, grown a face, a grey face, tired and furrowed. I hesitate. He pulls off his cap. A bald head shines in the moonlight.

'Se-ven-ty?'

The grey face contorts with pain.

'I am fifty!' he shouts. 'Fifty! D'you hear? I'm not old. I'm in my prime. I'm not *old*.'

I cannot think of anything to say, but he doesn't expect any answer. He seems frantic. Desperate words, unspoken for years, pour over me. The party ... promotion ... parades ... the Fuehrer ... infallible ... then war ... wounded ... disabled ... the collapse of the Reich ... home ... useless ... authorities ... committees ... a home for the aged ... finished ... nothing to do ... years drag on ... years still ahead ... years ... useless ... pointless .... hopeless .....

I have no words, but I give him my attention, all of it, and for a moment in that ghostly square he is not pointless, not hopeless. He begins to grope, to clutch ... not with this hands, but with his mind.

'If I had had someone to pull me up again ... just someone to live for .. to bring me back ... a woman!'

But I have nothing to say to him.

'Perhaps you know someone ... a woman ... Don't you know anyone who can help me? ... a woman ... like you.'

I draw away from him.

'I don't know any women here. I don't know anyone. I've got nothing to do with here any more. Just returned a few hours ago ...'

'Returned from where?'

'Oh, from abroad.'

He becomes very still. He looks at me.

'You Jewish?'

'Yes.'

Simply that! Don't explain your duality. Don't get further involved. Don't ... but he won't let go.

He has pulled himself up, very close to me now. His fingers clutch at my arm. He is right, there is still power in those hands.

'It is *you* I need! *You* I've been waiting for! *You*! A Jewess. A Jewish woman. You must help me to be once more the *German man I used to be*.'

I wrench myself free. The ice-cream in my hand is melting away. Chilly drops trickle down my wrist. I toss the shell-shaped wafer, half finished, on the ground.

Too late. It's no use. I cannot turn back time for him or the others. Why didn't they think of it—*then*!

With the man still so close I feel very remote. No longer part of the square, only part of the world I have just come from. I'm a visitor now in a dark town at night; only aware of the cold—while he cries to me for his manhood.

A cloud has moved across the moon and the square grows darker. The man rises and I hope vaguely that he will go away, but I know that our moment of parting has not yet come.

He slowly goes down on his knees and takes both my hands into his. We remain this way for a long time. How long? I don't know. Maybe minutes, maybe hours, a tiny second in eternity? He watches my face while I look up to see the night clouds drifting and floating in the wind.

Someone famous once wrote 'There are no innocent victims.' But it is also what he is telling me. Is this what I have come back to find out?

It is good that he should look at me for his look holds the promise of my freedom. Freedom to be what I am, freedom to feel what I feel, freedom to make choices, and freedom to share in his guilt and his anguish.

I lower my eyes to look into his and shake my head at him with a regretful smile.

'It's all right you know,' I say, 'all right', as if soothing a child. 'But you see, I left Berlin years ago and I'll leave it again very soon, only this time I shall remember. You're on your own, like the rest of us, and yet we're all in this together.'

I don't think he understands what I'm saying, I'm only just beginning to myself.

I free myself from his grasp, reach for my purse and hold out some notes.

'Here, take this. It's not much, but it's all I've got with me tonight. It'll buy you a meal and also a drink. Drink it to me. And remember me. I'll remember you when I face the others tomorrow, and all the days of my life.'

He murmurs his thanks and shrinks back into age as I rise and walk slowly away. Away from my square, away from the past and away from this Nazi—my first.

My first, but by no means my last, for there was still another to come.

I had met Wolfgang von Oppen, Jane's German agent, over dinner on our second night in Berlin. He stared at me across the table. 'Haven't we met somewhere before?' But this was quite impossible.

'I know your face,' he kept repeating, until we found that we had spent some years under the same roof, studying at adjoining schools and sharing our recreation yard each day during the midday break. We had never spoken, but Wolf had carried the image of my face for all those years. He had lived around the corner from our house, and, had I stayed in Berlin, we could easily have met as teenagers and fallen in love.

The parallel in later life was even more surprising. Wolf had flown a Messerschmidt at the same time as Desmond flew a spitfire in the RAF.

It was inevitable, I suppose, that we should now fall into a time warp. All at once we were sixteen, holding hands. We wandered through streets and parks and many of the places we would have wandered through together then and did all the foolish things that teenage lovers do.

Once, I'm afraid. I nearly burst out laughing. Stark naked, Wolf almost clicked his heels. 'It is only right and proper,' he informed me solemnly, 'that you should know I shot down three Spitfires in the war!' It did not matter. We were only acting out a fantasy.

After a week of playing might-have-been, Wolf drove me to the airport. 'Can't you stay? Must you really go away again?'

But the moment to leave my city had come once more. This time I thought my heart would burst. This time I knew I was leaving for good and now I would always remember leaving Berlin.

Of course I could not have known when I travelled there on a whim how profoundly the visit would change me. I had found and acknowledged my roots and would never again deny that I was born in Germany. This had a positive effect on my work and particularly my solo career which lay ahead. I next went to act for Philip Saville in a play by Murray Shisgal at the Arts Theatre and subsequently in his television extravaganza *His Polyvinyl Girl* with John Fortune and Nyree Dawn Porter. It was John Fortune who almost unwittingly pointed me in a new direction.

Rehearsal for *The Unknown Woman of Arras*, 1948 (*below left*), with Michael Cacoyannis (*centre*), later the film director Michael Yannis; and (*below*) its director David Tutaev.

Agnes at the poolside in Monte Carlo in 1952 with Claus von Bülow (*left*) and (*above*)Victor Sassoon.

Agnes and Desmond Leslie with Titus the owl in the Long Gallery (*top left*); Agnes catching raindrops in the Long Gallery (*top right*); Agnes asleep in a Venetian baroque bed, Wordsworth's Irish harp beside her, in the Red Bedroom (*above left*); and Agnes ignoring Desmond as he emerges from the haunting cupboard in the Porch Room. (From a photo-essay by Hayward Magee taken at Glaslough for *Picture Post* in 1950.)

XIV

People often ask me how I came to do a one-woman show and I tell them that it all began by chance in a ladies loo. It had never occurred to me to be a solo performer and I never planned it until the day I was drying my hands in the washroom of what was then the Establishment Club in Soho.

Peter Cook, Dudley Moore, Jonathan Miller and Alan Bennett had hit London with their Cambridge Footlights revue *Beyond the Fringe*. They had been an overnight success and the West End had suddenly 'discovered' satire!! Now Peter had gone on to found the Establishment Club, where you could wine and dine while watching the latest satirical revue performed by John Fortune, John Bird, Lance Perceval and Roy Kinnear. It was considered the 'in' place of the day, but it reminded me of the cellar cabarets in Paris and Berlin which I had heard about so much from my father.

When Peter decided to add a female to his cast of four, he held auditions which went on for months. John Fortune, who knew I had been trained in the refugee cabarets that flourished during the war, suggested I should apply for an audition. On the final day only three people were left: myself, a lovely black jazz singer whose name I have forgotten and a teenage beauty—Carole Simpson. We had been given the actual particular establishment songs to learn, words by Christopher Logue and music by Stanley Myers who some years later wrote the haunting Cavatina for the film *The Deer Hunter*. Having sung my way through the required numbers, I went upstairs to wash my hands. I was feeling depressed, not because I thought I had not done well enough, but because I knew I would not get the job. I may have been the one who had been raised in the tradition of the show they were casting, but I was nearing forty and was far too old to stand on that tiny stage with four Cambridge graduates in their early twenties. It would look incongruous, I was well aware of that. In the washroom I was approached by a woman who handed me her card.

'I am a reporter,' she said, 'and I have been sitting in on all the auditions. If you are chosen, ring me up and I will do a big spread on you.' I was shaken. Apart from being terrifying, auditions are very personal, private affairs. To know that someone from the media had actually witnessed them, seemed to me as if somebody had been watching me on my wedding night! I drew myself up to my full height and said haughtily, 'Thank you very much, but I am not here for this job.' 'Really!' said the astonished journalist. 'Then why have you been auditioning so many times?' 'Oh,' I said, 'I want to do my own show here at the Establishment—a solo evening!' 'Splendid, splendid—what is your theme, your title?' I had to make a quick reply. I remembered the song I had used for the other auditions. 'It will be all based on the songs of Bertolt Brecht and Kurt Weill,' I said hastily, hoping to make a quick getaway.

The reporter called after me: 'That should be very interesting! Keep my card. Give me a ring when it happens and I will write about you then!'

Seventeen-year-old Carole Simpson got the job, as I expected, but I do remember that on my way home from the audition I asked myself: What have I said now? Is this what I would really like to do? Why ever did I say that?

As soon as I got home I telephoned some of my closest friends. 'What would you say if I told you I am going to do a solo show based on the works of Bertolt Brecht?'

Without exception they told me I was off my head!

'Who do you think would go to the theatre, pay good money at the box office and sit for two hours watching you up there all on your own?'

That did it! Had they told me it was a splendid idea, I should never have attempted it. But I never could resist a challenge! I set to work. I researched the Brecht material, picked what was most personally appealing to my own thoughts and feelings, decided to use as many different composers as was possible for variety's sake—Dessau, Eisner, Spoliansky, Asriel—took my savings from the bank, engaged an accompanist and began to learn. Cassette recorders had not been invented. I had to work with the live pianist. It took me the best part of five months to put together a programme. The notes for it I wrote into our laundry book.

Armed with it I went to see Peter Cook at the Establishment. He remembered me. I waved the blue booklet and told him that it contained the bones of a Brecht Evening I was hoping to perform at his club. 'Why don't you let me have the place for a Sunday night?'

Peter glanced at the laundry book. Then he took out his diary. 'How many Sunday nights do you want?'

'One!' I said quickly.

'It seems to me,' said Peter, 'that you have done a considerable amount of work. Why don't you do two nights, 4 June and 11 June?' And so it was agreed.

When I got home I went straight to bed. My temperature was over 103. My mother came to nurse me. She was puzzled. 'What ever has made you so ill?'

'I have pushed against so many doors for so many years and now a big one has opened before me and I have fallen flat on my face.'

After a week I went back to work. I now taught myself twenty-six separate items but had no idea whether they would fuse into a workable show, so I picked up some coloured cards—black for drama, blue for whimsy and pink for comedy. I laid them out on the floor so that they made a balanced pattern. I wrote the name of my pieces on these cards and made out my running order according to the pattern. I used this method only for the first few years. By now I know instinctively which item is to follow which.

Someone suggested I consult Martin Esslin, the head of BBC radio drama and a Brecht expert. We had never met, but when I telephoned him he came over to our flat and I performed for him. He made only one suggestion. 'Sing "Surabaya Johnny" in German'. Then he asked how many performances I expected to give.

'Two!' I said proudly. Martin shook his head.

'My dear girl,' he said, 'you'll be doing this for the rest of your life.'

Peter Cook put Nicholas Garland, the director of the Establishment shows, at my disposal. Unfortunately it was now a little too late for him to teach me how to put over the songs. I had worked too many months with the material. Nicholas had recently been directing the young Carole Simpson for her debut at the Establishment.

'What Carole does', Nicholas told me, 'is to simply stand there, sing and click her fingers—like that. Why don't you try it?'

I did not feel that I could perform songs like 'Surabaya Johnny' simply by clicking my fingers and began to feel unhappy about rehearsing with Nick. Besides, I found him irresistibly attractive, a situation which was fraught with danger. I confessed all this to Jane. 'You've got to stop working with him,' she told me.

'I can't. What would I say to Peter Cook?'

A few days later Jane rang me. 'I met your Nicholas Garland last night,' she said. 'He is attractive, but I told him you were not happy working with him. He said that he would resign immediately.'

'How could you!' I cried in despair. There were only three weeks to go.

I badly needed someone to light and stage my show. Fortunately two very professional men now came to my aid.

I begged our friend Ernest Berk to take over the staging of my show. Ernest, a dancer, had lit and directed many dance shows in his time. He agreed, and we began rehearsing seriously at the Establishment. Just as fortunately Seán Kenny, the brilliant stage designer from Portroe, County Tipperary, who was to die so young, had his studio on the first floor of the Establishment building. I slipped upstairs one day and asked his advice. He was generous enough to give it free of charge.

'Why do you want to be carried on stage in a trunk?'

'I, er, I just thought it would be nice,' I stammered.

'Forget it. What is your motivation for starting the show on top of a ladder?'

'I, er, I thought it might look unusual.'

'Forget it' said Seán. 'Find something simple you can sit

on from time to time and just get on with it. Slides are OK, Brecht himself used them a lot.'

When I had lunch in Renée's kitchen the following day I noticed the two plain wooden stools we were sitting on. It turned out that she had brought them home from Brecht's own kitchen in East Berlin. Of course she gave them to me there and then. Seán Kenny approved heartily.

'Yes,' he said, 'they are perfect. They can be so many things. Just stools, or put side by side, a bench; on top of each other a pulpit. Splendid, that solves your problem.'

I used the stools for countless shows until the day I left one behind at the Abbey Theatre in Dublin. Before I could retrieve it, it had been incorporated into an elaborate wooden set designed by Bronwen Casson for a production of *The Three Sisters*.

Halfway through rehearsals workmen arrived at the Establishment, ripped out the central heating system and proceeded to install a new one. They made a lot of mess and noise and it became very difficult to work there. Apart from the timing of this, there were other obstacles which seemed to have been put in our way deliberately. Some subtle forces were at work to put me off rehearsals. Insecure as I was anyway, I needed encouragement for my project, not sabotage. Or was I becoming paranoid?

Bruce Kopp, the catering manager at the club, took me to the bar and bought me a drink. 'I've watched some of your rehearsals. You'll be fine, besides Peter is counting on you. It's his business partners who are doing this. They didn't approve when he gave you the place without seeing the show. If you want me to be blunt and honest, they think of you as a schmaltzy continental lady, a threat to the reputation for satire we have established here. But don't worry. It will all work out.'

I wrestled with myself for several days and nearly put off the show altogether, but in the end I persevered.

There was a curtain at the Establishment and I was thrilled when, after the dress rehearsal, Peter Cook's face appeared through it from the auditorium. He had watched with apprehension without telling me beforehand, but he looked extremely pleased.

'It's a *show*,' he cried.

'What did you expect?' I said, but I was only too well aware of the anxiety he must have been suffering.

Two of my actress friends who were 'resting' agreed to help with the production. Paddy Webster did some research at the British Museum and came up with some horrendous World War II photographs for the 'Song of the Nazi Soldier's Wife'. They were made into slides to go with Michael Spoliansky's charming little tune I intended to use instead of the harsher original music. They made a poignant contrast.

Janice Cole proved useful in other ways. She worked hard at publicizing the evenings, particularly amongst our friends and acquaintances, and this paid off handsomely. When I suggested to the Establishment to raise the price of their tickets for me everyone was doubtful, almost shocked, but to our amazement both evenings were sold out.

On the night of my first performance I was so terrified that I could not produce the off-stage whistle I had intended for my entrance. My lips were simply too dry. The pianist, part of the trio I was using, blew his tin whistle shrilly. This was my cue but no answer came from me as I walked on stage in the dark.

I took up my place by the lantern slide Seán had made, the lights went on and the band struck up 'Lily Marlene'. I could almost hear the 'management' groan.

I flared my nostrils in typical continental, schmaltzy fashion and began to sing ...

'Underneath the lantern by the barrack wall
Stands a Chelsea Pensioner and answers nature's call
And all the people rush to see
How far that poor old boy can pee ... ee,
Yes, even Lily Marlene, yes e...ven Lily Marlene.'

A great big roar came from the auditorium. I stepped forward and began my show in earnest. It had worked. And so did the show the following Sunday. I was only sad that Peter was not there to see it all. He had taken the resident company to New York and left behind a new quartet of Cambridge graduates in their place. They had opened just before me but had not been well received.

Unbeknownst to me, Bruce Kopp had taped my show. He

sent the reel to Peter in New York and suggested that I should replace the undergraduates. Peter agreed and so it was that I became the first solo performer at the Establishment Club.

For the next three weeks I appeared twice nightly, dressed, as before, in black woollen skirt and jumper.

Nicholas Luard, one of the 'management', sent me a letter of apology for the 'sabotage' and it was agreed that the new magazine they were launching at the time would be printed in my dressing room. We had quite a celebration when news came in that W.H. Smith had reluctantly agreed to carry this publication. It was called *Private Eye*, and, like me, it is still around today.

When three weeks were up a young management team, Farjeon and O'Donoghue, offered me a season in the West End. I rang Dr Czech, the Brecht agent, to tell her my good news. I was told that she had sold the performing rights to the Broadway hit *Brecht on Brecht* with Lotte Lenya, Kurt Weill's widow, to someone else, a well-established West End company, and could not allow me to appear anywhere with Brecht material before *Brecht on Brecht* had completed its London run.

'Then why did you let me get this far?' I cried.

'How could I know you would get this far? Better people than you have tried a Brecht solo and never brought it off.'

That seemed to be the end of all my dreams, but destiny had other plans.

Jack McGowran, who had been booked to do his Beckett show late night at the Grafton Cinema for the Dublin Theatre Festival, cried off and Brendan Smith, the festival director, was looking for a replacement. Seymour Leslie, Desmond's uncle who had once been so opposed to our marriage, graciously sent him my reviews, he made me an offer, and Dr Czech agreed to 'look the other way'.

I set off for Dublin with my management and Ernest Berk, who had staged the show for me in London, took me to the Grafton Cinema on his motor bike. When we arrived in Grafton Street we found that the cinema, which showed cartoon films during the day, had little if any facilities for us. A small platform designed by Michael Scott had to be built at vast expense. On the night before we opened, Ernest had to rehearse the cinema projectionist in a complicated lighting plot he had devised especially for Dublin.

We left the place at five o'clock the next morning, grey with exhaustion. 'Goodbye,' we called to the projectionist. 'Have a good rest. We'll see you later on.'

'Oh no you won't,' he shouted back. 'It's Monday now. I shan't be back tomorrow. My colleague Maguire is on call tonight.'

Ernest sent me to bed, and stayed behind to deal with this unexpected crisis. He must have done well, because I found nothing wrong with 'Maguire's' lighting when I went on that night. Waiting for the show to begin, I could not hear much noise from the auditorium. No wonder—only seven people had turned up and they were friends of mine. On Tuesday there were seventeen but on Wednesday, when the notices came out, you could not buy a seat. After that, for the rest of the week, there were queues all the way down Grafton Street.

I went to endless parties and other jollities at the Festival Club. It was only the second year of the event and everything was new and fresh. My show, entitled *Savagery and Delight*, was voted the best foreign show that year. I had a wonderful time. But even so, my fondest memories are those of the cleaning ladies who turned up every night after *Bugs Bunny* and *Mickey Mouse* to cleanse the place with anti-flea sprays. The Irish journalists somehow found out that I had been stopped from appearing in the West End. 'Why did Lotte Lenya forbid you?' I was asked. 'It was the management, not Lotte Lenya,' I always answered. 'I doubt if she has even heard of me.' It was the best thing I could have said at the time as it turned out.

Renée called from London to tell me *Brecht on Brecht* had opened at the Royal Court, but Lotte Lenya had far too little to do in it to compensate for the rest of the company. 'You'll be in the West End before they are,' she wrote. I could hardly believe it, but Renée, like Jane, usually knew what she was saying.

When I was home again, Lord Killanin, who was at that time the Chairman of the Dublin Festival, went with me to the Royal Court. Afterwards we 'went round' to see Lotte

Lenya. I had sent her a bouquet and she thanked me graciously. It was clear that she did not know who I was. When she took us to the door, she said: 'Oh and good luck—in whatever it is you do.'

As soon as I got home, I wrote her a letter and told her exactly what I did or rather what I had been prevented from doing. I enclosed some press clippings. Her answer came by return of post. 'Raum für Alle ist auf Erden'—there is room for everyone on earth—she quoted Brecht himself, and gave me permission to sing her husband's songs whenever and wherever I wanted to.

A young man came into my life who would become vital for my work. Michael Dress, all of seventeen years old, was the son of a clergyman and the nephew of Dietrich Bonhöffer, another Protestant pastor, who had been tortured and executed by the Nazis for his beliefs. Michael had come to London from Berlin to be with his friend and lover, the American/German Steven Vinaver, whom Oscar Loewenstein had commissioned to write a revue with music by Carl Davis, Steven's partner. I did not know that Michael too was a composer until he pressed a reel of tape into my hand and left in a hurry. He was too nervous to play his songs on the piano. The music was perfect, reminiscent of Kurt Weill.

Michael and I now started to work together on a new repertoire. He was a young man of many talents and capable, as no one had been before, of teaching me how best to put over this kind of song. Since all these songs were the work of published poets as opposed to genuine cabaret numbers that had to be topical, they do not date and I have been able to perform them to this day.

In 1962 I was asked to make a return visit to the Establishment, this time without the trio, but with Michael at the piano. I added a Brecht sketch, *The Jewish Wife*, to the programme and David de Keyser directed it.

One day during the three-week season the telephone rang at home. It was our young man at the box office.

'Do you know someone called Lotte Lenya?' he asked. 'She has just telephoned to book a table for tonight, but she's not a member so I could not take the booking.'

I arranged a table for her and there were orchids on it

when she came. The atmosphere was charged that night. There I was, up on stage, singing all the Brecht/Weill numbers Lenya had made famous—'Bilbao Moon', 'Surabaya Johnny', 'Pirate Jenny'—while she was in the audience. Everyone there knew exactly who she was. I was not half as nervous as I had expected to be.

Afterwards Lotte came to my dressing-room. I met her thirty-two-year-old second husband, Russel Detwiler. She was sixty-three at the time. She was introduced to Michael and asked if she could sing some of the songs we had worked on together. We promised to send them to her. When she got to the door, she gave me a roguish smile and said: 'Goodbye and good luck—in whatever it is you do!'

It was the last time I ever saw her in person. When I did my show in New York in 1977 she was too ill to be visited.

Another photograph now hung beside my own at the Establishment. The legend underneath said: 'Michael Dress, composer'. He made many useful contacts and went on to write music for plays and films. Unfortunately his success gave him the means to drink himself to death at the age of thirty-eight.

For me the early sixties were excellent years, perhaps my best. Desmond and I were happy together and there were, as far as I could tell, no other romantic distractions on either side. The children were growing up and were away at school, which gave me much freedom.

I had always wanted to write but was too intimidated when I married into a writing family; Papa Shane, Anita, Desmond and Uncles Seymour and Lionel Leslie had all published books. Even Marjorie, my mother-in-law, more courageous than I, had joined them with her *Girlhood in the Pacific*—for which Shane had written a foreword that she had promptly scrapped. Now I had time to write a little. My short piece about Berlin appeared in the *Cornhill Magazine* and when I watched a rehearsal of my play *Mr and Mrs Smith* at the Television Studios and saw the people I 'created' come to life, it gave me a feeling of God-like power.

Although I did not work much in the straight theatre, I was busy enough with my solo shows. Michael, Ernest and I went on touring dates to the Oxford Playhouse, the Traverse in Edinburgh, the Festival Club in York. The show gradually changed from being a pure Brecht evening. I found more poems by authors who had influenced Brecht, authors who were his contemporaries and authors who had obviously been influenced by him, such as Christopher Logue, Adrian Mitchell and Roger McGough. Michael set them to music and over the years I collected over a hundred items from which to choose.

My mother came with us on these journeys and spent happy moments every day in our hotel room, shortening the stems of flowers I had been given to make them last as long as possible. I had intended to take Janice Cole, who had been so efficient in helping me on my first Establishment show, along on this tour, only Janice seemed to have disappeared completely.

This mystery remained unsolved for quite some time, but one evening Renée came to our flat to talk to me in private. 'Did you know that Janice has had a child, a little girl, and her family refuses to let her bring her up at home? She boards her out with some woman in Hackney and is only allowed to take her to her parents' house for the weekend when the daily woman does not come and the neighbours are away. She tells me she hasn't the courage to move from home.'

'How old is the child?'

'Natasha is nearly two. It seems the father is a married man who does not want his wife to find out. With her mother's approval he did arrange an abortion but Janice ran away and hid somewhere in the country until after the birth.'

'Something will have to be done.'

Renée and I knew that Janice could not go on indefinitely denying her daughter an existence. She would have to leave home herself to bring her up properly. We began looking for suitable accommodation but this proved more difficult than we had expected. Whenever Janice carried the details of a prospective apartment in her handbag, her mother managed to sneak a look, contact the landlords and put them off Janice. Eventually we found a nice flat only a stone's throw from where I lived and Desmond took out the lease in his name. There was nothing Janice's mother could do about that and we were able to move Janice and Natasha there. The Actors' Benevolent Fund provided furniture and we provided moral support.

Unexpectedly one day the German government sent me four hundred pounds. It was some kind of compensation for missing out on 'further education' during the Nazi regime, and I knew just what to do with it.

Ever since I had spent a day on the Thames with the family in a hired motor launch I had fancied the idea of 'messing about in boats'. Desmond and I began to visit the small marinas that were springing up along the river banks. We saw many splendid yachts but, much as we longed to own one we had never been able to afford it.

Then one day, at Penton Hook basin, we saw a funny little boat for sale. She had been a lifeboat and had been converted to sleep at least four people. Small as she was, she was comfortable enough for a family like ours, with a galley, a wheel-house, a double bunk and two other narrow bunks astern. The present owners had done their best to make her look more like a car. They had installed a car's driving wheel, and her name, *Eiro 2*, was displayed on a car number plate. She was painted in colours more likely to be found on the walls of the Labour Exchange, but she was going for three hundred and fifty pounds and I bought her.

Over the next few weeks I spent many happy hours at Penton Hook on my own, turning *Eiro 2* back into a boat. I must have used gallons of blue and white paint, screwed in hundreds of screws and covered her deck with respectable vinyl sheeting. I bought an anchor, two metal oil lamps and, most important of all, a handsome steering wheel of brass. Our kitchen was raided for pots and pans and our linen cupboard for sheets and blankets.

When I was satisfied, we started out on our magical weekends or summer evening trips on the river and were joined by our friends on many occasions. They would drive to a pre-arranged spot along the river bank—Chertsey, Windsor or the Angler's Rest Hotel—and we would float quietly up or down the Thames or give wild parties, after which people could sleep off their hangovers in sleeping-bags or up on deck.

The boys adored these days and nights on *Eiro 2* and could bring their schoolfriends any time they wanted. We all became very efficient in navigating and working the locks and I do believe that we had quite a part to play in the sartorial reforms which gradually took place along the Thames. The first year we chugged along on *Eiro 2* the other river users would all be dressed in formal clothes. We were amused to see them handle ropes and work the locks wearing collars and ties and Sunday hats. We thought this rather silly and, ignoring the stares we attracted, would turn up in jeans and bikinis when the weather was fine and in anoraks when it was raining. In less than two seasons everybody followed our example and the atmosphere on the river became vastly more relaxed.

There is no doubt in my mind that David Frost's sudden rise to fame was also due to our boat, although he may not know it. Peter Cook and Wendy, his fiancée, came to spend a Sunday with us on *Eiro 2*. The arrangement was that they were to stay only until lunch was over because Peter had to be at BBC television for a pilot programme devised by Ned Sherrin. The day was fine and sunny, lunch had been particularly stupefying and Peter was determined to have a snooze. No matter how hard Wendy and I tried to rouse him, he simply would not move. 'They can get on without me,' he muttered and turned on his other side. Apparently they could—but only because David Frost, then unknown, happened to be 'hanging around' at the studio as he was wont to do at the Establishment, and stepped into Peter's role. The pilot was for 'That Was the Week That Was', only one of the most successful television programmes ever made by the BBC, and David Frost became a star.

One evening Desmond brought a young actress to the flat for drinks. On his desk stood a pair of priceless china owls of particular beauty, left by my brother-in-law Jack when he emigrated to Rome. We were under the impression that he had meant them as a gift, and the young actress was horrified when she noticed them. 'Don't you know that owls are terribly unlucky,' she said. 'You must never have them in the house in any shape or form.'

I did not get unduly worried that night, but was absolutely shattered when the girl was found dead in her bed the very next morning. I blamed the owls and from that moment I could hardly stand to look at them. I could not very well give them to anyone and pass on the bad luck. Putting them into a sale for someone else to buy seemed to me as irresponsible and I sold them for a song to a peddler who called at the door. Owls now became a source of terror, and strange as it sounds, whenever something bad happened between Desmond and me over the difficult years that followed, I would have come across the effigy of an owl somewhere a day or so before.

In 1963 I finally reached the West End with my solo show, *Savagery and Delight*. It opened at the Duchess Theatre off the Strand for a three-week season, under the management of Farjeon & Donoghue Limited, and Desmond, with help from Helen Strong, managed to raise some extra finance amongst our friends and also from film and theatre people such as Sidney Box and John Gale. I prayed that I would justify their trust.

I was reasonably confident on opening night. Michael Dress had orchestrated most of my songs and Renée had watched the dress rehearsal to check on everything. Desmond's speakers, which we had always used before, and which, for technical reasons, had not been installed in the usual place, were standing on stage for the technical run-through and were working well. It was therefore doubly dismaying when, a short time into the first half of the performance, I could feel that I was not reaching the audience in the stalls. Up in the dress circle, where Desmond was working the sound on a large console, the people responded, but down below they did not laugh, they did not cry and only clapped politely.

In the interval Michael Dress came rushing backstage. 'You've got to stop the show—we cannot hear you.'

I looked around for Desmond's speakers, but they were nowhere to be seen. A frantic search brought no result. Michael raced off to get Desmond, but before I could decide what to do, the houselights went down. The stage director had pushed the button that raised the curtain, the band struck up and we were off again.

I went through the second half in a daze and the rest of that night is still a kind of blur. I believe we had booked a large table in a restaurant to 'celebrate', but there seemed little to celebrate after the speaker fiasco and we sat and ate in silent gloom.

With hindsight I realize how foolish I had been to go on with the performance as if nothing was wrong. I should have told the audience. The critics too would then have known and not torn me to pieces.

When the reviews came out the next morning, my telephone never stopped ringing. It was the press, who dearly love a victim, to ask me how I felt. Desmond, like his speakers before him, was nowhere to be seen. I did some transcendental meditation and took the phone off the hook.

It turned out that in his haste to keep an important rendezvous after the dress rehearsal, Desmond had stored the speakers underneath the stage and had forgotten to bring them out again. It must have looked ludicrous when I walked from microphone to microphone, opened my mouth and produced little or no sound. Without amplification my natural voice, pitched low and soft for the microphones, hardly reached beyond the second row.

By the evening the speakers had been fixed to the walls and the show was working well. The houses were small after the reviews, but word went round that I was not as bad as I had been made out to be and we were, at least, able to finish the limited run.

On Saturday night Desmond did not come to pick me up at the theatre. This had never happened in all our years together and I was puzzled. I went home alone on the Underground and on the way stopped off at Fleet Street to get the Sunday papers in advance. These were important. Their reviewers hardly ever came on opening night and would have seen the show when the speakers were in place. I could not wait until morning to read them. As I walked down Fleet Street, I was joined by a young reporter who had recognized me. He offered to go into the press building and pick up the papers. 'I can get them quicker than you can,' he said and disappeared inside. When he came out again he was breathless with excitement.

'The place is in an uproar,' he cried. 'Someone has punched Bernard Levin on the nose on 'That Was the Week That Was.'

Bernard Levin's review of me in the *Evening Standard* had been particularly damning. Desmond had fumed about it all day.

'I hope it was not my husband,' I said jokingly. 'Let me have the *Sunday Times*. Let's see what Harold Hobson has to say.'

Hobson's review was marvellous, as I had hoped it would be. My young friend left me at the entrance to the Underground. He gave me his card.

'If by any chance it was your husband, do ring me up at once.'

When I reached our flat, there was a lot of noise coming from inside. Desmond, who opened the door to me, flushed and obviously delighted with himself, was entertaining half the journalists in London.

When I entered the reporters made a rush at me.

'Did you know?' 'Did you plan it together?' 'Was it a publicity stunt?'

I sensed danger. If they really thought I was involved, they would demolish what was left of me. I rang my journalist friend and he came straight over. He told his colleagues that he had been with me when I had heard the news and said he could vouch for it that I had been as startled as he had been. From that moment on the journalists became like so many nannies. They practically moved in with us over the next few days, interviewed us, photographed us, made sure that my make-up was all right, straightened out my dress and made me cups of tea.

Of course they wanted me to say how proud I was of my valiant husband, who had rushed to defend me. Secretly I could not see what was so valiant about shaking one's fist at Bernard Levin, whose review was justified under the circumstances, and I suspected that Desmond had acted not so much in my defence, but to allay his guilty conscience, and I was wondering who the person he had gone to meet before my opening night was, and where he had spent the following day. I was not to find out until a year later.

I had, of course, to pretend that I was grateful but I knew

that it would take many years to live this incident down. The publicity and the large photographs on the front pages were picked up abroad. The French papers reported it as a *crime passionelle* and claimed that Desmond had 'beaten up' my 'lover'—Bernard Levin—in a jealous rage. This was far from the press coverage I had dreamt of when I had planned my solo evenings.

Two unexpected events soon distracted me. First there was a curious letter from Anita asking Desmond to take over Glaslough altogether. Then I discovered that, after twenty years of marriage, I was pregnant again. For only the briefest moment I was dismayed. With both boys away at boarding school I had enjoyed my freedom and did not relish having to give it up once more, but then I wondered if this might not be the much longed-for daughter. I began to look forward to this baby. I called it 'Antonia' before it was born and refused to consider that it might be a boy. 'And if it is?' my worried friends would ask. 'Then I will still call it Antonia and dress it in pink,' I would answer.

Anita's letter was curious. It seemed that all she wanted in return for giving up Glaslough was Drumlargen, the piece of land in County Meath she had bought with the capital Jack had left for the running of the estate. It was there the Glaslough cattle were taken to be finished. Drum Largen— and whatever might be on the land there on the day of the take-over. Of course Desmond did not turn down the offer nor did he have any feelings of apprehension about having to run such a large demesne without the necessary capital. Years later when I was staying with Anita at Oranmore, she told me the story of the letter. In fact, she said, she had written two separate letters at the time. One, the one we received, offering us Glaslough, the other asking us to resign our shares in return for the sum of twenty thousand pounds. She had sealed the envelopes, handed them to Bill and asked him to post either of them. He could have not known which was which. Anita died in the late eighties firmly convinced that fate had caused him to post the 'wrong' envelope. She should have held on to Glaslough, she said.

It was in 1963 when Desmond prepared to take over the estate. I looked forward to this event with much anguish and apprehension. In spite of the Duchess débacle I was now in demand. Offers of work kept pouring in—quite possibly because of the Duchess debacle. Even a tour to the United States was mentioned. An appearance on David Frost's American programme was suggested. I had my doubts if David Frost would ever work with me now, but in any case, all these excitements would have to wait until I had produced 'Antonia'. After that, I would be ready for anything.

This was not what Desmond had envisaged when he accepted the Irish offer.

'If our marriage means anything to you,' he said, 'then you must give up the theatre and come and run this lovely place with me.'

It was the age-old feminine dilemma, but I could see his point.

Meanwhile the final break with my London life was fortunately postponed for a while because the baby was upside-down and I was forced to stay close to the hospital. Desmond had to travel to Glaslough without me. From there he wrote enthusiastic letters claiming that he was now truly a farmer because he had 'mud on his boots'. He did not mention that on takeover day the entire Glaslough herd and every working piece of farm machinery had been found on the land in County Meath, nor that there was no money with which to replace them. Even so, I felt that I was letting him down by not being there when he really needed me, and began to seriously consider risking a dash to Ireland. Help came from an unexpected source. Helen Strong came to tea and offered to travel to Glaslough in my place. It seemed the ideal solution. She knew the place well, having been there with us for countless holidays.

'I would be most grateful if you could go and cheer Desmond up at this important time,' I told Helen, and added jokingly 'as long as you don't run away with him.' We had a good laugh and Helen departed on the mail boat.

Apart from 'Antonia's' unfortunate position in my womb I was as fit and well with this pregnancy as I had been with the other two, even though I was by now forty years old. I designed yet another 'Chinese jacket' and worked almost to the last moment. Because of my age my Indian doctor, Chandra Sharma, had booked me into St Mary's Hospital for a Caesarean section on 1 November at ten o'clock in the morning. He had worked out this date and time most care-fully, according to his astrological charts, in order to give 'Antonia' the best possible horoscope. As was to be expected, the stars did not allow themselves to be dictated to in this manner and all Sharma's well-laid plans came to nothing in the end. Quite late I discovered that he had booked me into St Mary's Stratford East and not, as I had fondly believed, into St Mary's Paddington, which was only down the road from us. The London traffic was chaotic even then and it took hours to drive across the city. Who would be able to visit me in Stratford East? And I needed Desmond, who was to come home for the event, and my family by my side.

'This birth is off!' I cried and stormed out of the surgery.

Of course he reorganized everything at the last minute. He found me a bed in a small private clinic in St John's Wood which had an operating theatre, but he could not organize the surgeon he had chosen to travel to our side of town before two o'clock in the afternoon. 'Antonia' would have to grapple with her destiny without the benefit of Shandra's astrological manipulations.

On 1 November 1963, as I was being wheeled into the operating theatre, trying to be as calm as possible, the irate surgeon rushed past my trolley. 'You've really messed up my entire schedule,' he shouted at me. 'I hope you are proud of yourself!'

Somewhat shaken by this outburst I arrived in the theatre only to find the fuming surgeon and Sharma stripped down to their bare skins, wearing nothing but transparent plastic butcher's aprons. I quite expected to see these two hairy apes start jumping up and down with glee, sharpening gleaming butcher's knives.

An hour later, when I woke from my anaesthetic, a nurse handed me my apricot-coloured baby. A little jaundiced, but otherwise intact, Antonia had at last arrived.

We decided to have the christening in London and Helen travelled home briefly to be godmother. To celebrate the event she decided to throw a party at her house on the morn-ing of the ceremony which I could not attend. Desmond went alone and left me with all the preparations for our own christening party that afternoon. I recall trying to make the salads with one hand and dressing myself and the baby for church with the other. I was still clutching Antonia, who was not yet weaned, to my naked breast when I had to open the front door to Father Oswald Vanheems, who had arrived from Ampleforth to officiate at the ceremony. By the time Desmond came back to drive us there, I was furious and we had a row in the car in front of the church with our guests watching in amazement from the porch.

I should now have been able to concentrate on my move to Glaslough, but other events conspired to keep me in London for another month or so. The gods had picked on me to rescue Janice from total disaster and, having succeeded in this task, I had to stay on to see the situation through to the end.

In the final stages of my pregnancy, Janice had begun to act rather strangely. She would bring back baby clothes and baby toys such as rattles and teething rings from her shopping trips. At first I presumed these were intended for my expected baby, but I found that she was hoarding them carefully for herself. I began to understand that her closeness to me, a married woman who could be pregnant openly and proudly, contrasted cruelly with the furtiveness with which she had been forced to carry Natasha. Her love life, too, seemed unsatisfactory at the time. Bright and attractive as she was, she had no trouble finding intelligent men. Finding a husband was more difficult. Her anxiety about being a single mother invariably frightened her lovers away.

Perhaps I did not pay enough attention to her fragile state of mind. I was living in a rosy haze with my 'gift of love' in the cot beside my bed. People came to admire her and I even had a call from Cathleen Drogheda, who had seen our picture in the papers. Maureen, she said, was longing to see the child. Perhaps they could both come over for tea? I was thrilled. Had Richard lifted the 'cruel ban'? I made feverish preparations and dressed the baby in her prettiest clothes. I waited all afternoon but no Maureen ever showed. It was to be some time before I found her again in Dublin.

Meanwhile I got on with my packing. It was clothes and personal belongings to begin with: the dismantling of the flat would have to wait. Furthermore there was Desmond's music studio to be dealt with, and that would be a complicated business because he intended to set it up in the basement of Glaslough with all the equipment and the library of sounds which now numbered many hundreds of tapes. I welcomed any and every excuse to leave the flat intact for the time being. It was my life-line to my former existence and to my work and I dreaded being cut off from London.

On my last Saturday at home, Janice brought Natasha to the flat. Could I keep her over the weekend? she asked. I did not question her reasons. I knew she had recently had an upset over her current boyfriend. Perhaps she was hoping to make it up with him over the next two days. After settling both Antonia and Natasha for the night I sat down to watch the television. Suddenly I was overcome by a feeling of panic. Something somewhere was terribly wrong. I hastened to the nursery but the children were sleeping. There was a ring at the door. It was Janice's Spanish au pair. She said she was unable to get any reply to her knocking and calling at Janice's bedroom door. I snatched the keys from her hand, told her to stay and watch the children and raced across to Janice's flat.

I found her lifeless on the bed, empty pill boxes on the floor. I called for an ambulance but none was available. I tried to lift Janice but could not manage it. Then I remembered her lodger, a pleasant young journalist recently arrived from the country. To my relief he was at home and together we managed to haul Janice down three flights of stairs and into a taxi. In less than five minutes the taxi left us at our local hospital. While the doctors were busy with Janice behind the curtains at the emergency ward, the young lodger and I sat and talked in anxious whispers. I had taken full responsibility for Janice and refused to name any other relative because I knew her mother's appearance in this situation would have a disastrous effect on Janice if she came round.

I remember feeling very embarrassed when I talked to the lodger. What was this young innocent to think of the goings on in the wicked city? I could not have guessed that little more than a year would pass before Janice was married to the 'young innocent'—a marriage that has lasted to the present day.

In January 1964 there was little hope of such a happy ending. It was touch-and-go that Janice would survive the overdose and I was preparing myself for the eventuality of keeping Natasha as this had clearly been Janice's unspoken wish when she left her with me. After several anxious days, Janice regained consciousness but she seemed to be semi-paralyzed. The doctors assured me that this was not a permanent condition. I spent the next few weeks by her bedside, willing her to walk, and, above all, willing her to live again. I promised her that I would not leave for Glaslough until she was fit enough to be discharged from the hospital. I eventually set off for Ireland with Antonia in her carry-cot at the back of my car, several weeks later than Desmond had expected.

Once more I was leaving a country I had been happy in. Once more amnesia shrouded the details of my departure. I remember only the arrival at the docks in Belfast and the long drive to Glaslough. It was a route I had taken many times before, always in a happy holiday mood. This journey was different. While my baby slumbered peacefully, my feelings of doubt and apprehension grew with every mile we put behind us. I thought of the furniture at South Lodge bequeathed to Seán by Marjorie, of which we had been given the life use. Should I send it all to Glaslough when the flat was gone? Would it be safer with my friends and neighbours, Richard and Lydia Johnston in County Armagh? Safer from what? I could not say. I shocked myself with all this fear. What was it that disturbed me so as I sped towards my Irish home? I did not have to wait too long to find out.

At Glaslough Helen was firmly installed in my blue bedroom. No number of hints from me could dislodge her. Uncle Seymour's ominous warnings made me realize that she had been the mystery woman for whom Desmond has risked my performance at the Duchess Theatre and that she had convinced him I would never come to live with him in County Monaghan. After ten years in the shadows Helen was at long last asserting herself.

Our marriage limped along for another five difficult years and came to a painful end in 1969. I found myself virtually stranded in Ireland with the children. Since I no longer had the means to return to London I was forced to make a new life in Dublin, whether I liked it or not. To my surprise, I gradually found that I liked it.

POSTSCRIPT
The Story of the Jewel Book

The very week this book was to go to press, I received a letter from New York which foreshadowed the end of a story that had its beginning in my childhood days.

The story is about a book which, more than sixty years ago, my father had given to his partner Carl Meinhard for his birthday. It was one of a special edition, numbered, with the names of the subscribers printed at theback. It contained Heinrich Heine's story 'The Rabbi of Bacharach', with seventeen etchings by Max Liebermann, both of them artists of considerable distinction.

Meinhard obviously forgot who had given him this present, and handed it to my astonished father on his own next birthday. My father made no comment but had a small diamond set into the soft, yellow leather binding and gave the book back to his partner when his birthday came round again. Meinhard, who now realized his lapse, added an emerald to the diamond for my father's next anniversary. From then on the partners gave the book to each other every year, adding more precious and semi-precious stones until the cover was encrusted with them. I was shown the book once when I was seven and it made a lasting impression on me.

After several years it was decided to make this exotic exchange more official by adding a silver plate to the cover, giving the names and dates, and stating that the survivor should be the ultimate owner of the book. The two men handed it to each other in a ceremony at the Berliner Theater Club.

When the Nazis came to power Meinhard and Bernauer lost everything they owned except their lives. Meinhard fled to his native Czechoslovakia. My father emigrated to London and there the news reached us that 'Uncle Carl' had been picked up in his apartment and dragged to the concentration camp at Ravensbruck where he survived five terrible years of torture. He was saved from the gas chamber through the influence of his daughter-in-law, whose father was a German general.

When the war ended Uncle Carl wrote to us from Prague. He was planning to join his son and family in Buenos Aires, but everything he owned had disappeared from his flat during his years in the camp and he now had no suitable clothes in which to travel. I recall my father sending him a suit and some cash.

The two old friends unfortunately never met again, but kept up a regular correspondence, which eventually came into my hands. Carl Meinhard died several years before my father, and before sending the letters to the Bernauer archive at the Akademie Der Kunste in Berlin I read them through carefully. They were a touching record of their early days together, full of memories of small, private incidents and family matters with never a mention of any of their achievements, or their lost possessions. There was not a word about the 'Jewel Book' or its whereabouts. It had disappeared with everything else they had jointly owned.

Then in the early seventies, Dan Mason, a young American stage director, spent a holiday in Ireland. By an accident of fate he was introduced to me on his last day and our meeting resulted in his returning to direct me in several productions in Dublin and the forming of a firm and lasting friendship. There was nothing whatsoever to connect Dan Mason to my German past and yet it was he who was to play a vital role in this story.

After he directed Gerhardt Hauptmann's play *The Rats* off Broadway, he wrote: '... an old lady with a strong foreign accent came backstage to congratulate me on the production. She asked me if, by any chance, I knew you.' This was a very long shot indeed. 'She was delighted when I said I did,' Dan continued. 'She has known you since you were a small child. She is the widow of Hans Bartsch, your father's former literary agent, and she took me to see the book—you know the one with all the jewels on the cover ...' I hardly dared to believe that the lost jewel book had really turned up in a New York synagogue.

The next time I was in New York, Dan Mason took me to the Central Synagogue on 55th Street, and there was the book, part of an exhibition of Judaic Art, the odd man out amongst thirty-eight religious artefacts from European synagogues. I felt weak at the knees when I saw it there and had to sit down and ask for a glass of water. I also asked for the name and the telephone number of the curator of this exhibition and rang him as soon as I could get to a telephone.

At first Mr Schwartz, the curator, seemed delighted to speak to me, but soon it became clear that he was a very old man who had put a great deal of effort in obtaining these artefacts for the Central Synagogue from Europe. Eventually he told me that they had been brought to America by General Troper, the only Jewish general in the U.S. Army, after the war; that General Troper had died without an heir; and that Mr Schwartz had been able to persuade him in time to leave the entire collection to the Central Synagogue.

During Mr Schwartz's lifetime I made several unsuccessful attempts to find out how the general had obtained the collection in the first place and whether there was any chance of getting back my father's book. Of course I did not imagine that the general had simply 'liberated' all these precious items before returning home. I believe that he bought them from whoever had looted them. There have been many incidents of this kind connected with Jewish property, especially in the American art world.

When I sought advice, I was told that in each incident the original owners had been awarded the lost possession in court. I did not want to resort to legal action against the synagogue, which had acted in good faith, and was hoping that after Mr Schwartz's death the authorities at the synagogue would enter into a dialogue with me.

At first I did not get any reply but eventually someone wrote and offered me the book at a price. Unfortunately at the time I did not have the money and years went by without further contact—I was told that the book had meanwhile been removed from its place in the exhibition.

Last May I found myself once again in New York and telephoned the synagogue for an appointment with the present executive director, a lady called Livia D. Thompson. Miss Thompson turned out to be young and charming. She had never heard of the book, but listened patiently to my story. I told her that I could possibly raise the money to buy it back at this stage of my life and she suggested I send her all neccessary documentation to demonstrate that I was now heir to the book. She promised she would answer me if I did so, and also said she would start to look for the missing book.

Her answer reached me a few weeks ago: 'I am delighted to report that the Board of Trustees was moved deeply by your story and would like to arrange to return the book to you in an appropriate ceremony at Central Synagogue. We would also like to tell your story publicly because it is so moving and would like to arrange for you to have a chance to meet with the Jewish press while you are here to receive the book ... I am looking forward to seeing you again.'

I hope to travel to New York before the year is out.

Dublin, 3 August 1996

INDEX

Formia, 201
Fortune, John, 218, 219
Francis Goodheart Productions
  (Charlotte Francis & Geoffrey
  Goodheart), 63–5
Freier Deutscher Kulturbund
  (FDKB), 57
Friedman, Flossie, 65
Free German League of Culture, *see*
  Freier Deutscher Kulturbund
Freud, Lucien, 115
Frost, David, 231, 236

Gaiety Theatre, Dublin, 175–80
Gale, John, 232
Garland, Nicholas, 222
Gate Theatre, 103
Gee, Mr, 68, 69, 74–9
Geraldo, band leader, 66, 67
Gerson, Prager, Hausdorff, couturier,
  18
Getty, Paul, 169
Gibbons, Caroll, 83
Gielgud, John, 120
Glashütte, 24, 25
Glasgow, 109, 110
Glaslough, Co. Monaghan, 80, 102,
  104, 105, 113, 114, 135, 140,
  142, 195, 235, 236, 238, 240
Globe Theatre, London, 120
Goddard, Renée, 128, 129, 170,
  192, 211, 223, 226, 229; Michael
  (Mellinger) husband, 211
Goebbels, Joseph, 31
Gonda, Berzi, 26
Gonda, Gisela, *née* Bernauer, aunt,
  26
Gonda, Ilma (later Rosenber),
  cousin, 131
Goring, Marius, 101
Grass, Günter, *Onkel Onkel*, 21
Gotfurt, Fritz (originally Gotfurcht),
  57–9, 66, 67, 172
Gotfurt, Dorothea, 58, 59, 172
Grafton Cinema, Dublin, 225
Gregor, Nora, 21
Grigsby, Emily, 113
Gypsy Baron, The, 106

Hale, Sonny, 176
Hammer, Sigmund, 212
Harcourt Smith, Simon, 191, 194,
  195
Harrison, Mr, headmaster, 157, 173,
  192
Harvey, Lawrence, 150
Hauptmann, Gerhard, *The Rats*, 242
Hausdorf, Kurt, uncle, 48
Häusdorf, Martha, *née* Erb, aunt, 18,
  jewellery of, 75, 150
Headfort, Rosie (Boot), Marchioness
  of, 112, 113
healing power, 193, 194, 206
Hart, Vivienne Woollie, 113
Heartfield, John (formerly Herzfeld),
  59
Hebbel, Friedrich, 14
Heine, Heinrich, 240
Herz, Peter, 60, 161
Hindenburg, Marschall, 30; airship
  (Graf), 25
Hitler, Adolf, 29, 30, 39, 50, 52, 67
Hobson, Harold, 234
Hodgson, Joan, 192, 193
Hollywood, author does not go
  there, 110
Holmwood School, London, 39, 40,
  41 *sqq.*; Mademoiselle, 45, 46;
  Matron, 45
Hudd, Walter, 58
Hungarian nationality, 36–7, 52, 56

Ivy, restaurant in London, 71

'Jane' of the *Daily Mirror*, 46
Jennings, Humphrey, 71
Johnston, Lydia and Richard, 240

Karsavina, 183
Kastner, Erich, *Emil und die
  Dedektive*, 33
Kebbe, Charles, 85–9, 93
'Keith' (British Council), 143
Kempinsky, Della and Gerard, 67
Kemsley, Lady 61
Kenny, Seán, 222, 223, 224
Kiely, Maureen (Cusack), 103
Killanin, Lord, 226
Killick, Mr, 69

Kiepenheuer, publishers, 21
King, Commander Bill, 121, 142
Kinnear, Roy, 219
Kipling, Rudyard, 'If', 57
Kitchener, General, 113
Kopp, Bruce, 223, 224
Korda, Alexander, 110
Kösling, Hasso von, 49
Kyrieleis, Herr, barber, 10
Kneff, Hildegard, *The Gift Horse*, 33
Kölle, Herr, singing teacher, 34

Lalaingn, Count de, 122
Lanchester, Elsa, 171
Larsen, Egon (Lehrburger), 57, 67,
    96, 154
Latin Quarter, film, 102
Laughton, Charles, 171, 172
Lehmann, Beatrix, 58
Leigh, Vivien, 89
Lenya, Lotte, 226–8
Leslie, Anita, 80, 108, 115–6, 142,
    194, 195, 228, 235, 236
Leslie, Antonia, 235, 236
Leslie, Desmond, 49, 76, 77, 78 *sqq.*
    passim, 87, 89, 99, 100, 102, 103,
    104, 105, 106 *sqq.*, wedding, 108
    sqq., 116, 124, 125, 126, 131,
    139, 140, 146, 153, 154, 155,
    166, 167, 168, 172, 174, 175,
    181, 184, 185, 189 *sqq.*, 199, 204,
    205, 206, 208, 228, 230, 232,
    233, 234, 236, 237
Leslie, Sir John and Lady (Leonie),
    102; 'old Sir John', 104
Leslie, John (Jack), 80, 102, 106,
    107, 108, 126, 141–2, 144, 201,
    231, 235
Leslie, Lionel, 114, 228
Leslie, Marjorie Lady, 80, 101, 102,
    105, 108, 113, 114, 115, 119,
    126, 139, 140, 228
Leslie, Mark, 97, 157, 177, 192
Leslie, Seán, 97, 116–19, 124, 126,
    127, 136, 139, 140, 147, 153,
    157, 172, 192, 240
Leslie, Seymour, 80, 104, 225, 228,
    240
Leslie, Sir Shane, 80, 91, 102, 108,
    114, 119, 120, 139, 228

Levin, Bernard, 233–5
Liebermann, Max, 241
Lieder eines böen Buben, 13
Leinster, Raffaela Duchess of, 123
Ling, Dr, 82–3
Love Lies Bleeding, play, 72
Loewenstein, Oscar, 171
Loewenstein, Eileen, 176
Logue, Christopher, 219, 229
Lowe, Arthur, 150
Lowell, Robert, 115
Luard, Nicholas, 225
Luggala, Co. Wicklow, 115
Lustige Blatter, magazine, 14
Luther, Martin, 10
Lynn, Ann Lynn, 171, 205
Lynn, W. H., architect, 104

McGough, Roger, 229
McGowran, Jack, 225
McGuire, Eddie, painter 115
Mackintosh, Yvonne, 47
MacLiammóir, Mícheál, 103, 159
McNab, Robert, 97
Malik, Soviet Ambassador, 173–4
Manchester, 137–8
Marie, nanny, 167
Mario, Maestro, 65
Marlborough, Duke and Duchess of,
    135
Marschall, Herbert, 64
Martinez, Señor, 152, 153
Mason, Dan, 242
'Max', 161, 162
May, Joe, 21
Maytime, 18
Meinhard, Carl, 8, 14, 15, 16, 31,
    241, 242
Mellinger, Eva, 193
Melly, George, 174
Mermaid Theatre, London, 169
Messel, Oliver, 90
Meyer's Konverstions Lexicon, 12
Miller, Joan, 82–3
Miller, Jonathan, 219
Mitchell, Adrian, 229
Montague, producer, 109
Monte Carlo, 145 *sqq.*, 154 *sqq.*, 166,
    168, 189–91
Moore, Dudley, 219

Moore, Lady Patricia, 121
Moore, Patrick, 141
Moxon, Ollie, 175
Mr and Mrs Smith, play, 228
musique concrète, 134–6
Myers, Stanley, 219
My Hands Are Clay, film, 121, 132

Naples, 210–11
Neave, Rupert, 135
Nelson, Rudolf, 48
Nesbitt, Robert, 178
Neuhäusler, Margit, 35
Newton Longville, 85, 95
Niete Verhebst, film, 129
Nordmann, Paul, 12
Normann, Roger Graf von, 49

O'Brien, Kate, 124
O'Connor, Joseph, 133
O'Dea, Jimmy, 179–80
Oesterreicher, Rudolf, 36
Oppen, Wolfgang von, 217–18
O'Kelly, Seán T., 103, 140
One Girl a Day, musical, 210
O'Neill, Pat, 86
Oranmore, Oonagh Lady (*née* Guinness), 115, 181–2
Oranmore, Co. Galway, 142, 235
O'Reilly, Jojo(later Countess Sliwinska), 103, 182
OSS (Office of Strategic Service), 84, 86
O'Toole, Peter, 205
Ottoboni, Princess Giulia, 166
Oxford Playhouse, 228

Palladium, London, *Aladdin*, 176 *sqq.*
Palmer, Hilde, 86, 88, 89, 96, 106
Paramount, 23
Paris, 170–1
Parnell, Val, 177
Pascal, Gabriel, 89–90
Patch, Miss, 41, 45
Penton Hook, 230
Perceval, Lance, 219
Philipsky, Margaret, 163
Phillips, Sian, 205
Plotzensee, prison, Berlin, 98

Ponds cream, 123
Porter, Nyrée Dawn, 218
Possony, Ernst, 163–4
Post Office, The (Tagore), 158
Potasch and Perlmutter, 69
Potter, Maureen, 179
Private Eye, 225
Purna, Princess, 115

Q Theatre, 159

Radio Atlantik, 85
Rains, Claude, 89
Rattigan, Terence, *French Without Tears*, 82
Rauterkus, Pater, 35
Redgrave, Vanessa, 174
Reid, Dr Grantly Dick, 116, 117, 124
Reinhardt, Max, 15
religion, 11, 34, 35, 36, 114
Remarque, Erich Maria, *All Quiet on the Western Front*, 31
Roach, Hal, 179–80
'Roman orgy', 206–8
Rome, 142–5, 201
Rorrison, Professor Hugh, 57
Rotha, Wanda, 74
Rothchild, Baroness, 9
Royal Court Hotel, 197
Royal Court Theatre, London, 196, 226
Rubens, Bernice, 159
Rückert Lyceum, Berlin, 20
Rudolf Steiner Hall, London, 62
Rules, restaurant, London, 71
Russell, Bertrand, 174

Sacrifice (Tagore), 158
St David's, 198
St Martin's Theatre, London, 63, 160–2
Salomé (Oscar Wilde), 159, 163
Sassoon, Victor, 155, 166
Savagery and Delight, 226, 232
Saville, Philip, 170, 205, 218
Schanzer, Rudolf, 37
Schnabel, Stefan, 86
Schnitzler, Arthur, Liebelei, 125
Schöneberg, Berlin, 5, 32, 52, 53
Schtau Methode, 163